ex abundantia enim cordis os loquitur
Whatever is in the heart overflows into speech.
Luke 6:45, *The Living Bible*

For Talia, Trinity, and Lindsay

workplace writing

Marilyn E. Holt
Humber College

THOMSON
NELSON

Australia Canada Mexico Singapore Spain United Kingdom United States

Workplace Writing

Marilyn E. Holt

Editorial Director and Publisher:
Evelyn Veitch

Acquisitions Editor:
Anne Williams

Marketing Manager:
Cara Yarzab

Developmental Editor:
Klaus Unger

Production Editor:
Emily Ferguson

Production Coordinator:
Hedy Sellers

Copy Editor:
Claudia Kutchukian

Proofreader:
Liz Radojkovic

Creative Director:
Angela Cluer

Interior Design:
Pedro Gaudenz Pereira

Cover Design:
Pedro Gaudenz Pereira

Compositor:
Tammy Gay

Indexer:
Noeline Bridge

Printer:
Webcom

Printed and bound in Canada
1 2 3 4 05 04 03 02

For more information contact Nelson, 1120 Birchmount Road, Scarborough, Ontario, M1K 5G4. Or you can visit our Internet site at http://www.nelson.com

National Library of Canada Cataloguing in Publication Data

Holt, Marilyn E. (Marilyn Elizabeth), 1944-
Workplace writing/Marilyn E. Holt.

Includes index.
ISBN 0-7747-3421-3

1. English language—Business English. 2. English language—Technical English. 3. Business writing. 4. Technical writing. I. Title

PE1479.B87H65 2002 808'.06665
C2002-902315-7

Contents

Open 'till midnigt for you're convienience.

Preface

Communication is such a routine activity in our lives that we hardly pay attention to it. Successful communication, especially during the complex and difficult situations that arise at work, depends on our understanding of many variables: who? why? when? where? what? how?

Although employers want to hire people who write well, students often neglect writing courses, thinking that they are less important than program-related courses. Yet writing ability may be the skill that makes one student stand out from all the others. Think about it this way: Everyone in your program will graduate with similar program-related skills whether they are studying electronics, landscape design, culinary arts, photography, or computer science. If a company interviews several candidates with similar technical skills, that company will often hire the person who can communicate more effectively. "Excellent written and oral communication skills" is a phrase that appears over and over again in job advertisements. Furthermore, while writing skills may improve your chances of getting an entry-level position, they may well be the key to advancement once you are in the workplace. If you consider almost any field of employment, the time spent writing increases with the level of responsibility.

The good news is that writing is a skill that can be learned. Precise word choice, correct spelling, appropriate punctuation, grammatical sentence structure, and meticulous proofreading: These are tools that can make a rough draft lucid—even elegant. The bad news, of course, is that, like any skill, writing takes practice. Even those who seem to have a gift for writing must work hard to write well. Jacques Barzun probably said it best: Most people "do not want to write, they want to have written."

This book attempts to break out of the cycle of tiresome, somewhat cranky rules that may become outdated in the age of electronic communication. Should I write 12 Leacock Street or 12 Leacock St.? Should I centre it or put it to one side? Should I double-space? The almost universal availability of computers and word-processing programs means that our approach to creating a business document has to change. No longer can we simply proclaim only one correct way of formatting a letter or designing a title page for a report. Accordingly, this text focuses on guidelines and offers suggestions that will help you make intelligent choices. The text is designed to teach principles that apply whether the document is a résumé, a manual on the correct feeding of horses, or a response to a tender.

How This Book Is Organized

Workplace Writing contains 22 chapters and is divided into five parts. Each chapter ends with activities and exercises, and includes cross references to the 20 case studies that appear at the end of the book.

Communication

Part One deals with the fundamentals of all business and technical writing, including effective language use, accessible document layout, and graphics. The approach is not prescriptive; rather, the chapters present a wide variety of skills, or tools, that you can master along with suggestions on how and where to use them.

Correspondence

Letter writing was once an art. All too often these days, it has become either a chore or a rote task performed without thought. Part Two divides the business letter into two components: the template and the content. The template comprises all the elements that form the backdrop or canvas on which you place your content. Content is approached through the use of formulas. This section includes several types of letters not usually found in textbooks.

Short Documents

Part Three looks at several writing challenges that arise at work: summarizing lengthy articles; writing definitions, descriptions, and instructions; and preparing résumés, job descriptions, agendas, and minutes.

Reports and Proposals

Part Four looks at the purpose and preparation of these two specific kinds of documents. In addition, it gives a brief overview of skills that the report writer may require, such as preparing surveys, interviewing experts, and evaluating sources.

Roundup

Part Five is not a grammar or usage handbook. Instead, it looks at a series of topics that often present problems in workplace writing: numbers in text, parallel structure, active and passive verbs, and special punctuation marks.

Case Studies and Assignments

Many people do well on a writing exercise that requires revision of ten sentences containing errors. Yet the same people will turn around and make the very same errors in a paragraph or report. For this reason, *Workplace Writing* includes few practice exercises. Instead, writing assignments are based on case studies, most of these centred around the fictitious Ultimate Resort and Spa. Since a large resort functions almost like a small town, situations relating to this enterprise offer opportunities for students in most disciplines to try out their writing skills.

The case studies appear together at the end of the book since each includes more than one writing assignment, and thus cannot be attached to any one lesson or chapter. An index to the cases and a list of cases that are relevant to a topic at the end of each chapter allow instructors and students to find appropriate assignments.

In addition, I frequently recommend that students look for actual documents—reports, letters, agendas, etc.—that demonstrate the writing techniques described in the text. These will give you opportunities to evaluate the kind of real-world writing you are likely to encounter. Although names and some details have been changed, all of the examples used in this text are taken from real-life documents.

The Web Course Guide

Workplace Writing addresses the basics of writing that apply to all professions and includes examples and situations from various professions. The *Course Guide* is not an ancillary to the text in the traditional sense: it is not secondary to but rather forms an essential part of *Workplace Writing*. It provides materials, case studies, exercises, examples, and models for the major professional areas, thus enabling instructors to adapt the text to fit specific programs. All of this material is contained within a coherent whole—"The Ultimate Resort and Spa," a fictional workplace where all employees of all occupations are required to write various kinds of documents. This framework creates continuity between the text and the website, and it allows instructors to select cases to further customize the course to their needs.

Acknowledgments

I am truly grateful to the following people: Anne Williams and Kent Newell, who prodded me to get started; Klaus Unger, my editor, who was infinitely patient waiting for me to finish; Allison Roach, my high-school Latin teacher, who many years ago awoke in me the love of Latin and language; my students in many different classrooms over the years, who have taught me that successful communication requires laughter as well as perseverance; and finally, my dear family and faithful friends, who have always encouraged me.

The *Ultimate Resort* and *Spa*

1 2 3 4 5

Part One

Communication

Communication Theory

communication

The word *communication* originates from the Latin word *commun*, an adjective that means "belonging equally to more than one person." The Latin verb *communicare* means "to make something common to many, to share or divide something." Other related words in English are "communion," "communal," and "communicable." The term "communicate," then, implies not simply sending a message to one person, like shooting an arrow (although it certainly may mean that); more often it means making sure that many people share the same information, ideas, messages, or warnings.

Successful Communication

The little scenario outlined in Box 1.1 demonstrates a simple and successful act of communication. One party has a message and finds a way to send it so that the other party receives it, understands it, and responds appropriately. The message received is the same as the message that was sent. The actual feedback closely matches the anticipated feedback.

Box 1.1 ***Successful Communication***

A baby cries because it is hungry. → A parent wants the crying to stop. → The parent picks up the baby. → The parent feeds the baby. → The crying stops. → Baby and parent are both content.

In the workplace, you will spend much of your time determining how to communicate successfully. Sometimes you may hardly be aware of the choices you are making; other times, you may spend hours agonizing over the appropriate choice of message, tone, and medium. Any act of communication centres around two participants: the sender and the receiver.

The Sender

The *sender* begins the process. The sender may be a new customer, a speaker at a conference, or a friend in the cafeteria; an individual, a team, or a country; an artist, a musician, an architect, or an author. If you think about it, the sender of any message faces a daunting task. In the workplace, the sender has to

- decide exactly what message to send
- get the attention of the receiver(s)
- determine the best way to send the message
- recognize and overcome anything that might get in the way

In fact, those who send messages bear most of the responsibility for successful communication. This is why more textbooks are written for writers and speakers than for readers and listeners.

The Message

The *message* is any kind of information that needs to be conveyed: an idea, a thought, a feeling or emotion, a warning, a set of instructions, an apology, or an invitation. Messages vary greatly in complexity, from the cry of a hungry infant to a biogeneticist's explanation of how DNA works. The message may be original and creative—even noisy, like the promotion of a new car or the buildup to an election campaign. Other messages may be routine and repetitive, like the content of a month-end report.

Every message, of course, is not clear and straightforward. The idea in the sender's mind may be convoluted and hard to express, and the very same message may be worded differently at different times. At work, you will encounter a dizzying variety of messages and receivers. The hesitation (or paralysis) that hits when you try to write a report, an application letter, or a memo to your supervisor may indicate that the message itself is not yet clear in your own mind, it may mean that you don't yet know enough about the receiver, or it may mean that your communication skills need improvement.

The Receiver

The *receiver* (sometimes called the *audience*) is the person or group for whom the message is intended. The receiver may be a reader, a listener, or an observer; receivers may be in the same room or in the space shuttle; they may be surprised when they receive the message, or they may be waiting anxiously for it. Sometimes—for example, in a personal diary or an electronic daytimer—the receiver may actually be the same person as the sender.

To send a message appropriately, a sender should know as much as possible about the intended receiver(s). So the sender may spend several weeks doing formal market research to build an audience profile. Typically an analysis of a target audience looks for answers to questions such as those in Box 1.2.

Most of the time, however, we use a much less formal process for analyzing an audience. We tend to rely on instinct, feelings, or our past experience to help us prepare and send mes-

Box 1.2 *Building a Picture of the Target Audience*

- **What does my target audience look like?** Describe the audience in terms of age, gender, educational background, geographic location, socioeconomic position.
- **What's important to my target audience?** Are these people interested in buying a new sports car? fashion? health? ceramics? canaries? comfortable footwear?
- **Under what circumstances will the audience receive my message?** Will they be relaxing and watching television? Will they be in a high-pressure sales meeting? Will they be alone in an office?
- **What's the message for?** Is it designed to pass on information of general interest to many people? Is it just for one reader? Is it intended to sell something? to teach something? to warn? to entertain?
- **What knowledge level is my target audience at?** Do they already know a lot about this subject or am I introducing something new? Will they want to know about this?
- **What emotions will this message raise in my audience?** Will this message make them angry? fearful? enthusiastic? indifferent?

sages appropriately. We make small, almost unconscious assessments. For example, students in a new course confer with one another about how to prepare assignments appropriately for specific instructors. At work, we gauge our managers, coworkers, and employees by watching them, listening to them, and checking their body language. We are, in fact, constantly analyzing the audiences around us so that we can communicate effectively.

Inevitably, we will encounter a situation where we have to send a message to an audience that we don't know—someone in another department or company, for example. If we cannot learn about or assess our receiver directly, we can still make wise choices about the messages we send—choices that are based on our knowledge of how communication works.

The Medium

medius

Medius is a Latin word meaning "middle."

During a séance, a medium apparently acts as a go-between through which those who have died communicate with those who are alive. For Marshall McLuhan, the medium is the message. In the language of communication theory, the *medium* is the method of conveying a message from sender to receiver. The medium might be your voice, a letter, a hand signal, or a billboard. Artists might use canvas, steel, or umbrellas; musicians might use washboards, zithers, flutes, drums, steel guitars, or a full symphony orchestra. Sometimes the only medium you need is body language or a facial expression.

At work, the choice of an appropriate medium depends on many factors, such as

- location and number of receivers
- urgency or sensitivity of the message
- availability of equipment
- length and nature of the message
- need for a permanent record of the message

Every technological enhancement makes the choice of medium more complex. Box 1.3 lists just a few of the possibilities and variations involved when you have a message to deliver at work.

Box 1.3 *Choosing a Medium*

Deliver the Message by Voice

- Walk down the hall to the receiver's office.
- Make an appointment and go to the receiver's place of work.
- Make an appointment for the receiver to come to you.
- Call a meeting of all the receivers.
- Present your message at a conference.
- Make an announcement over an intercom.

Deliver the Message by Telephone

- Call and speak directly to the receiver.
- Call and leave a voice mail message.
- Call and leave a request for the receiver to call back.
- Use a conference call to reach several receivers.
- Use a speakerphone to include several receivers and senders.

Deliver the Message in Writing

- Write a memo and send it through interoffice mail.
- Write a letter and send it by mail.
- Send the memo/letter using e-mail or an attachment to e-mail.
- Fax the letter or memo.
- Distribute the information in a handout.
- Post information on a bulletin board—wall-mounted or Internet.
- Publish an article, or book, or pamphlet.
- Use an overhead projector.
- Use a multimedia presentation.

Encoding

Encoding means taking an idea or message and putting it into a form (some type of symbols or signals) that will be understood by the receiver. It's a process carried out—usually unconsciously—whenever we communicate. Encoding involves choosing from many possible symbols, styles, techniques, and media depending on the capabilities, knowledge, and purpose of the sender and the characteristics of the audience.

The term "encoding," of course, implies using a code. On the one hand, encoding can restrict communication—that is, it can prevent all but a few receivers from understanding a message. On the other hand, encoding can help to make a message accessible to a specific target audience or to as many people as possible.

Magazines, movies, newspapers, and retail stores all provide good examples of encoding for specific receivers. Notice how publishers design magazines so that they appeal to women, men, teens, sports fans, artists, gardeners, or mountain biking enthusiasts. Walk through your neighbourhood video store and you'll notice that comedies are usually packaged in light colours with bright graphics, while thrillers and horror movies more often use very dark packaging—black, dark green, and purple.

The same message can be encoded in entirely different ways for different audiences. You can see clear examples in the public library. Pick a topic such as volcanoes. You will find books on volcanoes that are suitable for children, teens, general readers, and advanced readers. You may find websites, descriptions of science experiments, articles in encyclopedias, and descriptions in tourism pamphlets, all devoted to volcanoes. All of these use the medium of print; each uses a different form of encoding.

Both the medium and the encoding involve *how* you send your message. The medium refers to your choice of conveyance. For example, will you speak or write your message, post it on a bulletin board, buy airtime on a local radio station, or design a package around it? The encoding involves all the signals you actually decide to use in the preparation of the message: small letters or big, loud voice or soft, pale colours or dark, animation or photography, formal language or slang.

Part of the reason audience analysis is so important is that it helps the writer choose appropriate encoding for the message that needs to be sent.

Direction

Communication moves in three different directions: upward, downward, or lateral [horizontal] (see Box 1.4). *Upward communication* means that the receivers have decision-making power. People who are above you on an organization chart are the people you report to, such as managers, supervisors, and employers (see Figure 1.1). Remember that communication with customers and clients, because they have the power to purchase or not to purchase, is also upward communication.

Box 1.4 *Communication Moves in Three Different Directions*

Upward

Please see me at four o'clock today. ✗

Would you be able to see me at four o'clock today? ✓

May I see you at four o'clock today? ✓

Downward

I'd like to have the results of the survey by Friday. ✓

Send me a quick e-mail if you feel you can't meet this deadline. ✓

All employees should submit their vacation requests in writing. ✓

I'll get back to you sometime. ✗

Get me some sort of answer. ✗

The entrance to parking lot B will now be limited to those who have cards that allow in and out privileges in the four parking lots in addition to parking lot B. This will be effective today. ✗

Lateral or Horizontal

Let's get together at four. ✓

I'll stop by at four. ✓

Can we arrange to have parking cards issued to all the sales staff? ✓

I still haven't received the new Guest Registry Totals for the month of January. Can you send them over today, Yuri? I have to finish my month-end report. ✓

At an early age, we learn to adjust our language and tone for upward communication. For example, we usually speak differently to our boss than we do to our coworkers. Similarly, we would not use imperative wording ("Send me the memo by noon") when communicating upward. Instead, we might choose a softer wording that makes a request ("Could I see the memo by noon?").

Downward communication is communication with people who work for you or who are below you on the company's organization chart. Don't make the mistake of thinking that the terms "upward" and "downward" indicate a difference in respect or politeness. "Talking down" to your staff, for example, is a good way of cutting off communication altogether; similarly, adopting an artificially ornate style merely to impress someone you work for will only make you sound pompous.

Figure 1.1 *The Ultimate Resort and Spa Organization Chart*

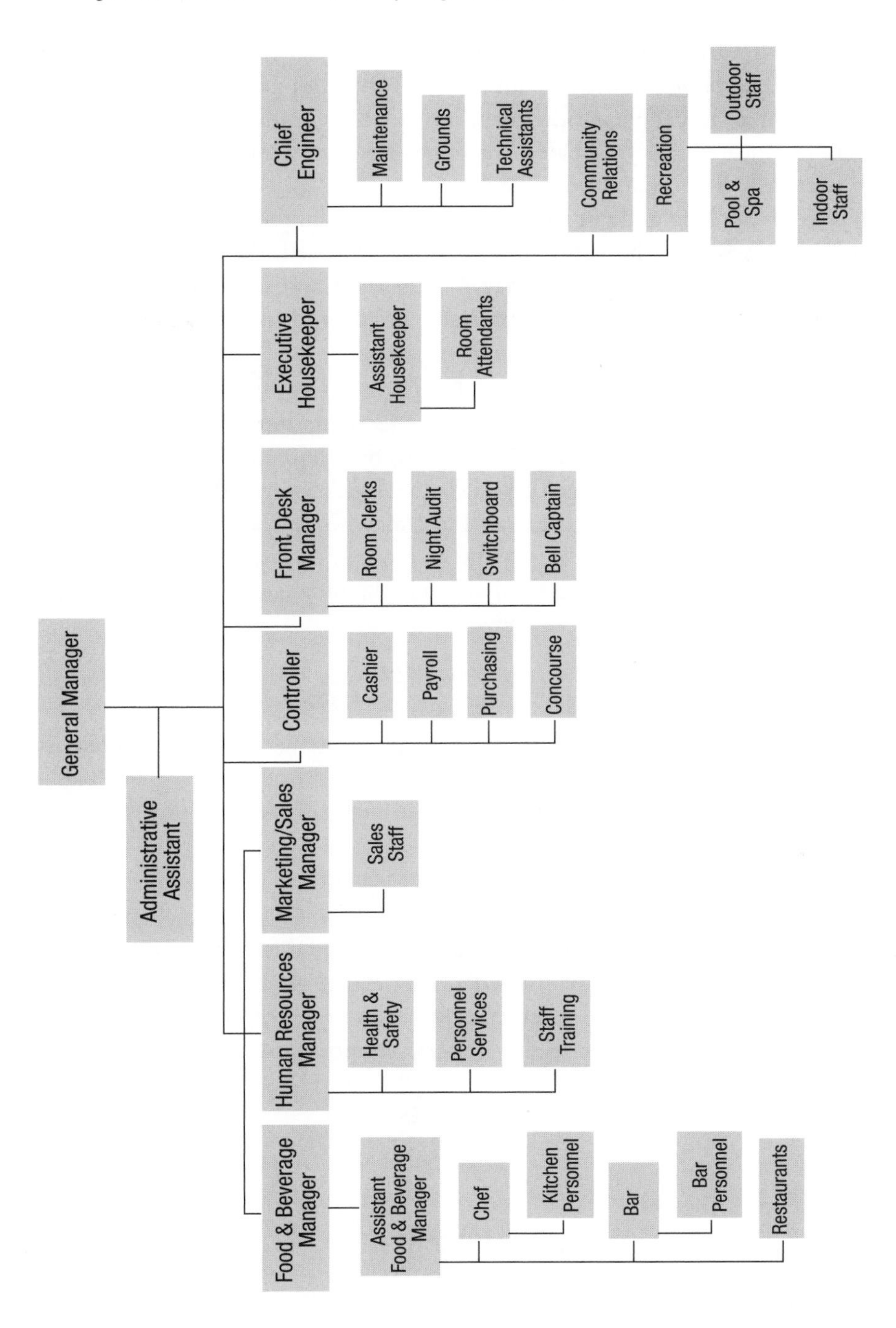

Employees sometimes complain that managers either do not communicate at all, or if they do, they send messages that are vague or confusing. A good rule, whether communicating upward or downward, is to send the kinds of messages you yourself like to receive.

Lateral or *horizontal communication* is directed to colleagues and those around you who have the same job or to people in other departments and companies who have about the same level of responsibility as you. Lateral messages often use a more colloquial, informal language, especially if you know your receiver well.

Of course, there are no hard and fast rules here. Depending on the size of the company, the number of employees, and the nature of the people involved, the level of formality may always be open and easygoing or it may remain rigid and impersonal. The best guideline is to maintain a tone that feels comfortable to you and to your audience.

Decoding

Receivers decode messages. *Decoding* involves not just receiving but also understanding. For example, students may hear what a professor says, but they must also understand, digest, remember, and apply the message. If you stand a block away and wave your hand at me, I may be receiving some sort of message, but I may not know exactly what you're trying to tell me. Furthermore, although the same memo may be distributed to hundreds of employees, all employees will not necessarily decode the message in the same way.

The Two-Way Process

The process of communication works somewhat like a tennis match. In fact, we often use the terminology of tennis when we say to a person, committee, or company, "The ball is in your court." This means we have delivered a message and now we're waiting for action or a response of some sort.

Anticipated Feedback

Consciously or unconsciously, senders usually anticipate specific feedback to their messages. The response to a message may be immediate or delayed. Sometimes, even while a sender is transmitting a message, the receiver may begin to respond. Table 1.1 shows examples of communication in progress. The senders are anticipating specific feedback.

Table 1.1 *Senders Anticipate Specific Feedback*

Sender	Receiver	Message	Anticipated Feedback
politician	voters	vote for me	gets elected
advertiser	TV audience	buy this product	consumers buy product
defence lawyer	jury	my client is innocent	jury decides not guilty
student who writes assignment	professor	here's my best work	gets A+
manager who sends out memo	department employees	meeting on Thursday at 10:00	staff comes to meeting

Actual Feedback

The actual feedback, however, is not always the same as the anticipated feedback. In Table 1.2, for example, the third column shows that something has caused the actual feedback to differ from what was anticipated.

Table 1.2 *The Actual Feedback Is Not Always What Was Anticipated*

Sender	Anticipated Feedback	Actual Feedback
politician	gets elected	someone else elected
advertiser	consumers buy product	no one buys
defence lawyer	jury decides not guilty	jury decides guilty
student who writes assignment	gets A+	gets C–
manager who sends out memo	staff comes to meeting	most staff do not attend

Barriers to Communication

Any factor that delays or blocks successful communication or causes the actual feedback to differ from what was anticipated is an obstacle that needs to be recognized and either accommodated or eliminated. Even though a sender may make careful encoding choices, barriers may still make the receiver's attempt to decode the message difficult or impossible.

Barriers may be physical, psychological, emotional, environmental, cognitive, or cultural. Moreover, they may originate with the sender, the receiver, or some other source entirely.

Sometimes it's easy to discover why communication was not successful: The Internet connection was down, the print on the overheads was too small, costs were calculated incorrectly. More often, however, determining the reason for communication failure presents a challenge. Why wasn't the proposal accepted? What does this memo mean? Why aren't applicants submitting their forms correctly? Why wasn't my call returned?

The study of communication could well be described as the study of barriers. Table 1.3 shows that pinpointing the reason for a communication problem can be a complex process. Although we may identify a barrier (for example, a classroom that's too cold), we then have to determine the reason for that barrier (a technical problem with the furnace? a failure to inform maintenance staff? a student with a fever?). We might discover more problems—each of which has its own origins. The forward movement of communication can stop if we spend too much time going backward to seek the source of every barrier. An experienced and competent communicator is one who has learned not to repeat past mistakes and who continues to enhance the skills that will avoid future pitfalls.

Table 1.3 *Identifying the Barrier Can Be a Complex Task*

Problem	Result	Possible Barrier
The room we held the meeting in was too hot. I was sleepy and didn't pay attention.	I didn't hear the date for the next meeting, so I missed the meeting.	environmental
I didn't get any sleep the night before the exam.	I failed the exam.	physical
The customer spoke too quietly.	The bank teller performed the wrong procedure and the customer got angry.	environmental, cognitive, perhaps physical
The résumé had three spelling errors.	The applicant does not get the job.	cognitive
The print in the catalogue was hard to read.	Sales are poor.	technical
The report was very confusing.	The manager didn't bother to read it. The employee who wrote it missed a chance for promotion.	cognitive
I'd had a fight with my parents, so my mind was wandering.	I read the report but didn't pay attention to what I read.	emotional

Activities and Exercises

Throughout this text, as you read and try the various exercises and assignments, take the time to consider alternative media. For example, you may be asked to write a letter, but would a telephone call be more appropriate in the given situation? Could the information be delivered as an e-mail? Whenever you decide that a different medium would work well, try it.

1. Think of a work experience you have had that involved a communication problem. Write a short paper describing the situation and analyzing it according to communication theory. Your paper should incorporate concepts such as sender, receiver, anticipated and actual feedback, and barriers.
2. A customer named Franco Bialli comes into the bank to make a payment on his credit card by cheque. He is angry about the long wait in line and speaks sharply to the teller, who is fairly new at the job. The teller, upset by the angry customer, becomes a bit distracted and, by mistake, thinks Mr. Bialli wants to deposit the cheque into his account. She finishes the transaction quickly to keep the line of customers moving. When he receives his updated passbook, Mr. Bialli becomes even more annoyed.
   a. Discuss what has caused the problem.
   b. Suggest some ways this problem could have been prevented from occurring in the first place.
   c. Decide on solutions that can solve the problem now that it has happened.
   d. The bank has a policy that requires a short written account of any incidents where customers become upset. Write up a brief report on this incident.

For further assignments dealing with the content of this chapter, see case studies 1, 2, 9, and 20 starting on page 275.

Clarity

chapter two

When I ask students to name characteristics of good writing, the most frequent responses I hear are "clear" and "to the point." Yet when I ask them what makes writing "clear," they usually have trouble explaining what they mean. Clarity is best understood in terms of what's *not* there: no ambiguity, no impediments, no errors. Clarity is a lot like fresh air: you notice it only when it's not there.

Think about the word "clear" in other contexts:

- If a window is clear, it's clean, *easy* to see through, and not streaked.
- If a road is clear, it's unobstructed, allowing you to reach your destination *quickly.*
- If you clear a piece of land, you remove trees, rocks, roots—anything that prevents you from farming or building *efficiently.*
- If the air is clear you can breathe, and what's more, breathing can even be *enjoyable.*
- If your cheque clears the bank, you know that sufficient funds were there, so that the transaction could be completed *successfully.*

Clarity in communication means that the audience can complete the decoding process easily, quickly, efficiently, and enjoyably—in other words, successfully. Although a reader must be appropriately equipped to decode a message, the responsibility for clarity lies principally with the person initiating the document: the sender. Clarity, along with that elusive "to-the-pointness," arises from three elements: precision, conciseness, and coherence.

Precision

Clarity begins with *precision*—the absence of vague, fuzzy language and poorly structured ideas. In casual conversations, vague language works fine. You say, "It's hot," "Get me some pins," or "That's a bad idea" without worrying about specifics because you assume the person who is with you understands what you mean. In business and technical documents, however, vague, obscure, or inexact language can be annoying, time-consuming, and costly.

If the following examples were part of a business report or a letter to a client, think how many different interpretations would be possible:

> It's a bad idea.

This statement could mean

- We can't afford it.
- I disagree with you.
- That product is too expensive.

Some of the equipment needs replacing.

This statement could mean

- The chef wants a walk-in refrigerator.
- The overhead fans are squeaking.
- You need two new broilers and a thermostat on the main oven.

To produce clear business and technical writing, get into the habit of using precise terminology for modifiers: avoid the habit of using general terms that need further explanation. Here are some examples:

- "Reliable" can mean
  - always completes required tasks correctly
  - punctual
  - trustworthy
- "Strong" can mean
  - weather-resistant
  - dishwasher-safe
  - able to lift 200 kg
  - assertive
- "Nice" can mean
  - cooperative
  - quiet
  - uncomplaining

Similarly, avoid exaggeration—especially overusing qualifiers such as "very," "so," "quite," and "extremely." If you use them too much, they lose their impact, with the result that you have to use them even more. In the following examples, the right-hand column conveys a more precise meaning:

I am extremely sorry. → I am sorry.

absolutely free → free

Concepts such as time and measurement should be expressed in precise language whenever possible, as in the following examples:

I need an answer as soon as possible. *(by 4 p.m. on Friday? before June 1st?)*

The surface of the wood was pretty hot. *(34°C? smoking?)*

We need narrower tubing. *(22 mm? $\frac{1}{2}$"?)*

Table 2.1 shows other examples of vague language and how they can be revised to produce a clearer message.

Table 2.1 *Vague versus Precise Language*

Vague	Precise
Everyone was late.	Twelve people were late.
We should include some employees in this discussion.	We should include two of the dining room staff and at least one person from maintenance in this discussion.
You can prevent the problem by adding liquid.	You can prevent the problem by adding a few drops of ice water.
I have a lot of experience with computers.	I worked on the help desk at Kovax Industries for four years.
Some customers were inconvenienced by the change of date.	Some customers had already booked transportation for the conference. When we changed the date, they lost their deposit.

Using precise language means that your word choices fit both the audience and the occasion. Language is a living entity that adapts constantly to changing environments. Accordingly, professional jargon, slang and street talk, clichés, buzzwords, short forms, and a variety of other forms of expression continue to develop in various environments.

Jargon is a vocabulary that is specific to one profession and that outsiders will likely not understand. Box 2.1 shows examples of jargon from three disciplines—you can probably think of many others. Inexperienced writers sometimes use jargon, thinking that it will impress people, but throwing terms at readers that they do not understand is a waste of time and is just plain rude.

Slang, which tends to be a spoken rather than a written language, is similar to jargon because it is understood only by members of certain groups. Slang often assigns new meanings to old words; it changes almost constantly. The slang you use today may mark you as an outsider tomorrow.

Clichés become clichés through continual use—some would say overuse. In writing, they come to our minds easily because they are so common. For example,

cold as ice
sick as a dog
at the end of my rope
high and dry

Box 2.1 *Professional Jargon*

Jargon from the Advertising Industry
DTC: Direct-to-consumer; refers to advertising, such as print ads and TV commercials, that is targeted toward consumers.

Interstitial: Refers to Internet advertisements that appear in separate windows while a new, lead webpage is downloading.

Jargon from the Hairstyling Trade
Texturizing: Thinning the hair to make it look fuller and give it more body.

Slicing: Angling the scissors to give cut hair a wispy effect.

Jargon from the Forestry Industry
Knuckleboom: A hydraulically operated loading boom whose mechanical action imitates the human arm.

Salvage Cut: To harvest dead or damaged trees or trees in danger of being damaged in order to save their economic value.

Wolf: A large, rough tree that is not good for lumber.

cliché

The word *cliché* is the past participle of the French verb *clicher*, a term that was used in the printing industry to refer to a metal proof or cast. The expression "cast in stone" denotes a similar idea.

The language of business also tends to rely on a kind of cliché that is not just an aphorism or popular saying. For example, how often have you used or read the following expressions?

Sorry for any inconvenience.
Feel free to call.
I beg to differ.
Please be advised that....
Please find enclosed....
Have a nice day.
Valued customer

The negative aspect of clichés is the loss of meaning that accompanies their familiarity. In business and technical writing, avoid clichés as much as possible. Instead, aim for language that expresses your ideas more precisely and demonstrates that you are not just putting down words without thinking.

Conciseness

conciseness

In Latin, *concis* is an adjective meaning "cut up." Conciseness denotes brevity and exactness—an important combination. It implies, in fact, that something has been cut to exactly the right length.

Achieving Conciseness through Deletion

Editing and revision—the keys to concise writing—involve deleting as well as adding material.

Wordiness weakens the impact of any message. You can reduce or eliminate wordiness by learning to recognize it when you see it. Don't use five words if one will do. Four words may not make much difference as an individual example; however, if every sentence you write contains four extra words, five pages of writing can quickly turn into ten pages and more.

Reducing the length of a sentence intensifies its message. Quite simply, short sentences are more emphatic. Of course, you do not want to pile many short subject–verb sentences on top of one another, as in this example:

> Dr. Barbara Wilke is the main speaker. She is head of psychology at Harvard University. The subject of her talk is "The Bereaved Child." Her work in this field is notable. She has published more than 100 articles. You are cordially invited to attend. ✗

Nor do you want to confuse your reader by cramming too much information into one monster sentence like this one:

> Package Plans can be offered to an advertiser who purchases two prime-time spots per week in a popular sitcom series but the company may also be required to purchase equivalent time in a prime-time Canadian series and/or equivalent time during daytime periods subject to the decision of the network. ✗

Aim for the middle ground. Here are some guidelines to keep in mind regarding sentence length:

- Be cautious about exceeding 20 words per sentence.
- Include no more than two independent clauses in a sentence.
- Include no more than two subordinate clauses in a sentence.
- Focus on only one main item of information per sentence.
- Avoid sentences that you cannot read aloud without stopping for a breath.

Here's an example of how using these guidelines can improve writing:

Wordy

Basements consist of concrete floors that are cold and hard. They never really get a chance to heat up. Most people assume that if they put down carpeting they are creating sufficient insulation and warmth. This, however, is not the case. There are insulators created for the purpose of flooring that require you to build up the floor by a couple of inches by means of wood flooring above the insulation. Though this is almost a necessity it is not often considered and more often than not, it is seen as too expensive and time-consuming to be worthwhile.

Concise

Basement floors are cold and hard. Carpeting alone will not provide sufficient insulation and warmth. For proper insulation, you should build a wooden subfloor above the concrete and lay the carpet on that. Many people think this step is too expensive and time-consuming, but it greatly increases the insulation value.

Redundancy

Redundancy is like clutter: It is needless wordiness that gets in the way of the real message. See Table 2.2 for some examples.

Table 2.2 ***Learn to Recognize and Avoid Wordy and Redundant Expressions***

Instead of	Use
10 a.m. in the morning	10 a.m.
at the present time	now
if at all possible	if possible
If you would be so kind as to give us your response at your earliest possible convenience....	Please let us know as soon as possible.
in view of the fact that	because
in spite of the fact that	although

Sometimes, to make a letter or report look more impressive, writers will intentionally fill up pages with words. What they may be doing, however, is simply restating the same information with different or superfluous words. Read the following example. Notice how the repetition clouds the meaning instead of clarifying it.

> It is important for us to address the issue of safety in the school parking lot. The school has never before experienced so many cars in the parking lot so the issue of safety has not previously been addressed. At this week's meeting we will address the safety issue and establish some guidelines for ensuring the safety of all students, staff, and parents in the school parking lot.

Expletives

If you look up the word *expletive* in the dictionary, you'll probably find it defined as a swear word or exclamation of some sort. It has an additional meaning in the study of writing: It refers to a particular way of putting together a sentence—usually starting with the word "it" or "there" followed by some form of the verb "to be." Instead of using these wordy expressions, make your sentences shorter and more emphatic. Notice the difference between the two sets of examples in Table 2.3.

Table 2.3 *Taking Expletives Out of Sentences*

With Expletive	Without Expletive
It is important to look both ways before you cross the street.	Look both ways before you cross the street. *or* You should look both ways before you cross the street.
It shouldn't be necessary to remind him twice.	We shouldn't have to remind him twice.
It was Jake who found the missing armadillo.	Jake found the missing armadillo.
There are many people who think I'm positively irresistible.	Many people think I'm positively irresistible.
There will be at least three people arriving late.	At least three people will arrive late.

Achieving Conciseness through Addition

In all business and technical writing, clarity needs to be carefully balanced with brevity. Shorter is not always better: If your message is so short that your receiver has to ask for more details, time has been wasted, not saved. If brevity gives your writing an abrupt, impersonal, "grocery list" tone, it may have a negative effect on your receiver and on the response you receive. Depending on the form and purpose of your document, you may want to add material to facilitate the reader's understanding.

Definitions, for example, may appear as part of the text, as footnotes, or as a separate list in a glossary. Used appropriately, definitions allow a wider audience to understand your document.

Background material helps to bring readers into the picture quickly by providing context. You might use a few sentences or several pages—the length depends on the type of document or the subject you are writing about.

Summaries (especially in longer documents) refresh your reader's memory by pulling together the main points in the preceding paragraphs or pages. Although they add to the length of a document, they ultimately make it more concise since many readers may choose to read only the summaries.

Appendixes in reports and proposals add data that is related to your topic but not of interest to every reader. Like a summary, an appendix may increase the size of a report, yet it speeds up reading by distinguishing optional material.

The following is an example of how adding material achieves precision:

Skiing is becoming more popular among all ages.	Skiing challenges every age group and offers excitement, exercise, opportunities to meet new people, and fun at every skill level.

Coherence

Coherence is the glue that holds your writing together. Imagine what would happen if you bought your textbooks unbound, as stacks of separate pages. Within a very short time, the pages would become unreadable, would get mixed up, or would be lost. The binding of a book allows the reader to use the material easily and get the message it contains efficiently. Similarly, the glue of syntax and logic holds your writing together.

Syntax

syntax

The word *syntax* is derived from two Greek terms: *syn*, a preposition meaning "with" or "alike," and *taxis*, meaning "classification." Syntax now refers to the way words are arranged to produce a clear meaning.

Look at the following group of words:

the from fairway yesterday was a window by hit broken the golf ball

Given a few minutes, most people will not have too much difficulty making these words into an intelligible sentence:

Yesterday, the window was broken by a golf ball hit from the fairway.

This sentence is fairly simple—easy to read and understand because we have a basic grasp of how words go together in English. Our understanding arises from our knowledge of syntax and punctuation. So we would not likely organize the words like this:

The hit window a golf ball by the fairway was broken from yesterday.

or like this:

The window broken was a golf ball by hit the fairway from yesterday.

As we grow up learning a language, we automatically learn an accepted order for various kinds of words. Thus we usually say

the small wooden ladder

instead of

the wooden small ladder

In fact, these two groups of words mean something quite different: The first implies that there may be two wooden ladders, one smaller than the other. The second, less likely expression, seems to mean that there are two small ladders, only one of which is wooden.

Business and technical documents do not require special or unusual syntax. Documents are clearest when the language works the way the reader expects it to work.

Logic

A logical order and layout of information also improves clarity. Most types of writing rely on a recognizable order to accommodate readers. Mystery stories, for example, save the vital information for the very end; romances rely on a twist of character or plot to weave their spell; newspaper stories use the familiar pyramid approach, moving from headline to ever-expanding detail.

Placement, or layout, plays just as important a role as organization. For example, in a newspaper, the story above the fold on page 1 carries more weight than an item in the middle of page 20. Readers are more likely to see and remember information found at the beginning or end of a document than information in the middle. The logical arrangement of a business document relies on these same guidelines.

Use familiar formats as much as possible. This concept covers every detail of your writing, from a conventional salutation in a letter to the use of a familiar font. Oddball features may occasionally add an interesting note, but often they have exactly the opposite effect.

Begin with what's known and then add what's new. This guideline applies at the sentence level as well as in complete documents. Avoid making your reader backtrack to find explanatory material. In the following sentence, for example, readers must wait until the last three words to learn what the message is actually about:

> This memo will outline two important new steps that must be followed by all staff who wish to request a leave of absence.

Put the main point or the big picture up front, and then add supporting details. Depending on the document, you might do this in a few opening sentences, an abstract, or even an informative title. A workplace document should not be a mystery story.

Activities and Exercises

1. Investigate some current vocabulary variations by answering the following questions. Try to use your own definitions rather than relying on a dictionary.
   a. Define *jargon*, and provide three examples of jargon from your particular discipline.
   b. Define *slang*. How are slang and jargon similar?
   c. Give some examples of current slang. Why is this difficult to do?
   d. Give some examples of slang that is outdated.
   e. Define *buzzword*. What buzzwords are popular today?
   f. Good writers who have taken the time to think about their readers know that there are appropriate places—even in business writing—to use terms and expressions such as

   warm and fuzzy
   groovy
   fuddy-duddy
   slammer

   Look for examples of colloquial language in business or technical documents. Are they appropriately used? Do you think they are effective? Why or why not?
2. This chapter mentions the derivation of the word *cliché*.
   a. Why is the term so apt when applied to writing?
   b. Clichés creep into the language mainly through speech. Why are they used so much in political speeches, news broadcasts, and everyday conversations?
   c. From the following list of expressions, select ten that you often use or hear. Replace them with carefully chosen words or phrases that would suit a business or technical document. Try using them in an appropriate sentence.

   a crying shame
   hard as nails
   the bitter end
   keep your eye on the ball
   stick to your guns
   in the final analysis
   something's fishy
   burn the midnight oil
   let bygones be bygones
   don't rock the boat
   winner takes all
   shape up

the powers that be	the pits
when all is said and done	if you can't stand the heat

3. Improve the clarity of the following memo by substituting precise language, omitting any redundancy, and improving the order of the information:

TO: Mark Tisdale, Head of Development

FROM: Andrea Radojkovic

DATE: December 1, 2001

RE: Deadline

Certain materials needed to complete work on my project arrived a week later than anticipated so work could not start until only one week ago. As you know in our conversations, it will take approximately two weeks to totally complete the project. But we are understaffed at the time and it will take longer than at first estimated. I am just so very sorry for any inconvenience our department is causing the company and I guarantee that we are working as hard and as fast as humanly possible to complete this job. I hope you understand that we are up against the wall here and will extend our deadline.

4. Revise the following paragraph, omitting wordiness, correcting any grammar and punctuation problems, and putting the main focus at the beginning:

For over 20 years, teachers and parents have expressed concern over those children whose parents stop their cars in the centre of the parking lot and send their children unaccompanied across the parking lot toward the playground. While one car stops even for one minute, five or six others may be forced to wait in the parking lot. Parents anxious to get to work then open their doors and release their passengers to save time when the way is clear and they are able to proceed. Children dart between the waiting cars unaware of the dangers this action entails. Because this occurs not in a designated driveway but in the school parking lot, there is the added hazard of drivers leaving the parking lot unable to see the children who may be walking across the lot. The longevity of this problem is evidence that the above-mentioned carpool habits are ingrained in the drivers who bring children to the school. Regulations and policies have little effect, as enforcement is difficult for the one teacher who is on outside duty before school. Additionally a question of immediate convenience (dropping off the children mid-lot) often overrides the question of safety.

5. Look up the derivation of the word "bombast" and its current meaning. Find examples of bombast.

For further assignments dealing with the content of this chapter, see Case Study 4 starting on page 278.

Confidence

Written language is far more than just black marks on a page. Language can startle you with sudden, beautiful metaphors, or with expressions that fill you with awe or anger; language can move you to tears or bore you to tears. It's all just words—but by using words, writers sculpt meanings and pictures that change the mood and the mind of the person who reads them.

Strength

Confidence normally implies *strong* feelings. If you are indifferent about or uninterested in something, you rarely display a confident attitude about it. Furthermore, you usually know when someone else sounds interested, and you can recognize the signs when someone is bored or dismissive. Whether you are writing a letter, memo, or report, you can assess the receiver and context and adjust the sound of your document to suit the situation.

We all have ideas about displaying confidence in face-to-face encounters: a firm handshake, eye contact, a smile, a voice that doesn't shake. When a document must speak for you, you can translate that confident manner into writing by demonstrating strength, positive feelings, and sound knowledge through the effective use of language.

Achieving a Confident Sound

To achieve a confident, affirming sound, use active verbs. Avoid relying on the weak linking verb "to be." Use shorter rather than longer sentences, and common, concrete nouns rather than obscure words. Table 3.1 gives some examples.

Achieving a Passive or Impersonal Sound

Occasionally, you may want to put some distance between yourself and the message, especially if you are conveying unwelcome news. Not surprisingly, the principal method of achieving this sound involves using the passive voice (see Part Five: Roundup), as in the following examples:

A decision will be made this week.

These instructions need to be followed.

Table 3.1 *Choosing Strong Verbs*

Weaker	Stronger
I am an honours graduate and was the class valedictorian.	I graduated with honours and delivered the valedictory speech.
The cost of registration is about $600 depending on the league. Included in that fee are a $30 insurance fee and a $150 entry fee.	Registration costs about $600 depending on the league. That fee includes a $30 insurance fee and a $150 entry fee.
In my research, I was trying to find out how important it is to have a bookstore right on campus.	I was investigating the importance of having a bookstore on campus.
The attached files are representative of the best work I can do.	The attached files represent my best work.
A new chairperson will be chosen by the committee this week.	The committee will select a new chairperson this week.

You can strengthen (or weaken) the effect by using weasel words and modal verbs.[1] A weasel is an animal that we usually think of as a bit sly, slippery, and hard to hang onto. A weasel word is a word or phrase that allows a writer or speaker to escape from total frankness or commitment. Weasel words are common in advertising and politics. Here are some examples:

Flakies are *part of* a complete breakfast.

Sudso *helps* colours last longer.

This product *may* contain peanuts.

We *hope to* review our results early in the new year.

I *think* your car needs a new transmission.

Using expletive constructions along with the passive voice makes writing sound even more distant and formal. Use full names and titles for people instead of personal pronouns. You can also add formal or even archaic words to heighten the effect. Look at the examples in Box 3.1:

[1] Modal verbs have only one form and are followed by the infinitive form of the verb. Examples of modals are *may, might, should, could, can, would, ought, need,* and *must.*

Box 3.1 Using Passive Voice and Expletives to Create Impersonal Language

It is possible a decision will be made this week.

It is to be decided this week.

Mr. Harold McQuillen will be appointed chairperson.

It is important that these instructions be followed.

The appointment of Mr. Harold McQuillen to the position of chairperson is hereby announced.

It is with pleasure that the appointment of Mr. Harold McQuillen as chairperson is announced.

It is mandatory that the directives elucidated in the personnel literature be observed by all corporate associates.

Achieving an Approachable, Personal, Informal Sound

To sound friendlier and more personal, choose shorter sentences and use first names, contractions, and even colloquialisms:

Ted, please try to arrange a meeting with our reps in Thunder Bay.

I'm happy to announce that Hal is our new chairperson.

Read the employee handbook carefully. It contains lots of helpful stuff.

Positive Language

Understanding and using *positive language* will help you to encode messages, even negative ones, in a way that expresses confidence. Box 3.2 presents two scenarios you may have experienced. What sorts of feelings do situations like these raise in the receivers? How can the senders adjust the encoding so the messages will elicit a more positive response?

Box 3.2 Negative Messages

Example 1

A parent arrives home from work after a frustrating day and the ensuing "conversation" sounds something like this:

"You didn't hang up your coats."

"Stop fighting with your sister."

"The radio's too loud."

"I told you, you couldn't."

"Stop doing that."

"No. You can't."

"I don't want that bike in the driveway."

Example 2

A student gets a major assignment returned covered in red pencil marks, x's, a list of all the errors, and a very low mark. No other comments appear on the assignment.

Classes in effective parenting recommend that a parent should intentionally plan and use positive and encouraging remarks when meeting the family after work. This practice can change the whole tone of a household. Similarly, effective teachers tell students what they have done well as well as what needs improvement.

Most people react better to positive suggestions and ideas than to negative ones. The opposite is also true: attitudes usually become negative in response to negative language. We all like to hear about what's good, not just about what's bad. We all want to know what we can have and can do—usually before we know what we can't have or can't do. We want to hear about what we've done well, not just about our mistakes.

Some words and actions just seem to carry their own negative or positive overtones. some examples in Table 3.2.

Table 3.2 ***Positive and Negative Language and Gestures***

Words with Negative Overtones ☹				
no	unfortunately	regret	lack	penalty
fail	weak	never	poor	argue
careless	you misunderstood	he claims	broken	forget
serious	waste	at a loss	disappointed	delay
problem	late	delinquent	wrong	deny

(continued)

Table 3.2 *Positive and Negative Language and Gestures* (continued)

Actions with Negative Overtones ☹				
shrugging	not looking someone in the eye	walking away	slouching	rolling eyes
snickering	shaking head			
Words with Positive Overtones ☺				
yes	vacation	paycheque	immediately	perfect
correct	improved	better	satisfied	guarantee
bonus	sale	congratulations	generous	thank you
appreciate	honest	approve		
Actions with Positive Overtones ☺				
nodding	smiling	firm handshake	leaning forward	applause
eye contact	hugging			

Some less obvious words also project a negative tone. Notice how the underlined words in the examples in Table 3.3 produce a negative effect that doesn't really need to be there. A few minor changes alter the tone without changing the meaning.

Table 3.3 *Avoiding a Negative Tone*

Negative Tone
I hope my qualifications might be suitable for this job.
Unfortunately, we are not open on Saturday.
I'm just a part-time student.
More Positive Tone
I am confident that my qualifications are suitable for this job.
(If you're not confident, how will the reader be?)
We are not open on Saturday.
(This is a fact—a company policy—not an unfortunate one.)
or
We are not open on Saturday, but we are open until 10 p.m. on Thursdays and Fridays.
(Offer an alternative.)
I'm a part-time student.
(Again, this is a fact; it does not need to be devalued.)

The language skills discussed here are not meant to encourage artificiality in your writing. Positive language should not be used to deceive or mislead readers. If a mistake has been made, if an event will not take place, or if the answer to a request is "no," this information must be clearly communicated. Yet even a mistake or a refusal can be conveyed in language that helps to minimize negative feelings. See some examples in Table 3.4.

Table 3.4 *Making Weak and Negative Messages Stronger*

Negative Overtones
The glass is half empty.
We regret to inform you that you failed to complete the application process on time.
We will not be able to accommodate you before June 13.
Only a few students failed to qualify.
I don't think this wall can be painted because the piano is in the way.
More Positive Language
The glass is half full.
Your application arrived after the closing date.
The earliest date we can accommodate you is June 13.
Most of the students were successful.
We might be able to paint this wall if we can move the piano.

Activities and Exercises

1. The following short document is a student summary of Crist Inman and Cathy Enz's "Shattering the Myths of the Part-Time Worker" (*Cornell Hotel and Restaurant Administration Quarterly*, October 1995, pp. 70–73; see pages 57–63 for the full article). It demonstrates many errors.
   a. If you were an instructor or supervisor receiving this document, what positive comment could you give to the student who wrote it?
   b. What errors in accuracy can you find?
   c. Choose one paragraph and revise it, correcting spelling, grammar, and usage errors.

Shattering the Myths of the Part-Time Worker

Background and Purpose

There is a general perception among managers that part-time workers are lacking in work ethics, competence, acceptance of company beliefs and have a higher rate of absenteeism. These beliefs have led to them being classes as inferior employees and therefore they tend to receive lower wages and little or no benefits.

Chris Inman and Cathy Enz have laid the groundwork to help managers understand why these perceptions have come about. They have categorized them as "Myths" and stated the facts based on a statistical approach.

Method

The food service industry is the focus of the study because a majority of the workers are on a part-time basis. A survey has been done using 125 employees selected from an established restaurant chain in NW USA of which 52 percent are part-time workers, and 50 percent women. A mix of race, age and type of job chosen at random.

The survey consist of questions asked on the following topics with part-time employment being the concept behind the questions:

- competency of part-time workers
- work ethics
- attendance
- acceptance/compliance with beliefs of the company
- operations value sharing

Each topic has a set of questions that have been evaluated using scales measuring the degree of agreement and/or importance of each question. For example using a scale ranging from very important to unimportant the "acceptance of company beliefs" was tabulated by asking specific questions about standard company beliefs like "cleanliness" and "customer service."

A statistical analysis using covariance was tabulated to determine the relationship between the above-mentioned questions and employee status (full-time or part-time), type of job, gender, age and race.

Based on the statistical data we found that

- Job type is significant to an employee's acceptance of company beliefs.
- Part-time or full time status is not a major contributor toward acceptance of company beliefs.
- Gender contributed toward attitude, value sharing, and attendance.
- Age did not play a significant role in any of the areas questioned.

The most noticeable outcome of the analysis is that job status does not significantly contribute toward any of the five areas questioned.

Discussion

Part-time workers contribute enormously to the food service industry by providing managers with flexible work schedules at lower wages and little or no benefits and compensation. Part-time workers, however have a high turnover rate. This is mainly because they are ill-treated not trained to do the job adequately or they find better opportunities. Our study has shown that perceptions are *Myths* that can be dismissed when the facts are highlighted.

The statistical analysis shows that job status does not contribute to either of the five areas relating to competence, work ethics, attendance, value sharing, and acceptance of company beliefs. Stereotyping of part-time workers has led to their reduced wage and negligible training; and due to these myths the industry is losing the money saved by lower wages and absent benefits because part-time employees have reduced efficiency and ill perception of management. This indicates a cycle that is only in the control of managers.

No studies or surveys are available to indicate that better benefits or increased wages to part-timers has improved the quality of business or reduced costs. Some companies such as Starbucks have provided benefit packages to their employees in the hope that it attracts the best employees in the market and reduces the rate of turnover and in turn reduces costs of training new employees.

Recommendations

Our study shows that part-time workers are just as good as full time employees, therefore tapping into their full potential can provide a company with a market advantage. Some things that are worth considering are:

- Offer a benefit/compensation package to part-time workers.
- Provide better training.
- Provide better opportunities for advancement.

A balanced combination of the above should help improve work attitude, improve efficiency and reduce the turnovers so that a company can gain an edge in today's market.

2. Revise the following messages so that they sound more positive:
   a. Convincing city hall of this idea will be a real problem.
   b. We will not be able to serve the special dessert you requested because the chef failed to order the fresh coconuts.
   c. The wedding will not be delayed if the bride does not miss her flight.
   d. Overcrowding in the cafeteria during construction will upset everyone. The renovations will not be complete until October.
3. The following memo was posted in a local automotive showroom. Prepare a revision using language that motivates and encourages rather than berates. Also look for ways to improve grammar, content, and layout.

TO: All Sales Staff
FROM: Sam Furedi
DATE: September 29, 2002
SUBJECT: Customers smoking in the showroom and in new cars

This is a reminder that under **no** circumstances is **anyone** allowed smoking in the showroom or in the new cars. Some customers have been getting away with this. If you encounter a customer smoking in the showroom, please remind them politely of the **no smoking signs** on all of our doors and ask them to finish and extinguish in one of the sand trays located at all entrances/exits outside before they come back in. If they are belligerent you may repeat yourself firmly or get me. Second hand smoke stinks up the showroom and makes the whole atmosphere of new cars on display feel and smell used. This is totally unacceptable. There is also evidence that clients have been smoking in new cars during test drives! THIS IS HORRIBLE FOR BUSINESS! These are new cars and **must** be presented as such. They must smell new during test-drives. Many customers love and look forward to that new scent. Please remind clients prior to a Test Drive that if they do smoke, we have a **strict policy** against this in the cars and showroom. They may have a smoke and a free hot coffee from our machine if they wish, outside next to a sand tray prior to the test drive or at any time during their visit. Larger *No Smoking* signs will be mounted tomorrow.

Smoking in the new cars or showroom will not be tolerated in any way. We are otherwise having a great season. Thank you everyone.

For further assignments dealing with the content of this chapter, see case studies 1, 3, 12, 17, and 18 starting on page 275.

Courtesy

As with clarity, you probably think about courtesy most when it's not there. Shoppers, for example, know about courtesy—or the lack of it—in salespeople, service, and follow-up. You've probably also experienced unreadable instruction manuals, abrupt and pompous form letters, and indecipherable legal documents.

courtesy

Courtesy is closely related to the term "curtsy." "Courtesy" denotes respect, thoughtfulness, and even elegance.

As a writer, you should treat your readers the way you would treat visitors to your workplace. You can apply some simple techniques to help make even business or technical writing relaxed, gracious, and just plain polite.

Use Conversational Language

You probably wouldn't wear a tuxedo to work and bow to your customers. Yet, all too often, writers feel that achieving a professional tone means using stiff and formal language. Sometimes this style of writing is called "businessese." If you find yourself trying to come up with a "$50 word," you're probably trying to use language to impress your audience—a practice to avoid. Aim instead for a style that sounds conversational, comfortable, and normal for you. One way to check your own writing style is to think about how you might speak during a business telephone call. Look at the examples in Table 4.1.

Many business and technical writers have difficulty realizing that the simpler expression is the better choice. The more common the word, the more people will understand what you are trying to say.

Preparing a rough draft of your work may seem like a chore, but it pays off every time. Failing to work from notes or to write a draft may cause you to omit important details or, maybe worse, to send a garbled message that sounds like the one in Sample Document 4.1.

Table 4.1 *Formal and Conversational Language*

Would you say This? or	This?
You are herewith requested to return the contracts to the undersigned.	Please send us the contracts.
May I take this opportunity to thank you for your kind communication of recent date?	Thank you for writing. *or* Thank you for your letter.
As per our agreement, all our efforts will be mobilized in order to expedite delivery at the earliest possible date.	As we agreed, we will do our best to deliver your order as soon as possible. (*or* by Friday July 6th)
We are in receipt of your letter.	We have received your letter.

garbled

Garbled is an apt term probably derived from the Italian term *garbeilo,* which means "waste" or "refuse"—specifically, the castoff material that was left over when spices were sifted. Save the good stuff; dispose of the *garbeilo.*

Focus on the Reader

A first draft may focus on what the writer knows, wants, or needs. *Reader-based writing* (sometimes called writing with a "you" attitude) is writing that focuses on the receiver's needs, attitudes, feelings, and wants.

Consider the pairs of examples in Table 4.2.

Table 4.2 *Writer-Based and Reader-Based Writing*

Writer-Based	Reader-Based
Our store is open until 10 every night.	You can shop until 10 every night.
I want to use my computer knowledge in this job.	Your company will benefit from my knowledge of payroll software.
I want some peace and quiet in this house.	You can play computer games if you turn the sound down.
We have been in the landscape business for 46 years.	The beauty of your home has been our concern for 46 years.

Sample Document 4.1 *A Garbled Message*

Highway 60, R.R. 2
Mirror Falls, Ontario L3R 4R4

Tel.: (705) 777-4000 Fax: (705) 777-4001
ultaspa@playground.on.ca

TO: Shift Supervisor

FROM: Arla Gwin

DATE: Feb. 12, 2002

SUBJECT: Reasons why the calling in process needs to be changed

Information provided to employees is encoded in both the mediums of print and that of voice, as employees are told by their training supervisor as to the policy and are responsible for reading the employee handbook that outlines the policy regarding sick calls. The problem that arose was that the crew would simply call their restaurant three hours prior to their scheduled shift and leave a message on voice mail informing management that they were ill. In the fast-paced restaurant environment it is rare that management has time to check the voice mail for messages. Several times the restaurant would be short-staffed during the peak hours. Management had no grounds to discipline employees for this action because the crew had never been informed that leaving a message on voice mail was not an appropriate way to inform of the inability to attend a scheduled shift.

Sample documents 4.2 and 4.3 are two versions of the same letter: the first is definitely writer-based, while the second, revised version focuses on the reader.

Sample Document 4.2 *Focusing on the Writer*

WEST LINE COMMUNICATIONS

Specialists in Long-Distance Savings
91 Riverside Drive
Windsor, Ontario N6T 4J4
(519) 555-2345

June 19, 2002

Mrs. J. Santana
Goldfinger Jewellers
1234 Estate Road
Amherstberg, Ontario
N6N 8L1

Dear Mrs. Santana

RE: Savings Card Inquiry

We have received your request for an analysis of long-distance sales figures. We want you to know that we will be in your area during the week of June 28.

We need to book a two-hour period in order to collect all the data we require. Our representative, Bob Markels, will process your data within two days.

We guarantee a result that saves our customers at least 17 percent per annum. In fact, usually we are able to produce a much greater saving.

We pride ourselves on our service and look forward to your business. We have enclosed two coupons for free multi-party calls.

Yours truly

Charles Nordal

Charles Nordal
President

Enc.: three-way coupon

Sample Document 4.3 *Demonstrating the "You" Approach*

WEST LINE COMMUNICATIONS

Specialists in Long-Distance Savings
91 Riverside Drive
Windsor, Ontario N6T 4J4
(519) 555-2345

June 19, 2002

Mrs. J. Santana
Goldfinger Jewellers
1234 Estate Road
Amherstberg, Ontario
N6N 8L1

Dear Mrs. Santana

RE: Savings Card Inquiry

Your request for a long-distance sales analysis arrived today. Your service representative, Bob Markels, will contact you and set up an appointment for the week of June 28th. You should plan on a two-hour time frame.

You will receive the results within two days. You have our guarantee of at least a 17 percent reduction in your long-distance costs; many customers experience even greater savings.

Thank you for contacting West Line Communications. Enclosed are two coupons for free multi-party calls. We look forward to serving you.

Yours truly

Charles Nordal

Charles Nordal
President

Enc.: coupons

Achieving a Reader-Based Sound

To make your writing sound more reader-based, look for the significant words and notice their position in a sentence. For example, Sample Document 4.2 uses the words "we" and "our" twelve times; Sample Document 4.3 uses the same words only two times. Sample Document 4.2 uses the words "you" and "your" only five times, while Sample Document 4.3 uses them nine times.

Sprinkling a few *yous* throughout a letter, however, will not necessarily make a document reader-based. You also have to consider what information is important to the reader. See Table 4.3.

Table 4.3 *Writer-Based and Reader-Based Information*

Writer-Based	Reader-Based
I have had 10 years' experience as a landscape architect, as you can see from my résumé.	My 10 years' experience as a landscape architect would enable me to make significant contributions to your property management department.
We need your confirmation by February 15th.	To allow time to prepare the meeting rooms as you requested, we need your confirmation by February 15th.

Electronic Communication

Electronic communication is changing so rapidly that no textbook is likely to be completely up-to-date with guidelines or advice on this subject. Courtesy, however, never goes out of date. The guidelines in this section can be applied to every form of 21st-century communication.

Fax

A fax requires a cover page that provides a clear context for the message it accompanies (see Sample Document 4.4). It should include

- the sender's name, company name, return address, telephone and fax numbers, and e-mail address
- the sender's job title and department, where appropriate
- the receiver's name, company name, address, and fax number
- the date
- the total number of pages, including the cover page
- a brief summary of the contents of the fax
- a contact name and telephone number in case the fax transmission is unsuccessful

Sample Document 4.4 *Fax Cover Page*

Highway 60, R.R. 2
Mirror Falls, Ontario L3R 4R4

Tel.: (705) 777-4000 Fax: (705) 777-4001
ultaspa@playground.on.ca

FAX TRANSMISSION

TO: Suma Inatamda
Atlas Foods
18 Shore Drive
Charlottetown, PEI
C4A 2P9

FAX NO.: (902) 866-5789

FROM: Allan Farnham
Manager, Catering Department

DATE: May 30, 2002

NO. OF PAGES (including fax cover): 6

MESSAGE

Confirmation documents for Order No. 24-664:

floorplan
cost estimates signed by client
tentative schedule
list of contacts

I'll be sending the final schedule by June 5th.

Please contact Elena at (705) 777-4001 if any pages are not clearly received.

A fax is usually used as a timesaver. Frequently, material that is faxed is later delivered in its original form as well. This is especially true with legal or official documents. The very term "fax" comes from the word "facsimile," which denotes a representation. So a faxed document is not, in fact, the *real* document. If you are faxing material, check first to make sure a faxed copy is acceptable. If you are signing a contract, the original should at least be kept on hand for verification later, if necessary. Sometimes you can fax a document so the receiver can begin working on a project with the assumption that the original is in the mail. Faxed documents should follow all of the usual guidelines for letters, memos, or reports (these will be discussed in detail in later chapters).

Voice Mail

The experience of becoming lost in a maze of electronic messaging annoys most people, but it's an experience that will probably not go away soon. The information and staffing requirements of most large companies today almost dictate that they use automated messaging for convenience, efficiency, and 24-hour service.

However, for a small business or your home telephone, if you anticipate business calls, you do have more control. Whether you are creating a voice mail greeting or leaving a voice mail message, keep in mind the things that annoy you and try to avoid them.

Creating a Greeting

A one-time, general greeting is the easiest to use. Keep it short—brevity is certainly appreciated by those who call long-distance—and informative. Businesses should avoid cute, lengthy messages with musical backgrounds. This is also good advice if you have applied for a job and given the employer your home telephone number. If possible, avoid saying, "I will return your call as soon as I can," and provide a more specific time frame. See Box 4.1 for examples of effective and ineffective greetings.

You might prefer to change your greeting every day to reflect your presence or absence at work. One problem with repeating the following kind of message is that its repetitive nature can result in your voice sounding boring and uninviting:

> Hello. You've reached Sam Wu on Monday, January 12. I will not be in the office until Friday the 16th. Please leave a message with your name and telephone number. I'll return your call after I am back in the office. If you need immediate help, press 0 and one of our receptionists will help you.

Box 4.1 ***Make Your Greeting Informative and Brief***

Hello. You have reached the voice mail of Alexandra Berringer in Accounting. I am either on the phone or away from my desk. Please leave a message that includes the date and time of your call. I will try to return your call within one day. If you need immediate help, press 0 and the operator will redirect your call. ✓

Thank you for calling Zappoli Industries. Please leave your name and telephone number as well as the time of your call. If possible, give us the contract number you are calling about. We will try to return your call the same day it is received. ✓

Hello. Thank you for calling Airwave Awnings. We are pleased to be the region's foremost suppliers of awnings, tents, window blinds, and canvas tarpaulins. Whatever your needs, you can be sure of the quality of our products. We're sorry that no one is available to take your call at the moment. However, if you would kindly leave your name and number, we'll get back to you. ✗ *(This greeting is too long and vague, and does not give a time frame for returning messages.)*

Repeated every few days, over and over, this message will become stale. Try changing the content slightly from time to time to prevent this problem. Adding some positive vocabulary, as in the following example, also helps:

> Hello. This is Sam Wu. Today is Wednesday, January 14. I am not working in the office today. However, if you leave me a clear message with your name and the time you called, I'll be glad to get back to you on Thursday. As usual, if you need immediate help, press 0 and one of our receptionists will redirect your call.

Leaving a Voice Mail Message

> Himynameiscarollneedsomehelploggingontothewebsitemyextensionis5623pleasecallmeback.

One of the more annoying situations in the workplace is an indecipherable voice mail message. In order to serve you efficiently, companies require the following information at a minimum:

- your name, title, and company—clearly and carefully spoken and spelled, if necessary
- your telephone number with an area code—again, spoken clearly and slowly
- any other relevant information, such as a file or account number or a product name
- a *brief* summary of the reason for your call *or* a specific request if it is brief
- the date and time that you called

If you have to leave a long message, make a couple of brief notes ahead of time so you can leave your information clearly and in a logical order. Perhaps the biggest mistake that people make with voice mail is speaking too quickly. If you read your message, you will speak more slowly. As a guide, consider that you should take approximately 30 seconds to leave the message in Box 4.2. Practising this timing will give you an idea of the rate of speaking that will accommodate the person who receives your message.

Box 4.2 ***Slow Down When You Leave a Message***

> Hello. I am calling from Circa Products. My name is Carol Schmidte, spelled S-C-H-M-I-D-T-E. It is 9:30 a.m. on Tuesday, September 2. We have received an overdue notice on our account, but we are missing the original invoice for our July shipment of ink. Please call me back. My number is 5 5 5 6 7 3 4, extension 3 3 0. If I am not here, you can speak with Hector Lorello at extension 3 3 5. Thanks. 'Bye.

E-mail

E-mail messages are so easy to send that it's hard to imagine their use will do anything but increase. Etiquette and common sense in the use of e-mail for business and technical communication should be no different than face-to-face messages. Remember that although e-mail is quick and easy to send, it carries the same impact as any kind of message. Don't use it without thought.

Look at the headings on most e-mails, and you'll see that they are essentially memos. They should be treated as such. Review the guidelines for setting up and writing appropriate memos (see Chapter 8). If your message is clearly a letter rather than a memo, consider preparing the letter as you normally would and including it as an attachment to the e-mail rather than simply keying it into the body of the e-mail.

Keep in mind that, since e-mail can be printed, it is a form of written communication. When you send e-mail, try to think of the things you yourself dislike in messages and avoid inflicting those ills on your receivers. Don't put anything in an e-mail that you wouldn't write on paper. Avoid using e-mail for any information that is highly sensitive or private or that is likely to upset your reader. If possible, don't rely on e-mail for messages that are urgent; a telephone call is more appropriate in these cases. Always think twice before you hit the Send button.

E-mail works well in situations where a series of short messages must be sent back and forth quickly. It is, of course, especially useful when both (or all) parties work online on a regular basis. Distribution lists can be timesavers, but check before using them to make sure everyone on the list is an appropriate receiver. If you receive a message that has been sent to a distribution list, check before you reply. Will your reply go to everyone on the list or just to the originator of the message?

As a receiver of e-mail, make use of available techniques for controlling massive volumes of messages. Use filters to eliminate spam (junk mail), and learn to create and organize folders for storing and organizing your messages.

Activities and Exercises

1. Revise and reorganize the memo in Sample Document 4.1. Prepare and send the memo to your instructor as an e-mail.
2. Revise the following messages to make them more courteous, reader-based, and conversational:
   a. We are so proud to announce the opening of our new cafeteria.
   b. We only rent power tools to customers who can demonstrate experience using them.
   c. It has been brought to my attention recently through several e-mails and telephone conversations that many of the employees feel management has not been communicating to the employees about the recent renovations within the Engineering Department.
   d. Utilize all possible personnel to achieve completion of the projects in the most expeditious manner possible.
   e. We have prepared and designed many new ideas that we think will be of interest to our customers.
3. Revise the following cover letter. Try to incorporate a more reader-based approach, and correct any other writing problems you discover.

> Dear Sir/Madam:
>
> I am a recent graduate of Alexandrian College. I attained a diploma in the three-year computer programmer analyst program. I would like to apply for the position of computer Programmer that I saw in the *Windsor Star.*
>
> In addition, I have contributed greatly to the City of Windsor's intranet by authoring webpages and publishing a user guide to the intranet's new software application. After working in the city hall and at the company of Networx as a data entry clerk, I was provided with enough knowledge in dealing with different office procedures.
>
> I am confident that the computer knowledge I attained from my education and the strong computer and mathematical skills gained form my past work experiences will be an asset to whichever company hires me.
>
> I have enclosed a copy of my résumé for your review. I can be reached any time at the number stated.
>
> I am looking forward to hearing from you.

4. Working in a small group, discuss what you know about "netiquette" for business communications. Some of the topics you might cover are

   - using short forms and emoticons
   - sending or receiving junk e-mail
   - using e-mail to solicit new business
   - using long distribution lists (many addressees)
   - deleting e-mail messages without replying to them
   - using grammar and spelling rules

   List five rules you think are most important. Share and compare your list with those of other groups.

5. Do this exercise with a partner. At a time specified by your instructor, call your partner and leave a clear voice mail message with the following information. You may invent the second and third items.

   - your full name
   - the name and telephone number of a business near your home
   - the name and extension number of an employee in that business

   Later, in class, compare the information you received with the message your partner actually left. If possible, practise this exercise in class with a tape recorder.

For further assignments dealing with the content of this chapter, see case studies 1, 2, 9, 12, 13, 14, 18, and 20 starting on page 275.

Choreography

Whether you are writing a short memo or a long proposal, part of your task is to arrange the content into an organized and accessible document.

choreography

Choreography is a wonderful term derived from two Greek words, *choros* and *grafo*, which mean "dance" and "write." Normally, choreography refers to the written arrangement of a dance; in this chapter, it refers to the arrangement of a piece of writing on the page.

Readers of English follow a top-to-bottom, left-to-right pattern. The eye focuses first on an area slightly above the centre and to the left. A page of a document can have three elements: text, graphics, and white space. If these three combine with balance and symmetry, they make a page inviting and accessible.

Page Components

Text is any part of the page that consists of readable language symbols: words and numerals.

- Ensure that the font you use is readable, familiar, and appropriately sized. Ask someone who wears bifocals to read your document if you have any doubts about the font size.
- Stick with two or three different fonts at the most. Incorporating too many different fonts creates a cluttered and confusing appearance.
- Use a *serif* font—one that has small strokes on the ends of the letters, like the font used for this book—for the main body of a printed document. Use a *sans serif* font (like this one) for main headings.
- Avoid using all capital letters for large blocks of text. You will just make reading difficult.
- Remember that text arranged vertically is very difficult to read.

White space is more than just what's left over after you've finished your writing. White space should not be an afterthought; it enhances the readability of any document. Without adequate white space, your document will look uninviting and boring, or even cluttered and confusing.

- Use indentation, centring, columns, and line spacing to avoid filling page after page with continuous text.
- Use headings and short paragraphs to break text into more manageable chunks.
- Use adequate margins, which act as frames for your text. They affect readability and can even set the mood for your document.
- Avoid automatically choosing justified alignment. Justification produces square blocks of text that may actually be harder to read, especially if your printer does not adjust the spacing between words appropriately.
- Use white space as a method of highlighting to direct the reader's attention to important details. Boxes or printed frames also draw the reader's eye to blocks of text, and they anchor graphics to the page.

Headings

We all crave organization skills when we encounter situations that seem scattered and confusing. So, for example, we try to organize

- our time, so we can get multiple tasks completed efficiently
- our closets, so we can find the things we want
- our files, so we don't lose important information

When we fail to organize, we end up with something that resembles the inside of our neighbour's garage.

Organization requires a structure or framework. Think of the closet organizers that are sold in home furnishing stores: they have many shelves, drawers, and modular sections so that an entire wardrobe can be not only neat but also easy to manage. Various frameworks are available to organize written material. To determine whether a framework is useful, think about why the following would *not* work:

- a telephone book in which the entries are organized by people's age
- a library where the books are arranged according to the colour of their covers
- a supermarket where the items are arranged alphabetically

The problem with these systems is that they do not match the intended use of the material.

- You use a telephone book to search for names, so the organizing scheme needs to use those names, and an alphabetical arrangement works best.
- In the library, you look for books mainly by subject, so the books are classified by subject. Supplementary organizing systems allow you to search alphabetically for authors and titles.

- In the supermarket, the arrangement becomes a bit more complex since items are arranged according to storage requirements (e.g., refrigeration), use (frozen vegetables, frozen desserts, etc.), and marketing considerations (impulse items closest to the checkout counters).

The key to a good organization scheme, then, is a structure in which all the items will fit so they can be easily found. Consider the following group of miscellaneous items:

red sock	ping-pong ball
mandolin	package of gum
coffee mug	pencil
flowerpot	telephone
teaspoon	dictionary
bath towel	

At first sight, organizing such a group might seem difficult or impossible. The key involves discovering categories that will bring together items with related uses. For example, you could create categories based on use (see Table 5.1).

Table 5.1 *Categories Based on Related Uses*

Household Items	Office Items	Recreational Items
red sock	pencil	mandolin
coffee mug	telephone	flowerpot
teaspoon	dictionary	ping-pong ball
bath towel		package of gum

Or you could create categories based on principal material (see Table 5.2).

Table 5.2 *Categories Based on Materials*

Ceramic	Wood	Fabric	Plastic	Paper
coffee mug	mandolin	red sock	telephone	package of gum
flowerpot	pencil	bath towel	ping-pong ball	dictionary
			teaspoon	

Or, you could create categories based on weight (see Table 5.3).

Table 5.3 *Categories Based on Weight*

100 g or less	101–200 g	201–400 g	401+ g
red sock	teaspoon	coffee mug	bath towel
ping-pong ball	package of gum	flowerpot	telephone
pencil			dictionary
			mandolin

Notice the following characteristics about tables 5.1 to 5.3:

- Each section deals with a feature that is similar, such as use, material, or weight.
- Items in each list relate to the heading directly above. If the tables were shelves and an item fell off, you would know which shelf to put it back on.
- Each category has more than one item in it. If a category is too short, it should be combined with another; if it is too long, it should be divided into more categories.

The same principles that apply to sorting objects on shelves apply to sorting information in a document. In a document, the shelves are created by headings.

Linear schemes, as the name implies, go in a straight line. Every item has the same value. These are fairly simple arrangements, often based on alphabetical, numerical, or chronological patterns. See Figure 5.1.

Relational (or hierarchical) schemes consist of two or more linear patterns used together, resulting in main categories and subsections of categories. See Figure 5.2.

Choosing useful headings is another method of greatly improving the readability of even the most complex document. Here are a few guidelines to keep in mind:

- The main headings should be *linear*; that is, each should have about the same importance in the document. All first-level headings should have the same importance, all second-level headings should have the same importance, and so on. Look at the headings in this book for examples.
- If a heading does not have enough information, it should be combined with the previous heading. If it has too much, it should be divided further into subheadings.
- The amount of information under each heading should be reasonably balanced. For example, try to avoid having one heading followed by pages of text, and the next heading followed by only one paragraph if the headings are meant to be equally important.

Figure 5.1 *Example of a Linear Pattern*

Mon. June 4	Fri. June 8
Tues. June 5	Sat. June 9
Wed. June 6	Sun. June 10
Thurs. June 7	Notes

Figure 5.2 *Example of a Relational Pattern*

I.
    A.
        1.
            a.
            b.
        2.
            a.
            b.
        3.
    B.

II.

Some writers like to set up their headings before they begin to write. This method may feel strange at first, but it does give you a useful grid into which to place your information.

- Use a combination of font changes and indenting to make each level of heading visibly different.
- Avoid using too many headings or too many heading levels.
- Review your list of headings apart from the rest of the content. They should provide a miniature overview of your document, much like a table of contents.
- Have at least *two* branches whenever you subdivide a heading; that is, every level should have at least *two* headings. Remember: Subheadings are divisions; you cannot divide something into only one part.

Table 5.4 and Figure 5.3 demonstrate how a series of linear headings develops into a relational pattern. A document moves from a *linear* to a *relational* set of headings when the material under the first level of headings needs more sorting. Figure 5.4 expands the grid further. If you convert it into a series of headings and paragraphs, it might look like the outline in Figure 5.5.

Table 5.4 ***A Set of Linear Headings***

Background	Method	Discussion
Purpose	Findings	Recommendations

Figure 5.3 ***Moving from Linear to Relational Headings***

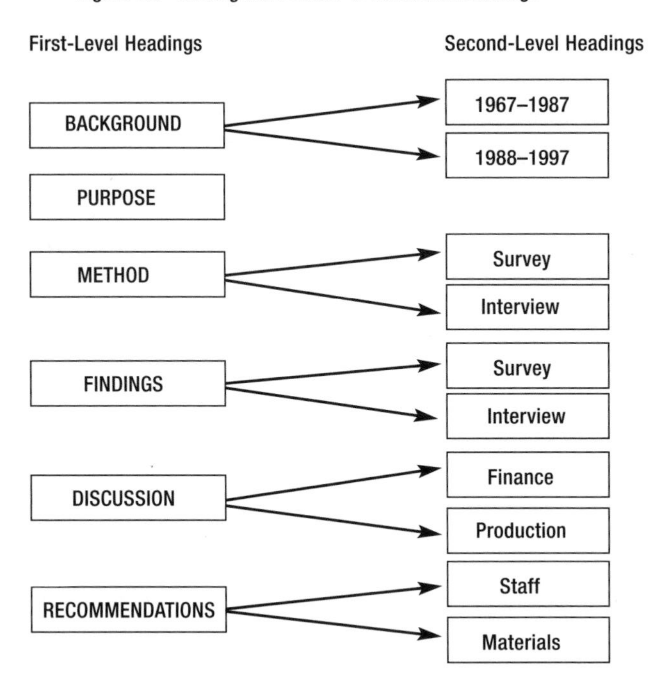

Figure 5.4 *Grid with Main Headings and Subheadings*

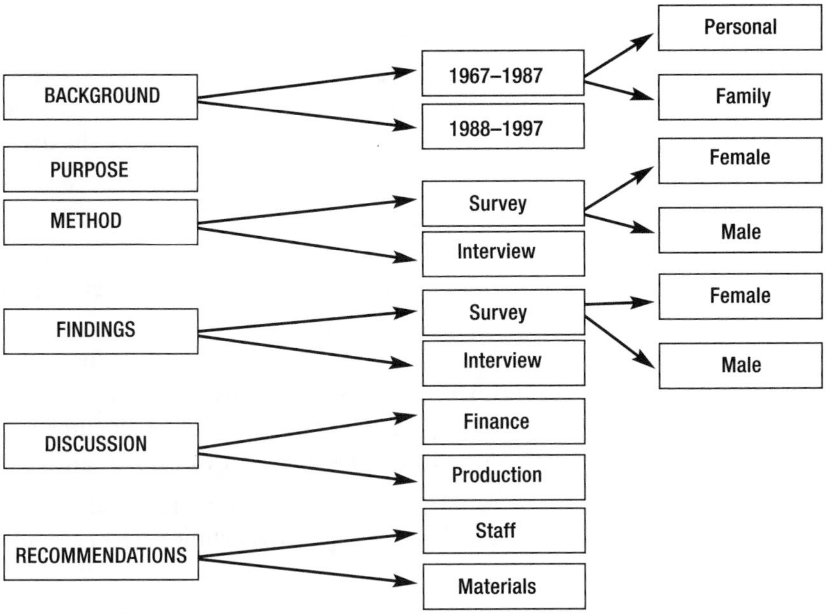

BACKGROUND
1967–1987
Personal
Family
1988–1997
PURPOSE
METHOD
Survey
Female
Male
Interview
FINDINGS
Survey
Female
Male
Interview
DISCUSSION
Finance
Production
RECOMMENDATIONS
Staff
Materials

Figure 5.5 *Outline for a Report*

- BACKGROUND
    - 1967–1987
        - Personal
        - Family
    - 1988–1997
- PURPOSE
- METHOD
    - Survey
        - Female
        - Male
    - Interview
- FINDINGS
    - Survey
        - Female
        - Male
    - Interview
- DISCUSSION
    - Finance
    - Production
- RECOMMENDATIONS
    - Staff
    - Materials

Cognitive Order

Organizing information requires both a cognitive (or logical) and a visual (or spatial) layout that allows easy access. You don't want content to just look good—you want it to make sense too. Determining the order in which to present your information can be daunting. As usual, the purpose and target audience for the document will guide the decisions you make.

- Purpose: Are you writing an annual report, a set of instructions for operating a lathe, a proposal to open a branch office, or a résumé? These and many other workplace documents have conventional systems of arrangement that readers expect to find.
- Audience: Who will the readers be, and how will they use the material? Is there one main piece of information your readers will want? Will they use your document as a frequent reference source? Will they compare it with other similar documents? Will they keep the document, pass it along to other readers, or discard it quickly?

The difficulty in making a choice arises from the fact that a document can always be arranged more than one way, so there will rarely be only one *correct* choice. Here are just a few of the possibilities:

- Spatial or geographical: This choice would work well for an atlas, a weather map, or a fire inspection report. The writer arranges information from left to right, north to south, bottom to top, or east to west.
- Chronological: The information moves from decade to decade, from morning until night, or from the most recent event to the earliest.
- Classification: A product catalogue might use this method: it distinguishes departments, products, or even positions within a company.
- Priority: The document starts with what's most (or least) important.
- Level: This method works for a textbook: it begins with the easiest material and moves to the most difficult.
- Process: The information begins at step one and works through all required steps in order.
- Problem and solution: The writer describes one problem or a series of problems and provides solutions.

Activities and Exercises

Working in a group, read the article by Inman and Enz that follows. Divide the information in the article under the following headings. You should be able to assign each piece of information to one heading.

- Background
- Purpose
- Method
- Findings
- Discussion
- Recommendations

Your instructor may ask you to rework the article in report format using your own words as much as possible.

Shattering the Myths of the Part-Time Worker*

by Crist Inman and Cathy Enz

Crist Inman, Ph.D., is an assistant professor at the William F. Harrah College of Motel Administration at the University of Nevada, Las Vegas.

Cathy Enz, Ph.D., is an associate professor at the Cornell University School of Hotel Administration.

The time has come to tap the hidden talents and unappreciated potential of part-time employees, but first it's necessary to shatter managers' widely held beliefs about part-timers' work attitudes and behavior.

Part-time workers are an essential and flexible source of labor in the food-service industry. Reliance on part-time workers helps fill shifts during peak business periods while allowing for smaller shifts during slow business periods. Not only do these workers permit flexible scheduling, but on average they are less expensive to employ because they typically receive lower wages and many firms do not provide them with benefits.

Roughly two-thirds of the food-service–industry labor force is part-time.[1] The Bureau of Labor Statistics has reported that about 20 million employees in U.S. businesses—20 percent more than a decade ago—work fewer than 35 hours a week. Of those employees, six million work in the food-service industry.

Employing part-timers helps reduce wage outlays, but these workers frequently have high turnover rates. Often part-time workers simply move on to a better opportunity elsewhere, which may be another job in the food-service field. Frequently, however, they quit their jobs because they feel that they are unappreciated or, worse, ignored, and because they do not receive adequate training.[2] We feel that the beliefs some managers hold about part-time workers—often based on myth—contribute to the workers' dissatisfaction and turnover and cause managers to underuse them.

---

*Source: *Cornell Hotel and Restaurant Administration Quarterly,* October 1995, pp. 70–73. Reprinted with permission.

In this paper we offer a strategically useful view of part-time workers in the food-service industry and make suggestions for maximizing their impact in an organization.

The Myths about Part-Timers

The reader may recognize some of the following myths about part-time workers compared to full-time workers: they are inferior; less hardworking; less concerned with product quality, cleanliness of the operation, and cost control; and higher in absenteeism.

Such negative views are vividly captured in a study of managerial beliefs about part-time workers.[3] Open-ended interviews with 82 managers, union officials, and workers from a variety of industries, including food service, revealed that many managers have bought into the myths, believing part-time workers have less experience, fewer abilities, lower work standards, and less loyalty to their position and to the company and are more prone to absenteeism, tardiness, and theft than full-time workers. Many managers view part-time workers as less competent, less work-oriented, less reliable, and less committed to organizational values and philosophies.

Shattering the Myths

In a recent study we explored whether the negative stereotype of part-time workers was accurate. We found that critical work attitudes and behavior were as strongly exhibited by part-time workers as by full-time workers.[4]

The widely held belief that part-time workers have less commitment, less competence, and less willingness to work hard than full-time workers may be the result of historical stereotypes and self-fulfilling prophecy. The benefits they bring to the firm are twisted into an indictment of their abilities and attitudes. Those views may become institutionalized in the firm's recruiting, training, and management practices and compensation policies. Thus the actions of managers may make it more likely that part-timers will respond negatively.

Since, in fact, employee work attitudes do not vary with employment status (see the box on the next page), food-service firms that assume the worst of their part-time labor force are wasting resources. What they gain by using low-cost part-time workers may be lost through high turnover that results from treating them as less capable than full-time workers. By one estimate, the cost of replacing a single hospitality employee is at least $1700.[5] A wiser strategy for the food-service industry would be to stop underusing part-time workers and take better advantage of the scheduling flexibility they can provide.

Value added. Part-time workers should be treated as valuable assets. Starbuck's, the now-famous coffee shop chain, has carved out a profitable niche in the food-service market by doing just that. The company offers its

A Study of Part-Timer Attitudes

Our study contrasted the work attitudes of part-time and full-time food-service employees. We collected data from 125 employees in a full-service restaurant chain in the northwestern United States. Part-timers constituted 52 percent of the sample. The sample was evenly split between men and women, who were predominantly white and single. The typical tenure with the chain was two years, and respondents expected to stay with the company for an average of three years. The average employee had some college training.

We explored whether work attitudes and behavior vary depending on employment status. To test the assumptions we believe are prevalent in the food-service industry, we conducted a multivariate analysis of covariance on the sample responses. We controlled for age, gender, race, and job type to avoid the confounding effects of those factors.* We tested these managerial assumptions:

- Part-time food-service workers are less competent than are full-time workers.
- Part-time food-service workers have a weaker work ethic than do full-time workers.
- Part-time food-service workers have more absenteeism than do full-time workers.
- Part-time food-service workers have a lower level of acceptance of the organizational beliefs of restaurant cleanliness, cost control, honesty in guest relations, quality presentation of food and service, and high food quality than do full-time workers.
- Part-time food-service workers have a lower degree of value similarity with management on the values of efficiency, profits, adaptability, ethical behavior, company stability, quality, and service than do full-time workers.

The survey asked several questions on each of those topics. Work ethic was measured using an eight-item scale. The instrument captured the degree to which the respondents expressed a strong desire to work hard. A seven-point Likert-type scale was used, with the scale ranging from "completely disagree" to "completely agree." A work-ethic score was computed by summing the eight items in accordance with previous approaches.

---

* At the editor's suggestion we conducted the same analysis adding a further control to tenure in the job. Surprisingly, the results were unchanged.

(continued)

Competence was measured using a 12-item scale that captured the degree to which respondents viewed themselves as capable of performing their job.

To measure perceived absences, respondents were asked to indicate how many days they were absent from work for any reason except vacation in the previous year.

Acceptance of company beliefs was measured by asking respondents to indicate the degree of importance they attached to six widely articulated company beliefs or standards, using a seven-point Likert-type scale ranging from "very unimportant" to "very important." The beliefs included items such as the importance of food quality, restaurant cleanliness, cost controls, honesty in guest relations, and presentation of food and service.

To measure operating values, respondents were asked to indicate the degree to which they were similar to top management in six operations values (using a scale of value agreement developed by author Cathy Enz). Specific organizational values included efficiency, quality and service, profits, adaptability, ethical behavior, and company stability. The seven-point scale ranged from "very dissimilar" to "very similar."

The results may surprise food-service managers: we found that all the assumptions were wrong (see table, below). In short, part-time workers were not different from full-time workers on those five important measures of work attitude and behavior.

Some of the related findings are also interesting. Job type had a significant influence on acceptance of company beliefs. If there are certain jobs in which pockets of counterculture develop, and there are more part-timers in those jobs than in other types of jobs, that may be a source of the assumption that part-timers have inferior work attitudes. Nonetheless, our study provides evidence that it is not the work status but the job itself that influences the worker's acceptance of company beliefs. Gender was another source of difference in attitudes. Age, on the other hand, did not account for any differences in attitude or behavior, and neither did tenure in the job.

Most important, we found that an employee's status as a part-time or full-time worker did not account for any differences in the five attitudes. The desire to work hard, skill levels, loyalty to the restaurant, and absenteeism were not significantly influenced by the employment status of workers.

—C.I. and C.E.

(continued)

Multivariate Analysis of Covariance, F-Values

Independent Variables	Full-Time vs. Part-Time Work Status	Type of Job	Controlled for Gender	Age	Race
Acceptance of company beliefs	.77	2.6*	.87	.84	.85
Work ethic	.77	.69	.89	.83	.83
Competence	1.42	1.33	.90	.74	.79
Operations value-sharing	1.33	1.37	2.1†	1.62	.86
Absenteeism	.8	1.22	1.22	.70	1.20

* $p < .01$
† $p < .05$

Note: The only significant differences in worker attitudes were based on job type in the acceptance of company beliefs and gender in the sharing of operations values.

part-time employees high pay (by industry standards) and health benefits. Starbuck's proclaims that doing so differentiates it in the labor market, allowing it to hire the best workers.[6] That has made Starbuck's one of the fastest-growing, most profitable chains in the industry. Other firms are doing the same; for example, this year Hardee's made all its part-time workers eligible for health-care benefits.[7]

While there are no statistics available on how many food-service establishments provide health-care and other benefits to part-time employees, it has been estimated that in all industries combined, fewer than 25 percent of part-time workers receive health-care benefits, and fewer than 20 percent receive life-insurance benefits.[8] One way for food-service companies to differentiate themselves in the part-time–labor market may be to do exactly what Starbuck's and Hardee's have done: offer the benefits that part-time workers need.

Staying on Top of the Market

To use part-time workers as a competitive advantage, firms should follow the following practices.

- **Revise compensation strategies.** We found from our study that work attitudes and behavior did not differ based on work status. If part-timers' work is as valuable as is full-timers', basing wage differentials solely on the number of hours worked can send the wrong signal to the workforce. Firms in many industries have adopted pay programs based on knowledge and skills. That concept makes sense, and food-service firms should also offer incentives for *any* employee to provide improved customer service. Such a compensation system would not only be fair, it would also send a signal to all employees that it is ability, not employment status, that matters. It would also help firms attract and retain part-time workers with the strongest skills.
- **Provide adequate training.** While training is more costly on a per-hour-worked basis for part-timers than for full-time associates, the cost of not providing enough training—or not providing it at all—is even higher. As long as part-timers stick with the job, the overall training costs are diminished. Many firms provide part-timers minimal on-the-job training, and that can frustrate the undertrained workers, their co-workers, and the customers. The result can be high turnover and other forms of resistance among the part-time workers, thereby increasing the per-employee cost of selection and training.[9]

  One alternative is to have part-timers participate in the segments of the firm's formal training program (if there is one) that cover critical skills. Another alternative that some firms have developed for part-timers is a home-study course that teaches basic job skills, appropriate attitudes for various service situations, and ways to deal with the most commonly encountered on-the-job problems. Such a program can have a high payoff for a firm that has a substantial number of part-timers on its staff. Both alternatives let part-time workers know they are important members of the team and send a message to the other workers that management considers part-timers valuable.

- **Develop clear communication channels.** Typically, communication channels are opened during the recruiting process, when the interviewer explains what the job entails and what skills are needed. Those channels must be kept open. Part-time workers must be included in the day-to-day communication process. Job-related suggestions, announcements, firm news, and training updates should be directed to the entire staff. Part-time workers should not be ignored.
- **Open up the possibilities.** Part-time workers should be considered for some jobs that have traditionally been reserved for full-time workers. Many of the jobs in a typical food-service establishment should be within the reach of capable part-time workers who are paid a fair wage and properly trained. Full- and part-time workers have similar work-related values, beliefs, and behavior. Therefore part-time workers should have access to more jobs and responsibilities than are now within their reach.

- **Offer benefits.** Firms should look closely at the costs and advantages of offering health-care and other benefits to part-time employees. In a study of part-time workers in fields similar to food service (health care and retail), employees stated they wanted more vacation leave, merchandise discounts, and sick leave. The top three benefits that employees did not currently receive but wanted were cash bonuses, medical insurance, and sick leave.[10]

  While there are obvious differences in cost between leave benefits and medical insurance, withholding benefits from part-time employees is not likely to be a viable tactic in the future. The competition for part-timers will probably force food-service firms to consider offering some or all those benefits.

Competitive Advantage

Full- and part-time workers have similar work-related attitudes and behavior. Recognizing that fact will be an important step in developing new management strategies in the food-service industry to accommodate shifting demand patterns and shifting demographics.

The time has come to tap the hidden talents and unappreciated potential of part-time workers. They may be the most critical ingredient for gaining a competitive advantage. **CQ**

References

[1]National Restaurant Association and Deloitte Touche, *Restaurant Industry Operations Report* (Washington, DC: National Restaurant Association, 1993), p. 5.

[2]Mike Duff, "If You Notice Part-Timers Leaving, It's Too Late," *Supermarket Business*, Vol. 44 (May 1989), pp. 90, 115, 140. This story reports the results of a Cornell University survey of part-time employees in the food industry.

[3]Chris Tilly, "Dualism in Part-Time Employment," *Industrial Relations*, Vol. 31 (Spring 1992), pp. 330–347.

[4]C. Enz and C. Inman, "A Comparison of Attitudes and Work Practices of Part-Time and Full-Time Workers in the Food Service Industry" in *1992 Annual CHRIE Conference Proceedings* (Washington, DC: CHRIE, 1992), pp. 19–21.

[5]John J. Hogan, "Turnover, and What to Do about It," *Cornell Hotel and Restaurant Quarterly*, Vol. 33, No. 1 (February 1992), p. 40.

[6]Barbara Presley Noble, "At Work: Benefits? For Part Timers?" *New York Times*, August 16, 1992, Sec. 3, p. 23.

[7]Beth Belton and James Overstreet, "Take This Job ... Please!: Bidding War for Workers Stirs Creativity," *USA Today*, October 10, 1994, p. 1B. For other interesting examples outside the industry, see also: Samuel Greengard, "Leveraging a Low-Wage Work Force," *Personnel Journal*, January 1995, pp. 90–102.

[8]H.B. Williams, "What Temporary Workers Earn: Findings from a New BLS Survey," *Monthly Labor Review*, Vol. 112, No 3 (March 1989), pp. 3–6.

[9]For an interesting investigation of the various forms of resistance, see: Craig C. Lundberg, "Forms of Resistance by Temporary Hospitality Employees," *Hospitality Research Journal*, Vol. 18, No. 2 (1994), pp. 127–135.

[10]Helen I. Doerpinghaus and Daniel C. Feldman, "Employee Benefit Packages for Part-Time Workers," *Benefits Quarterly*, Second Quarter, 1993, pp. 72–82.

For further assignments dealing with the content of this chapter, see Case Study 14 starting on page 299.

Graphics

chapter six

Graphics such as illustrations, photographs, drawings, tables, and graphs appear in business and technical documents for two reasons:

- to clarify information—that is, to help the reader understand complex or detailed information more easily
- to speed up comprehension—a well-produced graphic will often reduce the amount you have to write, thus reducing the amount your audience has to read

Any graphic you use should be measured against these two points. Avoid using graphics merely as filler or decoration. The ease with which graphics can be produced on computers makes this a very real temptation.

Once you have decided to use graphics, plan how to incorporate them into your document effectively by considering their appearance, identification, and placement.

Appearance

- Put a frame around your graphic to separate it from the accompanying text.
- Label clearly: Labels should be horizontal and large enough to read comfortably.
- Judge the size of your graphic carefully; avoid using a full page for a simple graph or diagram.

Identification

- If your document contains only one graphic, it does not need a number. If your company has a rule for numbering graphics, follow it. Otherwise, the conventional system is as follows:
  - Tables are numbered consecutively: Table 1, Table 2, etc.
  - All other graphics are numbered consecutively as Figure 1, Figure 2, etc.
- Refer to the graphic, using its number, in the accompanying text.
- Provide a short title that emphasizes the main point of the graphic.
- Document the source if you have used a graphic from an outside source. You may need to obtain permission to legally reproduce someone else's work.

Placement

- Place graphics close to the text that describes them, preferably on the same page and following, not preceding, the relevant text.
- Avoid placing graphics all together at the end of a document unless they are part of optional material in an appendix.
- If a full-page graphic is to be placed sideways on the page (run vertically rather than horizontally), place it so the document is turned clockwise for reading.
- Avoid interrupting text with graphics; finish a paragraph so the logic of the text remains clear.

Types of Graphics

The types of graphics you use in a document depend on the information you are presenting. This section presents some common categories of graphics and the types of information they are best suited to.

Graphs

To compare data at a fixed point in time or at regular intervals, use a bar graph. Bar graphs may be horizontal or vertical; see Figure 6.1 for an example of a vertical graph.

Figure 6.1 *Vertical Bar Graph*

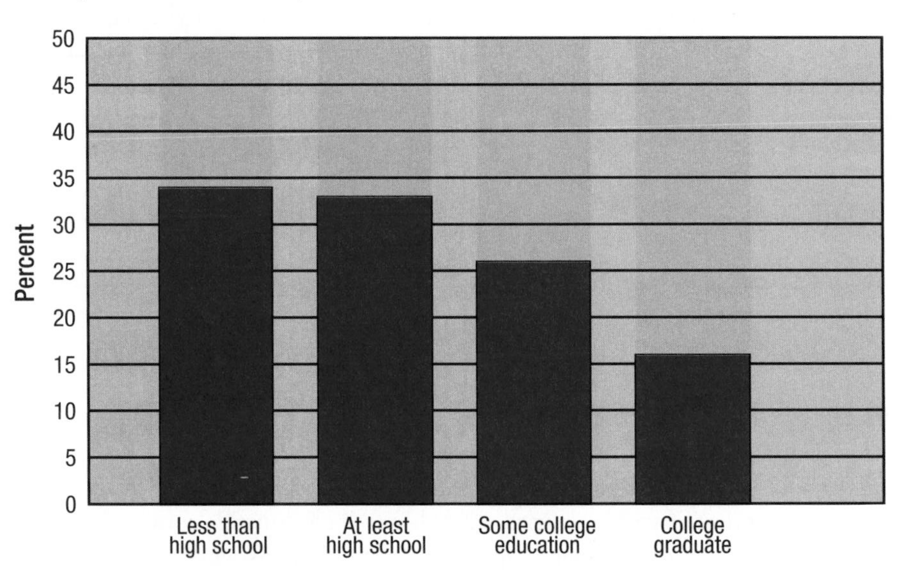

To show how data changes over a period of time, use a line graph. Figure 6.2 shows a simple graph with only one curve, but line graphs can include multiple curves. Make sure you distinguish different curves clearly for the reader; to do this, you can use different shades of grey or different colours or different line patterns (e.g., solid line, dashed line, dotted line, etc.). If the graph will be too cluttered with labels identifying the various curves, you will need to provide a legend to help the reader.

Figure 6.2 *Line Graph*

Percentage of Cigarette Smokers with at Least Some College Education

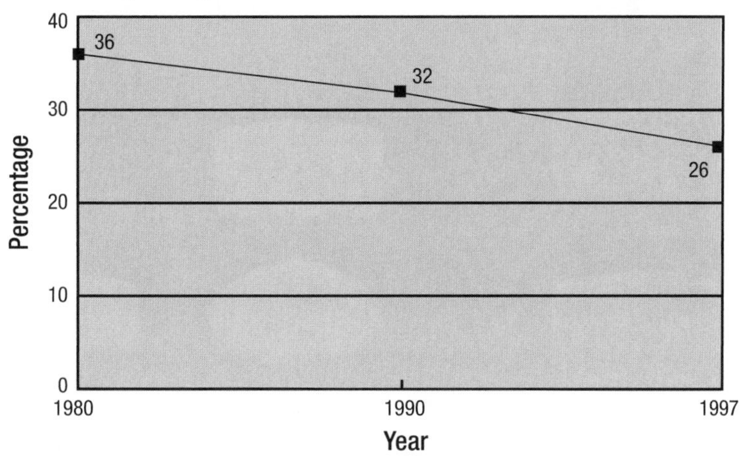

To show how a whole amount is divided into parts, use a pie graph (see Figure 6.3).

Figure 6.3 *Pie Graph*

Number of Smokers in Canada by Education Level, 1994–1995

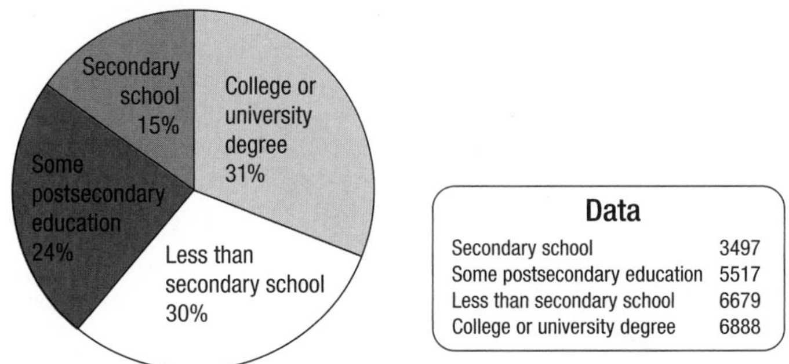

Source: Based on data from Health Canada, "Smoking behaviour of Canadians," *National Population Health Survey—Supplementary Tables 1994/95* (Table 4). Retrieved May 4, 2002, from http://www.hc-sc.gc.ca/hpb/lcdc/bc/nphs/tabls945/tab4_e.html.

Charts

To display how a process works or to clarify a complex process, use a flow chart (see Figure 6.4).

Figure 6.4 *Flow Chart*

If the washer will not operate, follow the steps outlined in this chart.

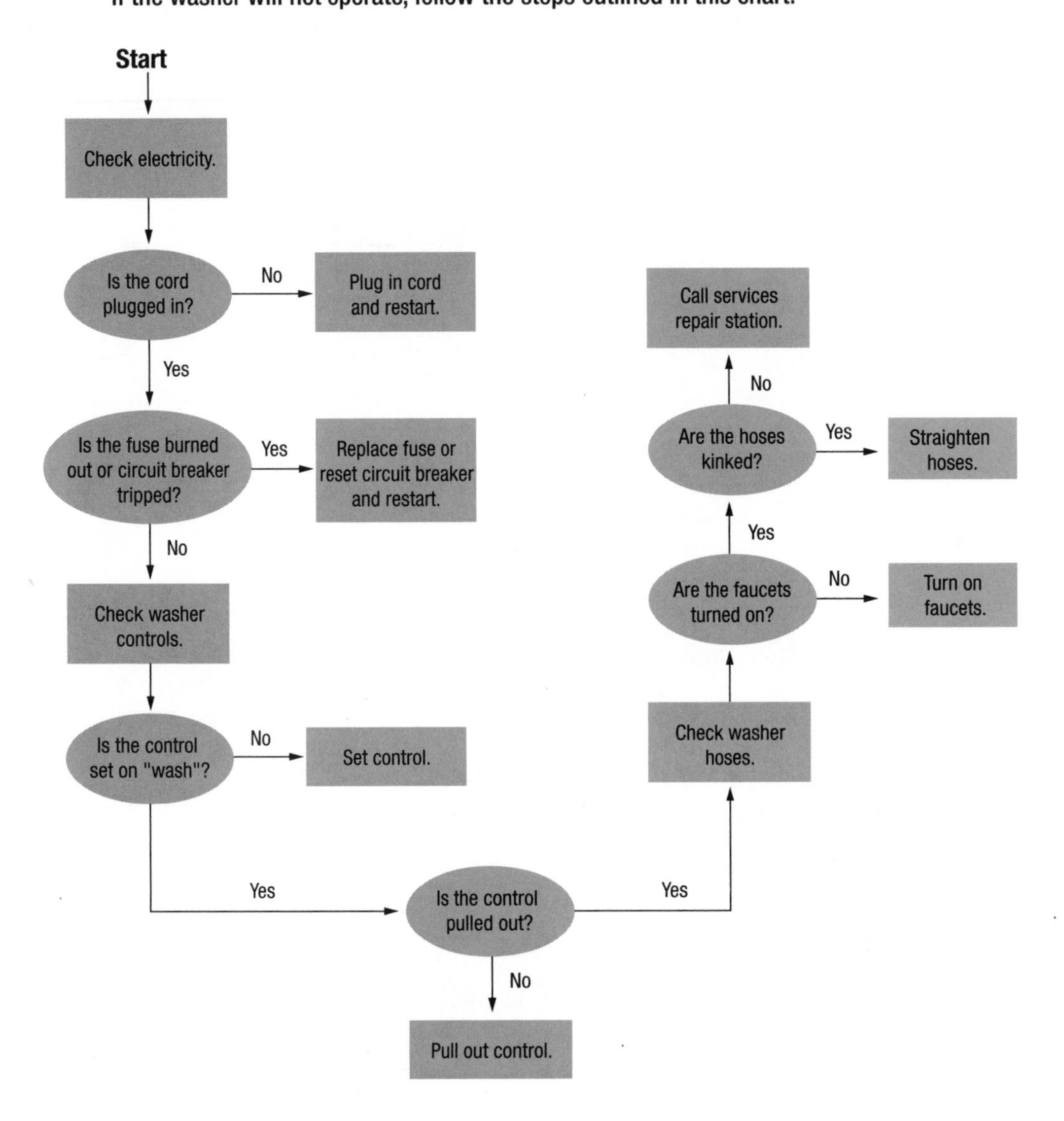

To display numerical data in different categories, use a table. Avoid overusing tables, however—they tend to be boring and difficult to read. Use them to highlight important information (see Table 6.1).

Table 6.1 *Table*

	Actual	Budget	Variance	Forecast	Variance	Last Year	Variance
Sales	75 606	39 033	36 573	50 407	25 199	29 908	45 698
Average Cheque (include all meal periods)	8.51	11.35	–2.84	10.82	–2.31	9.97	–1.46
Covers (include all meal periods)	2 199	768	1 431	1 025	1 174	776	1 423
Labour	1 115	673	442	336	779	694	421

A table that displays descriptive rather than numerical data (i.e., words, not numbers) is sometimes called a matrix (see Table 6.2).

Table 6.2 *Matrix*

Legal Interview Questions

Requirement	Can Ask (if a job requirement)	Cannot Ask
Ability to work overtime	Are you able to work extra hours during the week on a regular basis?	Have you made daycare arrangements? *(Makes the assumption that if the candidate had children it would affect his or her ability to work overtime.)*
Eligibility to work in Canada	Are you legally eligible to work in Canada?	Are you a Canadian citizen? *(Citizenship is not relevant.)*
Minimum level of education	Have you completed your high-school diploma?	What high school did you attend? *(This could uncover religious background.)*
Ability to travel	Would you be able to travel outside of the province from time to time?	Are you married? *(Makes an assumption that being married would influence ability to travel.)*

To produce a clear schedule for a long-term project, use a Gantt chart (see Figure 6.5).

Figure 6.5 *Gantt Chart*

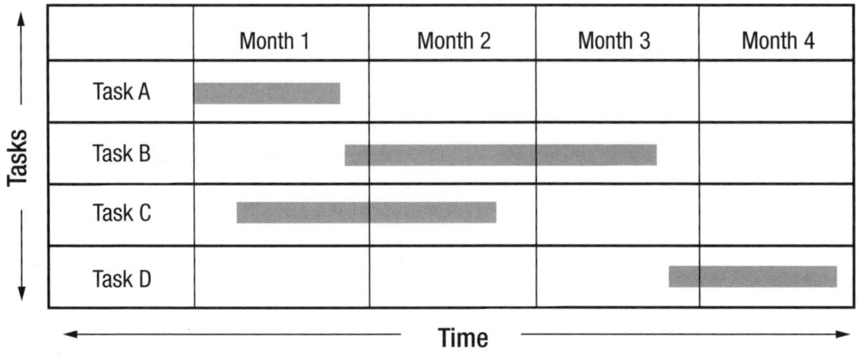

	Month 1	Month 2	Month 3	Month 4
Task A				
Task B				
Task C				
Task D				

Tasks

Time

Photographs, Drawings, and Diagrams

To show what something looks like, use a photograph, drawing, or diagram.

A photograph gives the most realistic view of how an object, person, or place looks. However, it can also leave out important information, such as small details, the inside of an object, and so on. Photographs of specific people or objects can be difficult to find or take yourself (e.g., if you need a photo of an urban street but live in a rural area). As well, it is difficult to present business services and abstract concepts in photographs—what would a photo of "life insurance" look like, for example?

Drawings can be used to overcome some of the limitations of photographs. They can show a little or a lot of detail. Because they can show perspective, drawings can also present information that is impossible to show in any other way—think of a cross-section of a mountain, for example.

Conversely, diagrams tend to simplify an object and use stylized shapes to get a message across quickly. Think of the well-known "no smoking" sign that has become almost universal: a cigarette in a circle with a line through it.

Figures 6.6 to 6.8 show three different ways of presenting what a sailing yacht looks like.

Figure 6.6 *Photograph*

Source: Benelux Press/PhotoDisc

Figure 6.7 *Drawing*

Figure 6.8 *Diagram*

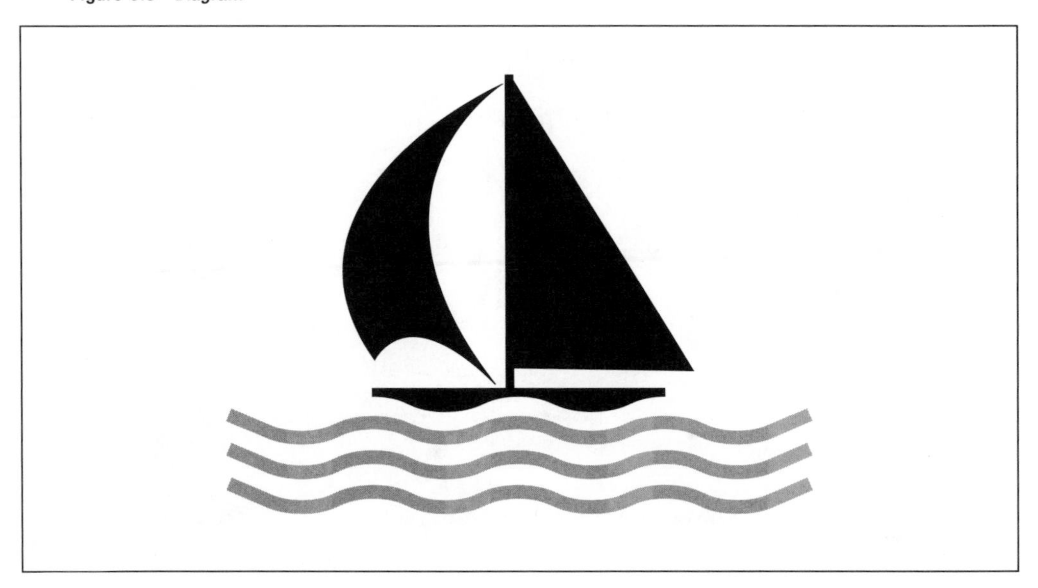

Activities and Exercises

1. Bring to class any workplace documents you can find (form letters, insurance policies, résumés, etc.). Discuss the effectiveness of the layout, font, and graphics.
2. Below are the results of three surveys on the language abilities of Branchton College students:

1982

89 percent were fluent in English
31 percent were fluent in English and French
40 percent were fluent in English and at least one language other than French
21 percent did not speak English at home

1992

81 percent were fluent in English
51 percent were fluent in English and French
61 percent were fluent in English and at least one language other than French
36 percent did not speak English at home

2002

70 percent were fluent in English
51 percent were fluent in English and French
65 percent were fluent in English and at least one language other than French
40 percent did not speak English at home

Prepare appropriate graphs to show the following information. Use a clear title for each graph.

a. Show the change in the percentage of students who were fluent only in English from 1982 to 2002.
b. Show the distribution just for the year 1982.
c. Compare the percentages of students who spoke more than one language fluently in 1982 and 2002.
d. Show how the percentage of students who did not speak English at home increased over the 20 years.

3. Use a flow chart to demonstrate the process you use to prepare an assignment in one of your classes, from the moment you receive the assignment until you hand it in. Compare your completed flow chart with those of classmates.
4. If you are working on any group assignments at present, prepare a Gantt chart to show the distribution of tasks or your schedule for getting the assignment finished.

For further assignments dealing with the content of this chapter, see case studies 5, 8, 12, 13, and 14 starting on page 280.

The *Ultimate Resort* and *Spa*

1 2 3 4 5

Part Two

Correspondence

A Business Letter Template

chapter **seven**

template

A *template* was originally a pattern for testing accuracy of form in woodworking.

Just as a pattern helps a woodworker achieve a level of consistency and accuracy in manufactured items, a template gives you a consistent background for all your business letters. The *template* is the collection of elements that set up the page on which you write your letter—in other words, everything but the actual message of the letter. Of course, your workplace may already use an established pattern, which you should follow.

Template Elements Above the Message

The following elements, which appear at the top of the letter, provide the context for the letter.

Letterhead

The *letterhead* contains information about the sender of the letter. Normally you will find the company's name, mailing address, telephone and fax numbers, e-mail address, website, and other related information, such as a company logo or slogan. Letterheads may be centred or off to one side. Sometimes they are even printed across the bottom of the page.

If you are writing personal letters from your home address (for example, a job application letter), you should provide your own address. Until recently, the format shown in Sample Document 7.1 was recommended, with only the writer's home address and the date at the top.

Sample Document 7.1 *Appropriate Format for Personal Return Address*

17 Roehampton Street
Windsor, ON
N6M 4T7

March 21, 2002

Simon Amberley
Building Supervisor
The Ultimate Resort and Spa
Highway 60, R.R. 2,
Mirror Falls, ON
L3R 4R4

Dear Mr. Amberley

Thank you for taking the time to speak to me last Friday about the maintenance of public swimming pools.

Your comments about the insurance requirements and chemical levels were interesting and helpful. I was not aware that so many regulations were involved.

I'm going to follow your suggestion and look up some of these statistics for my report. I'll send you a copy of my report when I finish it.

Yours truly
Ben de Roget
Ben de Roget

With the help of computers, however, many writers choose to design their own personalized stationery (see Sample Document 7.2)—maybe even a different letterhead for every letter. If you decide to design your own letterhead, here are a few guidelines to keep in mind:

- Don't let your letterhead overwhelm your letter. You don't want your reader to be distracted from the main message of the letter.
- Make your letterhead complete—include phone and fax numbers and e-mail address.
- Use the same letterhead if you write again to the same company.

Sample Document 7.2 *Example of Personalized Stationery*

Ben de Roget
17 Roehampton Street
Windsor, Ontario N6M 4T7
E-mail: bdr@ymail.ca Tel.: (519) 555-7329

March 21, 2002

Simon Amberley
Building Supervisor
The Ultimate Resort and Spa
Highway 60, R.R. 2,
Mirror Falls, ON
L3R 4R4

Dear Mr. Amberley

Thank you for taking the time to speak to me last Friday about the maintenance of public swimming pools.

Date

The use of numerical dates has become a subject of debate. Depending on where you live, for example, the date 06 04 02 could mean June 4th or April 6th. In the workplace, easy and accurate recognition of correct dates is vital. To avoid misinterpretation, write out the name of the month as shown in sample documents 7.1 and 7.2. Reserve the numerical date for printed forms that provide the required spacing—for example,

(_ _/_ _/_ _ _ _)
d d mm y y y y

Inside Address

Here is where you identify the receiver of the letter. Use as much information as you have: name, position or title, and complete address, including postal code. The receiver's name and position may be first, or they may come after the address with an "Attention" heading. This is also the format to choose if you don't know the name of your receiver but you do know his or her position. Ideally, the inside address should match the address that appears on the envelope. See Box 7.1.

Box 7.1 ***Formats for the Inside Address***

Mr. Jack DeMarsh
Walter Beer Construction
12 Finn Ave.
Toronto, ON A9B 4P4

Allan Nyfield
Promotions Manager
The Ultimate Resort and Spa
Highway 60, R.R. 2
Mirror Falls, ON
L3R 4R4

The Ultimate Resort and Spa
Highway 60, R.R. 2
Mirror Falls, ON
L3R 4R4

Attention: Allan Nyfield, Promotions Manager

Salutation

salutation

In Latin, *salutare* means "to greet or salute"; *salus* means "safety" or "welfare." The *Oxford English Dictionary* uses the expression "customary formula" in defining the greeting expressed by a salute. The implication is that the salutation should be recognizable—something your reader finds familiar.

The *salutation* greets the receiver. It seems a small part of a letter, yet it involves some critical choices if you want to appear courteous and appropriate. Even in the 21st century, the familiar salutation in business letters is still "Dear" followed by the receiver's name. Some companies, however, are choosing to substitute the salutation line (see sample documents 7.3 and 7.4).

Sample Document 7.3 *Subject Line Used in Place of Conventional Salutation*

Francis Dreyfield

12 Depalma Ave. Mactier, NB B2B 4N4
fdreyfield@monctoninfo.com
(506) 515-5679

July 15, 2002

Metallica International
P.O. Box 1200
Red Deer, AB A6R 1L1

Reference No. CDD-200

I am enclosing my résumé in response to your advertisement for a Business Evaluation Professional.

Sample Document 7.4 *Attention Line Used in Place of Conventional Salutation*

Francis Dreyfield

12 Depalma Ave. Mactier, NB B2B 4N4
fdreyfield@monctoninfo.com
(506) 515-5679

March 28, 2002

Creiff Pharmaceuticals
1200 Yonge Street
Toronto, ON M2C 5L9

Attention: *Manager, Clinical Data Management*

Please accept my résumé in application for a Clinical Data Management Assistant position.

Courteous business writers take the time to check—and double-check—that they have spelled the receiver's name correctly and used the appropriate title. Avoid the outdated, generic use of "Gentlemen" or "Dear Sir." "Dear Sir/Madam" and other indefinite terms such as "Dear Friend" have also fallen out of favour.

Use only the information you know for sure—don't guess. For example, don't assume that J. Imrie is Mr. Imrie, or that Renata Gundt wants to be addressed as Ms Gundt. In such circumstances, the correct salutation is *Dear J. Imrie* and *Dear Renata Gundt.*

Often when you are responding to employment ads, you are not given a specific name—for example,

> For immediate and confidential consideration, send résumé and covering letter to the following address:
>
> Reference No. CDD-200
>
> **Metallica International**
>
> P.O. Box 1200
>
> Red Deer, AB A6R 1L1

When you are given clear instructions, you are wise to follow them. For the above example, use the form shown in Sample Document 7.3, where the subject line replaces any salutation. If you know only the person's title, you might use the attention line alone as shown in Sample Document 7.4.

To Whom It May Concern

Use this salutation only in special circumstances. It is suitable for a document going to a reader or readers you have no way of identifying. For example, if one of your employees asks you for a letter of recommendation that she can show to various unspecified, prospective employers, use "To Whom It May Concern" in your letter (see Sample Document 7.5). If you are sending a copy of a report to several organizations and do not know who the appropriate recipients are, this salutation is also appropriate. The expression is also often used in legal documents. Do not use "To Whom It May Concern" when you could actually learn the name of your recipient—it should not substitute for a telephone call or some research.

Subject Line

If you have written mostly personal letters before now, you have probably not been in the habit of using subject lines. A subject line is useful in a business letter or memo for several reasons:

- It tells the reader quickly what the letter is about. As a result, your letter may be handled more quickly.

Sample Document 7.5 *Appropriate Use of "To Whom It May Concern" Salutation*

Highway 60, R.R. 2
Mirror Falls, Ontario L3R 4R4

Tel.: (705) 777-4000 Fax: (705) 777-4001
ultaspa@playground.on.ca

January 24, 2002

To Whom It May Concern

RE: Jenna de Santos

I am pleased to write this letter of reference for Jenna de Santos, who worked in my department at The Ultimate Resort and Spa for three years.

Jenna's responsibilities included assisting with strategic planning and marketing for all aspects of The Ultimate's convention and banqueting facilities. She consistently demonstrated superior ability to develop and carry out growth plans. Under her leadership, our sales increased 22 percent in 1999, 17 percent in 2000, and 40 percent in 2001.

During her employment here, Jenna demonstrated a consistent attitude of responsibility, authority, kindness, and good humour. Her integrity is a characteristic that allowed the rest of the staff here to relax, knowing with certainty that the work under her supervision would be handled completely and accurately.

We are going to miss Jenna. I personally wish she had decided to stay in Ontario, but I also understand her desire to move back to Saskatchewan. Whatever organization she works for will not be disappointed.

Hans Dieter

Hans Dieter
Manager, Reservations and Customer Service

- It provides vital information up front, such as a contract or file number.
- It helps to keep all related correspondence together, whether letters arrive in hard copy or by e-mail.
- It helps to keep you (the writer) focused, so that your letter deals with only one subject. If you try to cover two or more unrelated subjects in a letter, one of them may be overlooked and the letter cannot be filed appropriately. If you have a different item of business with the same company, write a separate letter.

Use a headline style for your subject line. That is, make it specific and short, aiming for a balance between a long expression and a generic term—for example,

Not Satisfied With Service ✗

Request ✗

Refund Request ✓

File No. C-6679 ✓

Your Letter Dated May 12, 2002 ✓

Template Elements Below the Message

Elements that appear below the message of the letter provide a suitable closing and direct the reader's attention to enclosures and other recipients.

Complimentary Closing

Various conventional and familiar closings are used in business letters depending on the formality of the situation. Avoid cute wording (e.g., Yours angrily); it is rarely effective in the workplace.

- "Yours truly," "Yours sincerely," "Sincerely yours," and just "Sincerely" are the most common. The addition of "very" makes these closings more emphatic.
- "Cordially" is a somewhat more formal term especially suitable for invitations, congratulations, and other positive news messages.
- "Regards" is less formal and suitable for occasions when your salutation uses only the first name of the receiver. See Sample Document 7.6.

If you have omitted a conventional salutation at the beginning of your letter, you may omit the complimentary closing. You'll see an example of this format in Sample Document 7.5.

Sample Document 7.6 ***Using "Regards" for the Complimentary Closing***

Timothy Haines & Associates
Water Consultant Engineers
Suite 400, 123 34th Street North
Calgary, Alberta A4T 2Y2
(403) 278-9126

June 12, 2004

Mr. Jack DeMarsh
Walter Beer Construction
12 Finn Ave.
Toronto, ON
A9B 4P4

Dear Jack

RE: File 12-601 Moog Creek Flood Plain

Here is the report you requested on the Moog Creek Flood Plain. I notice that we just managed to complete this work exactly six months from the date of your first letter.

As you suspected, the development of lands adjacent to Moog Creek would present a precarious environmental risk for the surrounding community. Pages 10 through 19 of the report indicate the month-by-month gradient calculations. Notice especially that the March–April figures rise sharply.

We cannot recommend construction in this particular sector.

The Department of Geology at the University of Guelph provided valuable assistance in this investigation. Dr. Fred Whitstone in that department would be a good contact for you.

Once you have had a chance to read the report for yourself, I'd be glad to sit down with you and review some of our findings. Give me a call any time.

Regards

Jaris Vonderveen

Jaris Vonderveen, P.Eng.

JV: lz

Signature Group

signature

The signature used to be called the "subscription," meaning, literally, "something written underneath." The signing of one's name adds authority to everything that appears above.

The *signature group* includes a handwritten signature, a typed name, and the title or position of the person signing. When you are signing your own letters, keep in mind that you are giving your reader a clue as to how you want to be addressed. If a woman wants to be addressed as Mrs., Miss, or Ms, for example, she can add that detail when signing her name (see Sample Document 7.7). Similarly, if you want to be addressed as Doctor or Reverend, then you should indicate this preference in your correspondence.

Some companies put the company name above the signature following the complimentary closing. This choice emphasizes to both the writer and the reader that the letter represents the company's words or decisions rather than just those of an individual.

Don't put the company name after your signature and title if it already appears in the letterhead. If you are writing a personal letter, avoid the temptation to invent a title for yourself—for example, "Angry Consumer."

Using "Per"

per

Per is a Latin term meaning "through" or "by means of."

Occasionally you may have to send a letter that has not yet been signed by the writer. If the writer is your supervisor or a coworker, you may sign the letter and send it by using "per." The correct procedure is to write the initials of the sender, add the word "per," then sign your name. See Sample Document 7.8, which indicates that Jane Seaton sent the letter but Harriet Elm signed it on her behalf.

End Notations

These details appear after the signature:

- identification initials
- enclosure note
- copy and blind copy information

Sample Document 7.7 *Indicating Your Preferred Form of Address*

E A S T

M E T R O

Minor Hockey Association

Box 12, Station A
Toronto, ON M2R 4R6
(416) 503-5336

February 8, 2003

Mr. John Halliwell
Banquet Manager
The Ultimate Resort and Spa
Highway 60, R.R. 2
Mirror Falls, ON L3R 4R4

Dear Mr. Halliwell

RE: Hockey Banquet May 29, 2003

For 12 years the East Metro Minor Hockey Association has held its season-end banquet in the Westview Room. You have always provided satisfactory, friendly, and competent service. This year, however, we have run into a number of problems, and I want to get the situation cleared up as soon as possible.

- Despite our several telephone calls to your office, you have not yet sent a confirmation of our planned date.
- You have also not provided information about costs and room layout.
- This morning when I called, the person I spoke to in Catering was abrupt (rude actually) and simply said someone would call me back. It's now 3:30 and no one has called.

If we cannot get confirmation details settled by the end of business hours tomorrow afternoon (Friday February 9), we will have to go elsewhere to make our arrangements. This would be a disappointment and a great inconvenience to us, and I'm sure it would prove embarrassing to your restaurant. Obviously there have been some communication problems among your staff.

I would appreciate a telephone call and a written response to this letter.

Yours truly

Alicia Dunmore

Alicia Dunmore (Mrs.)
Secretary

c: Eldon Winhauser, Team Manager

Sample Document 7.8 *Using "Per"*

UNDERHILL **Press**

3700 Anchor Hill Drive
White Rock, British Columbia
V2Q 6H4
(250) 737-1682

January 23, 2002

Mrs. J. Whitehall
37 – 4th Street S.E.
Calgary, Alberta
A7W 3R3

Dear Mrs. Whitehall

RE: Your Recent Letter

We cannot provide you with a set of writers' guidelines since our company no longer publishes works of fiction. Instead, we deal exclusively with colour photography and visual arts. You'll find enclosed a list of publishers that might be able to help you.

Thank you for your interest.

Yours truly

JS per Harriet Elm — assistant who signed on behalf of sender

(JS) — initials of sender

Jane Seaton — sender
Editorial Assistant

Enc.

Identification Initials

This type of notation at the end of a letter lets the reader know that a letter has been dictated or originated by one person and then typed by someone else. Normally the author's initials appear first, but the exact format can vary from company to company.

The practice is not as common as it once was. At one time, identification initials served a useful purpose when letters were drafted by a manager and then typed by someone in a typing pool. You'll see an example of them in Sample Document 7.6. The initials show clearly who prepared and who typed the document. If you type your own letters, don't use these initials.

Enclosure Note

If you enclose something in the envelope with your letter, type "Enclosure," "enc.," or "Enc." at the end and add a number if there is more than one item. For added clarity, always mention any enclosures in the body of your letter. See Sample Document 7.8 for an example.

Copy and Blind Copy Information

The notation "c," along with a name or list of names, indicates that copies of a letter are being sent to other receivers. The format used to be "cc," meaning "carbon copy," but these days most writers have never even seen carbon paper.

Occasionally, you may want to send a copy of your letter to an interested party without informing other receivers. This is referred to as a "blind copy." The notation "bc" naturally appears on only two copies of the letter—the copy you keep and the blind copy itself. In Sample Document 7.9, the writer is sending a copy to his new employer at the Wind Tower Hotel and to Ardra Hof, who helped him find this new position. For reasons of confidentiality, the writer is not letting his current employer know that he used an executive placement service.

References

Companies that handle hundreds of reports, proposals, and drawings may want to provide clear references to documents mentioned in the letter's content. A list of references following the signature group is the most convenient way to itemize this information. See Sample Document 7.10 for an example.

Second Page Format

Printed letterhead is not used for the second page of a business letter. For continuity and identification purposes, carry over enough information so the letter can be recognized if page 2 becomes separated from page 1: usually the receiver's name, the date, and the page number (see Sample Document 7.10). Be sure to indicate the number of pages in the complete letter. If, by chance, you are sending two letters to the same person on the same day and they both have more than one page, carry over the subject line as well.

Sample Document 7.9 ***Blind Copy Notation***

J.C. MARKOWITZ
1379 Plains Road East, Unit 90
South Beach, BC V5R 2R2

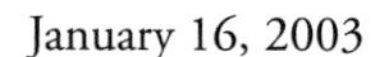

January 16, 2003

Allan Nyfield
Promotions Manager
The Ultimate Resort and Spa
Highway 60, R.R. 2
Mirror Falls, ON L3R 4R4

Dear Mr. Nyfield

I have recently received an offer to become the new Banquet Manager at the Wind Tower Hotel in Vancouver. As you know, I have been looking for an advancement opportunity for the last several months. This letter is to notify you that I will be resigning from The Ultimate Resort as of March 30, 2003.

Although I will be sorry to leave The Ultimate, I know that the training I have received here over the past four years has provided me with the vital experience required to obtain this new position. Thank you for all of your help and encouragement.

Yours truly

J.C. Markowitz

J.C. Markowitz

c: Mr. Len Finkleman, Wind Tower Hotel
bc: Ardra Hof, Executive Placements Inc.

Sample Document 7.10 *Using References in a Letter*

Highway 60, R.R. 2
Mirror Falls, Ontario L3R 4R4

Tel.: (705) 777-4000 Fax: (705) 777-4001
ultaspa@playground.on.ca

July 19, 2003

Mr. R. Ainsworth
Finkle, Morris, & Arzuro Contractors
1200 North Bridge Road
Mirror Falls, ON V3T 2R9

Dear Mr. Ainsworth

Proposal R19-33: Piping and Refitting of Pool and All Related Equipment

We have reviewed your proposal for our Mirror Falls location [1] and concluded that the proposal is consistent with the requirements [2].

Accordingly we ask you to proceed as outlined in both your proposal and the attached specifications. This approval includes the following:

- closing of the pool and all attachments on Oct. 9, 2003
- all demolition and removal
- fittings to be completed no later than Dec. 9, 2003

We require the signed copies of all agreements [3] before any work is completed. Mrs. O. Donegal of Donegal and Simms in Lakefield will contact you within two days to arrange for this.

Yours truly

N. Zaud

N. Zaud
Director of Building Services

c: O. Donegal; L. Simms

R. Ainsworth
July 19, 2003
page 2 of 2

References:

1. Tender 12R412. January 2, 2003.
2. Proposal R19-33: Piping and refitting of pool and all related equipment. February 12, 2003.
3. Contract 7121.061; Contract 912.061; Contract 0100.061; Contract 1233.061. July 19, 2003.

Layout and Punctuation

Textbooks on business and technical writing have traditionally provided detailed instructions about the spacing of various elements of the letter template: for example, after the date, leave four lines blank; after the last sentence, leave two lines before the complimentary closing. Now that a click of a mouse provides a clear print preview, such details are largely redundant.

If your letter looks all scrunched into the top half of the page, use the Enter key and space bar to rearrange it on the page. For a very short letter, use double-spacing to make the layout more appealing; for a very long letter, use single-spacing and move to a second page at the end, not the middle, of a paragraph whenever possible. Especially in long letters, use lists, bullets, indenting, and even headings to make the document more user-friendly.

Full-Block

The simplest layout is called the full-block form. You begin every line at the left side margin. Double-space between paragraphs. If you are writing a very short letter using double-spacing as suggested earlier, you may want to add an extra line between paragraphs. Most of the letter examples in this book use the full-block form.

Semi-Block

The semi-block layout differs mainly in the placement of the date, the complimentary closing, and the signature group: These three items are centred. See Sample Document 7.11.

Punctuation

Use no end-of-line punctuation in the letter template unless you are using an abbreviation. This style is called open punctuation and is certainly the easiest to remember. Most of the letter examples in this book use the full-block format with open punctuation.

If you prefer to use end-of-line punctuation, put commas after each line except the last of the inside address, and a comma after the complimentary closing. Use a colon after the salutation or attention line. See Sample Document 7.11.

Sample Document 7.11 *Semi-Block Format*

Highway 60, R.R. 2
Mirror Falls, Ontario L3R 4R4

Tel.: (705) 777-4000 Fax: (705) 777-4001
ultaspa@playground.on.ca

September 25, 2002

Mrs. Flossie Hall,
P.O. Box 503,
Fenelon Falls, ON,
K0M IN0

Dear Mrs. Hall:

RE: Your Letter of June 30, 2002

I am writing in regard to your recent visit to the Waterfall Room at The Ultimate Resort and Spa. Thank you for bringing your experience to our attention.

You are absolutely correct in saying that a certain level of service should be expected at The Ultimate. I pride myself on working in such a luxurious resort, as you do in staying here. The situations you speak of in your letter are not acceptable, and the management team will be targeting these areas immediately. The service you received comes nowhere near the service standards you should expect from our resort.

I would like to invite you to come again for lunch (on me) so that you can see the proper level of service we provide. Please call me at (705) 368-2511, extension 2313, and I will make the arrangements.

Sincerely,

Abby Lindow

Abby Lindow
Manager, Arcade Level Restaurants

Envelopes

Canada Post produces a booklet entitled *The Canadian Addressing Guide* [1] that provides instructions for formatting the address on envelopes in order to meet the requirements of automated mail-handling equipment. Here are a few of the specific requirements:

- The destination address should be written in uppercase and formatted with a uniform left margin.
- The municipality, province, and postal code should all appear on the same line.
- The postal code should be separated from the province by two spaces. It should appear in uppercase, with a space between the first three and last three elements.

Activities and Exercises

1. You may often have the most questions about setting up job application letters. The following items represent information taken directly from published job advertisements. Prepare the template you would use if you were going to reply to these ads. Make up any details about the positions that might be needed. Compare your versions with those of classmates, and discuss which seem the most appropriate.
   a. Interested candidates are invited to submit their résumé to

      Clinical Director
      Seamont
      6000 Empire Street, Fieldmont, Ontario N1Y 3R4

   b. Detailed résumés with supporting documentation will be received by the undersigned until February 19, 2002, at 2:00 p.m.

      K.J. Hearns
      Chief of Police
      Mirror Falls Police Services
      Box 600
      Mirror Falls, Ontario L3R 6Y1

   c. All applications, including references, should be addressed in confidence to

      The Search Committee
      National Ski Team
      466 – 3rd Avenue
      Ottawa, Ontario K1K 1K1
      or e-mail: adminnst@fortress.ca

   d. Please reply with résumé to P.O. Box 3695, The Daily News, 1200 Main Street, Whitehorse, YT Y1A 3L6.

---

[1] Canada Post. (2001, May). *The Canadian addressing guide.* Retrieved May 4, 2002, from http://www.canadapost.ca.

e. Please e-mail cover letter and résumé to SeeLane@exp.com.
f. Fax or e-mail your résumé to

Sam Fanecetti
Brandt Street Chrysler
400 Brant Street
Box 12
Mirror Falls, ON L3R 5Y6

g. Please apply in writing to Caroll, Faulkner, and Winston, Box 1600, Prairie Springs, AB A2B 3C4. Attention: Anne.

For further assignments dealing with the content of this chapter, see Case Study 14 starting on page 299.

Memos

memorandum

Memorandum is a Latin word meaning "it is to be remembered."

The conventional distinction between memos and letters has been the location of the receiver: Memos carry messages within an organization, whereas letters communicate outside an organization with customers, clients, and other companies.

Of course, there are some exceptions to this rule. For example, even within a company, if a message is extremely sensitive (such as a disciplinary measure or a termination notice), a letter is a better choice simply because it's more private and, legally, may appear more authoritative. For an example, see Sample Document 8.1. Moreover, the proliferation of e-mail, which takes the form of memos, means that memos now travel between companies as well as within them.

Length and Formality

Many writers think that memos, by definition, are shorter than letters, less formal, or less important—messages that are just dashed off by hand that can easily be communicated over coffee. This may be true sometimes, but not always. The length of a memo obviously depends on its content. A memo (or a letter) may convey a routine piece of information in a few lines, it may give important instructions that need to be posted, or it may describe a major organizational change and be two or more pages long. The formality depends not on the type of document (letter, memo, report) but on the sender (what style of writing does the writer feel comfortable with?) and the receiver (is it the company president? your coworker? the Governor General?).

The importance of a memo (or any other document) depends on the meaning of the information to the receiver. A short, informal memo such as the one in Sample Document 8.2 may be discarded immediately. A long memo with instructions that may be needed at a later time may be filed by some employees who will need to refer to it frequently, while others may post it on a bulletin board for general reading (see Sample Document 8.3). A short report giving important information, such as details about an employee injury, may be written in memo format and will likely be filed as a permanent record.

Highway 60, R.R. 2
Mirror Falls, Ontario L3R 4R4

Tel.: (705) 777-4000 Fax: (705) 777-4001
ultaspa@playground.on.ca

June 29, 2003

Mr. Wolfe Schmidt
Stewarding Department

Dear Wolfe

RE: Follow-Up Of Our Meeting Of May 12, 2003

The meeting on May 12, 2003, was held to discuss your attendance record for 2003. As of June 23, 2003, you have missed a total of 17 days of work.

Wolfe, as we discussed, this rate of absenteeism is well above the norm. During our meeting, I asked whether any problems were occurring, either medical or personal, that we would be able to assist you with. You advised that there was nothing. As you are aware, the hotel Medical Centre is always available to help you with any concerns.

I want to confirm that any further absences must be validated by a note from your physician. Your record will be reviewed again in December of 2003, and if your attendance record has improved, this letter will be removed from your personnel file.

If you have any questions, please contact me.

Sincerely

Eric Burton

Eric Burton
Assistant Chief Steward

c: Cynthia Woladjcek
Stanley Allen

Sample Document 8.2 *A Short Memo*

Highway 60, R.R. 2
Mirror Falls, Ontario L3R 4R4

Tel.: (705) 777-4000 Fax: (705) 777-4001
ultaspa@playground.on.ca

FROM the desk of ANIKA SCHEIM

TO: All Staff

DATE: June 6, 2003

SUBJECT: New Coordinator of Recreation

I'm pleased to introduce the new Coordinator of Recreation at The Ultimate.

CAROLYNNE O'SHAE has nearly 12 years of experience in recreation and leisure services. She has worked for the City of Regina Department of Parks and, most recently, spent three years as Cruise Director for WorldView Tours.

Carolynne is a former Olympian in show jumping and has great plans for our riding program. She has also been a soccer coach and instructor, and she holds the Royal Lifesaving Society's highest awards in springboard diving and swimming. In her "spare" time, Carolynne teaches tennis and squash to teens.

We know that Carolynne will be a wonderful addition to our staff here at The Ultimate. Stop by and say hello—and ask her about cruising the Caribbean for three winters. Tough work!

AS

Sample Document 8.3 *A Long Memo with Instructions*

Highway 60, R.R. 2
Mirror Falls, Ontario L3R 4R4

Tel.: (705) 777-4000 Fax: (705) 777-4001
ultaspa@playground.on.ca

TO: Department Heads, Assistant Department Heads, Supervisors, Coordinators

C: Health & Safety Committee, Incident Investigation committee, Human Resources

FROM: Ali Musifa AM

DATE: August 8, 2002

SUBJECT: New Accident Report Form

WE NOW HAVE A NEW ACCIDENT REPORT FORM, AND IT IS ELECTRONIC!

As of today, the accident report form has been updated and made available in electronic form. Here's how to access the new report form:

OPENING THE FILE

1. Click the Start button.
2. Cursor all the way up to FORMS. A list of programs will appear.
3. Cursor over to Microsoft Excel, and click.
4. When Microsoft Excel opens, click the File menu.
5. Scroll down and click Open.
6. Click the button beside Look in, and a dropdown menu will appear.
7. Select GROUP A.
8. Click Users.
9. Click Common.
10. Click FORMS.
11. Select the file Accident report.xls. A message will appear saying that the file is reserved and asking for a password.
12. At the bottom right, click the READ ONLY button, and the file will open.

When the file opens, you will notice that it looks very similar to the previous accident report form. To use the electronic form, simply click the cell beside the heading (e.g., Name), and type in the information.

Note: Some cells are protected. If you click a heading that belongs to these cells and try to type, you will get a message telling you this is not allowed. If you get that message, move to the next empty cell to the right.

Accident Report Form Information
August 8, 2002
page 2 of 2

For the sections with check boxes, move the cursor over the box you wish to select (a pointing finger will appear), click the box, and voilà, a check mark appears! Be sure to fill in ALL the information requested.

Saving the File

When you have filled in the form, you need to save it in your directory (if desired), and print one copy for your department head. To do this

1. Click the File menu.
2. Click Save As.
3. Give the file a name, and ensure that the Save in field says g:\ry-1\users\your id. (Your ID is your e-mail name. Mine is amusifa, for example.)
4. Click Save.

E-mailing the File to the Distribution List

1. Click the File menu.
2. Click Send.
3. Click Mail Recipient. The distribution list will appear. Select the appropriate recipients.
4. Click Attach File.
5. Select Accident.
6. Click Send and you are done.

For those of you who prefer, the form can always be printed and filled in by hand. Make sure copies are made and distributed to the distribution list within 24 hours. If you encounter technical problems, contact HELP Services directly (ext. 5400). If you have questions about when to use the form, contact Employee Health Services (ext. 2268).

Headings

Since memos are used so frequently within organizations, they omit the usual business letter features and use four basic headings instead:

- The *To* line replaces both the inside address and the salutation. The distribution notation (c:) can follow the recipient's name. Depending on the level of formality, you might use first names only or full names and job titles.
- The *From* line replaces the signature group, so the complimentary closing and signature are omitted. If you wish, you can initial the memo in a clearly visible spot, beside your name or at the end.
- The *Date* and *Subject* line work the same as they do in a letter.

To make all of the headings easily readable, use cues such as double-spacing, boldface type, or underlining.

Options

The structure of a memo is different from company to company. Sometimes memo forms are preprinted with the company name or the name of an individual (as in Sample Document 8.2). The order and position of the headings may vary.

While letters are usually addressed to an individual reader, memos may be directed to more than one person. If memos are routinely sent to lists of people, especially in a large company, a distribution list such as the one in Sample Document 8.4 may be used. The list, which is stapled to the front of the memo, helps the sender not to forget anyone and allows the receivers to know how the memo was distributed.

An extra heading, labelled "Action," may appear at the end of the memo. See Sample Document 8.5. This heading highlights the response required by the writer.

If the memo has items attached, add an "Attachments" heading. List the attachments, using brief names, and be sure to refer to them in the body of the memo. See Sample Document 8.5.

Sample Document 8.4 *Distribution List*

Highway 60, R.R. 2
Mirror Falls, Ontario L3R 4R4

Tel.: (705) 777-4000 Fax: (705) 777-4001
ultaspa@playground.on.ca

INFORMATION DISTRIBUTION

UR and S Correspondence Date: ______________________________
Subject: ____________________ File No.: ____________________

Immediate Distribution To

____
____
____
____

Action Required	Responsibility	Reference
Contact R.J. Milne for change of information.		

Distribution To: Admin	Front	Level 1	Level 2	Level 3
R. Marcelli	D. Canzoneri	A. Friars	S. Dadd	

R. Land ❑	E. Johanssen ❑	L. Milne ❑	S. Haddad ❑	R. Delvecchioni ❑
I. Zaccolo ❑	E. Friedelander ❑	J. Kannuck ❑	M. Hill ❑	J. Arnold ❑
K. Linnert ❑	J. Vello ❑	A. Smythe ❑	J. Sugarman ❑	A. Young ❑
J. Szabo ❑	O. Thielssen ❑	A. Langman ❑	B. Bowman ❑	W. Piekert ❑
N. Zaud ❑	S. Dernnan ❑	V. Suttgannussen ❑	C. Nauru ❑	L. Bouchard ❑
E. Moussino ❑	D. Foreman ❑	F. Pickering ❑	B. Eduster ❑	C. Canon ❑
BUILDING	**FINANCE**	**PERSONNEL**	**SERVICE**	**ADDITIONAL**
C. Winestone	J. Malkou	J. Bismonte	S. Edwards	N. Aburto
R. Brisebois	J. Yagultov	L. Wolecki	S. Duay	
A.L. Kasimov	D. Herrera	M. Mustapha	W. He	
J. Taylor	R. Joshi	D. Ying	D. Bismonte	
A.C. Kasimov	O. Latimer	F. Dramin	C. Ederlyn	
O. Peirera	J. Capparrone	M. Martin	L. Nickerson	
G. Sabatino	W. Williamson	Y. Orr	Y. Schembro	
R. Rhee	H. Nuosci	K. Wu	L. Iwosaki	

Sample Document 8.5 *Memo with Action Line*

Highway 60, R.R. 2
Mirror Falls, Ontario L3R 4R4

Tel.: (705) 777-4000 Fax: (705) 777-4001
ultaspa@playground.on.ca

INTEROFFICE MEMORANDUM

TO: R. WU, Head of Site Planning

FROM: J. RICKERT, Vice President

DATE: June 9, 2003

ATTACHMENTS: Request for power shutdown dated June 3, 2003

SUBJECT: Repair and Calibration of Alarm Systems

To complete the contracted maintenance of the site alarm systems, I have been told we require power shutdown for approximately two minutes (see attachment).

This downtime must not take place without due notification of all department heads and supervisors.

Given the 24-hour nature of this organization, a complete written plan and schedule must be submitted two weeks in advance of the work.

ACTION:
Submit detailed schedule for required downtime, including two alternate dates. Date required: June 14, 2003

JR

c: A. Ling
J. Jones
K. Delorme
J. Han
P.K. Murdoc
J. Elliot
A. Khan

Content

To organize your information in a memo, use the following formula:

1. Main point or purpose
2. Details
3. Action statement or request

Main Point or Purpose

Depending on the receiver and the context, your main point may be short and simple. For example,

> There will be a training session for the six new staff members on April 9, from 1:00 p.m. until 4:00 p.m., in the Lecture Hall on the third level.

For some readers, you may need to provide background or context to clarify the reason you are writing. If you can do so in a sentence or two, put this with your main point. Otherwise, think about using a "Background" heading so that readers familiar with the context can skip over it. For example,

> Human Resources has asked all departments to provide a half-day introduction for new staff. Accordingly, there will be a training session for the six new staff members on April 9, from 1:00 p.m. until 4:00 p.m., in the Lecture Hall on the third level.

Details

The details or discussion section of the memo provides all of the information needed to fully inform your reader. Make your memo easy to read by using short paragraphs and lists wherever possible. See Sample Document 8.6 for an example.

Action Statement or Request

Normally, your reader is going to look at the bottom of the memo with one question in mind: "What do I have to do?" Close the memo by answering this question. If you are writing to your staff or employee, this will take the form of a polite statement. If you are writing to your manager, you will want to turn this statement into a polite request. See Sample Document 8.6 for an example.

Sample Document 8.6 *Using Formatting to Highlight a Message*

Highway 60, R.R. 2
Mirror Falls, Ontario L3R 4R4

Tel.: (705) 777-4000 Fax: (705) 777-4001
ultaspa@playground.on.ca

TO: All New Staff

FROM: Erin Dubois, Assistant Manager ED

DATE: March 26, 2003

SUBJECT: Training Session

There will be a training session for the six new staff members on April 9, from 1:00 p.m. until 4:00 p.m., in the Lecture Hall on the third level.

This session will deal with communication barriers that you may encounter within the company and in your dealings with our clients. The following topics will be covered:

- *Cognition:* You will learn more about your responsibilities as outlined in your job descriptions and a staff training video.
- *Emotion:* You will have the opportunity to listen to one of the senior staff members whose job description is similar to yours. We'll try some role-playing too.
- *Vocabulary:* You will learn some of the hazards of occupational jargon and how to avoid misunderstandings with clients.
- *Listening:* You will get some practice in telephone communication and learn about the possible problems you may encounter.
- *Feedback:* You will have a chance to ask questions about issues that have come up during your first two weeks at The Ultimate Resort and Spa.

Please let me know by e-mail, before April 1, if you will be *unable* to attend. Otherwise, I'll see you there.

Activities and Exercises

1. Choose a topic for a short investigative report from the list below (or one suggested by your instructor). Prepare a plan of investigation that includes the following information:
   - the purpose of your investigation
   - a survey of at least 25 people
   - an interview with someone who has expert knowledge
   - at least three secondary sources
   - a timetable for your work

   Prepare a proposal memo for your instructor outlining the investigation you have planned. Your instructor may ask you to carry out the investigation and prepare the final report based on your work.

   Possible topics:
   - What is involved in starting a small art gallery or photography studio.
   - Compare the advantages and disadvantages of hair colouring done at home and at a hair salon.
   - Estimate the costs of buying and raising a puppy.
   - Assess wheelchair accessibility of various businesses in your area.
   - Investigate the involvement of high-school students in your area in extracurricular activities such as sports teams, clubs, band, etc.
   - Compare the kinds of music students in your college are interested in.
2. You work in the human resources department of a busy downtown hospital. Parking is always a problem. Hospital employees have a few parking lots available to them, but the cost can be as much as $14 a day. Lately, you have received complaints that employees have been using the lots reserved for customers of small businesses in the area.

   Prepare a memo for all hospital staff to be included with their next paycheque. Remind staff about several things: Public transit is still the best transportation method, small businesses nearby will have cars of hospital staff towed away, public parking lots have monthly rates that are slightly lower, and so on. Try to make your memo encouraging and helpful rather than negative and critical.
3. Prepare a memo for the staff of your workplace announcing details of an end of season get-together. This event might be a summer picnic for employees and their families or the annual New Year's party. Try to anticipate and answer all of the questions your employees will have.
4. Your brother is finally getting married. Unfortunately, he and his fiancée have chosen the Victoria Day weekend for the wedding. Since you work part-time at the Grow-Rite Garden Centre, you know it will be a problem asking for this very busy weekend

off. Write a memo to your employer asking for the Saturday and Sunday off. You may invent (within reason) any details that might help you be convincing.

5. The place where you work has been undertaking renovations in the engineering department. Employees are often becoming upset when they're asked, on short notice, to pack up their work and move elsewhere with little explanation. Write a notice to be posted for all staff that will effectively communicate the situation and what is needed of employees. You may want to include a schedule of renovation work so everyone will know how long the disruption will last.
6. Think of a situation you have experienced, as an employer or employee, when a clearly worded memo may have helped to avoid a problem. First, describe the situation briefly using the terminology of communication theory described in Chapter 1. Then, write the memo that should have been used.

For further assignments dealing with the content of this chapter, see case studies 1, 2, 3, 11, 18, and 20 starting on page 275.

Routine Letters

Many business writers have difficulty beginning a letter and organizing the message. Just as a template provides a consistent background for letters, formulas help you determine how to write and organize letter content.

In this chapter, you will find formulas that will help you to plan and write several different types of letters. Once you decide on the purpose of your letter, the formula will help you decide what information you need to include and in what order.

Positive Messages

You will probably use the *direct approach* most often since it works for most routine correspondence, including letters that

- ask for information
- provide information (positive or negative)
- apply for a job
- order supplies
- thank people
- extend invitations

Direct letters use a three-point approach:

1. State the main point.
2. Provide any necessary details.
3. Provide a goodwill closing.

You will notice, with this formula and all the others, that the number of steps does not necessarily correspond to the number of paragraphs in the letter. Instead, the parts of the formula refer to the order of the information.

State the Main Point

This step seems simple enough, but the beginning of any letter probably presents the greatest challenge to any writer. The mistake many writers make is thinking that they somehow have to work up to the main point. Quite the contrary—in a direct business letter, your very first sentence (or sentences) should clearly state the reason for writing. You may want to edit your sentence later, but begin by stating as simply as possible the purpose of your letter. To highlight the main point, try to limit your first paragraph to one or two sentences. Here are some examples:

> Thank you for the time you spent with me last Friday discussing my plans for a new course.
>
> Please send me information about the model X3-100 mountain bike.
>
> The Pharmaceuticals Division of Equex Products Limited would like to invite you to be our feature speaker at the annual Equine Veterinary Conference on May 12, 2002, in Winnipeg, Manitoba.
>
> I'm inquiring about your policy on accommodation of pets in the hotel.

Provide Any Necessary Details

Once you have informed your reader clearly about your purpose for writing, add whatever is needed to clarify, support, or strengthen your main point. Here is where you need to think about the feedback you expect and the information the reader needs in order to give you that feedback. Make sure your reader won't have to write you back to ask for further clarification. The sample opening sentences above might continue as follows:

> Your suggestions about the programs available at Campana College and Argyle University were very helpful. I didn't realize that the work I have already done in accounting would be so useful. I plan to contact both schools.
>
> I saw your presentation at the Canadian National Exhibition last August and was impressed by the many features of the X3-100. I currently own a 15-year-old Zuma bike, and I've been looking for a new one that is both lightweight and strong.
>
> The theme of the 2002 conference is Show Jumping. Your expertise in this field and your recent work on equine ligament injuries are internationally recognized, and we would be honoured to have you on the program.
>
> The conference runs from May 11 to 13. Your presentation would be scheduled to follow the Saturday night banquet in the Waterfall Ballroom on May 12.
>
> We will, of course, cover air travel expenses for you and a guest, as well as accommodation at The Ultimate Resort and Spa.
>
> We have a 10-year-old pure-bred French poodle who is accustomed to sharing our bed. She cannot possibly be left in a kennel.

Layout is as important in a letter as it is in any other type of document. Use short paragraphs and any other layout features that will help to organize your information clearly: indenting, centring, underlining, boldface type, and lists. Don't fall into the trap of thinking that a letter can only be written in long paragraphs. See Sample Document 9.1.

Sample Document 9.1 *Direct Letter with Formatting*

CANADA'S COLLEGE SKI TEAM

September 12, 2002

Mr. Allan Farnham
Catering Manager
The Ultimate Resort and Spa
Highway 60, R.R. 2
Mirror Falls, ON L3R 4R4

Dear Mr. Farnham

RE: 2003 Annual Convention

As discussed in this morning's telephone call, we would like to book the following dates and times for our 2003 Annual Convention:

> Opening Night Banquet
> Friday, February 1, 2003
> Snowtop Ballroom
> 5 p.m. until 1 a.m.

> Annual Meeting
> Sunday, February 3, 2003
> Eagle's Roost
> 2 p.m. until 6 p.m.

At present, the anticipated total attendance at the banquet is 120 people and at the annual meeting 60 people. We will confirm these numbers by December 1, 2002. Our menu and room arrangement requirements are attached.

Thank you for all your help and suggestions. We look forward to planning this event with you.

Yours truly

Jason Ridout

Jason Ridout
President

Enc. 2

CANADA'S COLLEGE SKI TEAM BOX 12 STATION A CALGARY, AB A2B 3C4

Provide a Goodwill Closing

Don't confuse the goodwill closing with the complimentary closing. The complimentary closing (Yours truly, Sincerely, etc.) is part of your letter template and may be the same in most letters you write. The goodwill closing, on the other hand, is a short comment related to the content of the letter. It is usually, but not always, a forward-looking comment; that is, it looks ahead in some way to a friendly and mutually agreeable business relationship. The goodwill closing may involve saying thank you, but avoid using "thank you" as a generic closing unless you are actually thanking the reader for something specific.

For the earlier examples, the goodwill closings might be as follows:

> I will let you know my final decision.

> Thank you for any information you can provide.

> If possible, we would appreciate receiving your response by October 1. We eagerly look forward to hearing from you.

> We would appreciate a fax or telephone call assuring us that Mitzie will be welcome at your resort.

Notice that these goodwill closings are not wordy, stiff, and formal. The language is conversational and does not needlessly repeat what has already been said. Immediately following this brief comment, the complimentary closing and signature appear.

Negative Messages

Of course, every letter does not convey positive or routine information. Sometimes you have to say no to a customer or staff member. Experienced writers know how to write refusal letters that minimize damage to relationships.

A well-written refusal letter could be called a "No, But" letter:

- *No* (we can't comply with your request).
- *But* (here's a suggestion that might be helpful).

Indirect Refusals

In the indirect approach, the main point—the actual refusal—appears near the middle of the letter instead of at the beginning. This strategy is not intended to hide the main message or "beat around the bush" before saying no; instead, it allows the reader some preparation time, no matter how slight, and softens the overall impact of the refusal.

Use the following formula when writing an indirect refusal letter:

1. Use a neutral opening that is relevant to the subject of the letter.
2. Explain the reason for the refusal or bad news.

3. State the refusal or bad news either clearly or by implication.
4. Add a forward-looking helpful comment or alternate suggestion.
5. Use a goodwill closing.

The Neutral Opening

Avoid starting a refusal letter with a comment that is misleading or completely unrelated to the situation:

> We were delighted to receive your letter. ✗ *(This sounds like the beginning of a positive, good news letter.)*

> The Ultimate Resort and Spa welcomes you to a world of relaxation. ✗ *(This sounds like the start of a sales pitch.)*

Refer instead to the situation at hand:

> Your inquiry about accommodation for pets arrived today. ✓

> Thank you for your application for the position of Chief Housekeeper. ✓

The Explanation

Begin the explanation right after your opening statement. Be honest and brief; avoid hiding behind vague company policies. Keep in mind the principles of positive, confident, and courteous language.

The explanation is often combined with the refusal—see the examples in the next section.

The Refusal

The refusal may be written out distinctly or it may be implied as part of your explanation. All of the following examples contain a refusal; three are implied and two are direct:

> We are looking for a candidate with considerable experience in reservations software and programming. Your work has been mainly in accounting. ✓ *(This is a clear explanation with some information that may be helpful to the applicant. The refusal is implied; however, it could also be added in a further sentence.)*

> I have already committed the month of May 2002 to a family event that will culminate in my daughter's wedding in New Zealand. As a result, I will not be able to accept your kind invitation. ✓ *(The reason and the refusal are clearly and politely stated.)*

> Local public health regulations do not permit pets of any kind in the hotel suites. ✓ *(This is a clear reason for refusing the guest's request to keep a dog in her suite.)*

If you had read the brochure more carefully, you would have noticed that we do not accommodate pets. ✗ *(This line insults the reader.)*

Applicants must have a two-year credit history to qualify for a loan. Since you have been in business for only six months, we cannot accept your application at this time. ✓ *(The final three words soften the refusal.)*

The Forward-Looking Helpful Comment

Your purpose here is to ensure that the letter does not end with the refusal. Move away from the bad news and provide your reader with a useful alternative, or look ahead to other possible business opportunities. Above all, do not insult or scold your reader, and avoid offering unrealistic compensation for the refusal.

In most cases, you should also avoid apologizing. If you apologize for acting according to your company's policies, you imply that those policies may not be well designed. Reserve apologies for situations where your company has made a mistake or caused a problem. Here are some examples of forward-looking helpful comments:

We will keep your application on file for the next 90 days. ✓ *(This is a conventional statement in a letter turning down an employment application.)*

If you had completed the next level of training, we might have been able to hire you. ✗ *(Written in the past tense, this statement sounds patronizing.)*

When you complete the next level of training, we might be able to reconsider your application. ✓ *(Here, looking ahead, the statement offers something useful.)*

Although pets cannot be accommodated in your suite, guests travelling with pets receive a 15 percent discount for boarding services at Wagging Tails Kennels. Simply notify our front desk when you register, and they will make all the arrangements for you. ✓ *(The hotel's policy is well thought out as it offers a solution to guests travelling with pets.)*

We are extremely sorry that we cannot accommodate your dog. Please accept the enclosed coupon for a free week's stay at Wagging Tails Kennels. ✗ *(The apology should not be necessary if the hotel's policy is well thought out. Also, the free offer may be out of proportion.)*

You should have read our brochure more carefully. ✗ *(Don't scold your client.)*

The Goodwill Closing

As in the direct approach, the goodwill closing completes a polite and businesslike letter. It should be brief and relate in some way to the subject of the letter. Here are some examples:

> Thank you for your interest in Ackerman Insurance.
>
> We look forward to your next vacation at Mirror Lake.
>
> Best of luck in your future plans.

Sample Document 9.2 is an example of an indirect refusal letter.

Direct Refusals

When you refuse a request, you can do it in two ways. With customers, clients, or strangers, you should normally use the indirect approach, since it helps to avoid offence or hurt feelings. In a few circumstances, you can convey a simple "no" in an adaptation of the routine direct letter.

Use the following formula when writing a direct refusal letter:

1. State the main point (refusal).
2. Provide an explanation.
3. Add the forward-looking helpful comment.
4. Provide a goodwill closing.

Notice that, although the order has changed, the steps remain essentially the same as for the indirect refusal. Sample Document 9.3 is an example of a direct refusal letter.

Table 9.1 should help you decide when to use the direct or the indirect refusal. If in doubt, use the indirect approach.

Sample Document 9.2 *Refusal Letter Using Indirect Approach*

Highway 60, R.R. 2
Mirror Falls, Ontario L3R 4R4

Tel.: (705) 777-4000 Fax: (705) 777-4001
ultaspa@playground.on.ca

October 1, 2003

Arla Heinz
127– 3700 3rd Street East
Nanaimo, BC V6T 7T1

Dear Arla Heinz

We have received your application for the position of Front Desk Manager at The Ultimate Resort and Spa.

Much to our surprise, nearly 50 applications arrived, and we have been impressed by the high calibre of all the candidates. In order to speed up the interview process, we have shortlisted approximately 15 candidates on the basis of education and past experience in similar resorts. Since your experience has been mainly in much smaller establishments, we have not placed you on our shortlist at this time.

We will retain your application for a period of six months in case a job opening occurs that might suit your qualifications.

Thank you for your interest in The Ultimate Resort and Spa.

Yours truly

Sandra Woodstammer

S.W. Woodstammer
Personnel Assistant

Sample Document 9.3 *Refusal Letter Using Direct Approach*

UNDERHILL **Press**

3700 Anchor Hill Drive
White Rock, British Columbia
V2Q 6H4
(250) 737-1682

January 23, 2002

Mrs. J. Whitehall
37 – 4th Street S.E.
Calgary, Alberta
A7W 3R3

Dear Mrs. Whitehall

RE: Your Recent Letter

We cannot provide you with a set of writers' guidelines since our company no longer publishes works of fiction. Instead, we deal exclusively with colour photography and visual arts. You'll find enclosed a list of publishers that might be able to help you.

Thank you for your interest.

Yours truly

JS per Harriet Elm

Jane Seaton
Editorial Assistant

Enc.

Table 9.1 *When to Use the Direct or the Indirect Approach*

Direct	Indirect
• receiver is well known to writer	• receiver is customer/client or someone you do not know
• news is minor or routine	• news is sensitive
• news is expected, may be a follow-up to a telephone call	• news is not expected, may be a shock
• reader will not be upset	• receiver may be upset or angry

Activities and Exercises

1. Working with a partner or in a small group, read through the recent Letters to the Editor section of a local newspaper. Spend some time discussing a few issues of current concern in your area, then write a short letter to the editor expressing your views. Actually send your letter by mail or e-mail to the newspaper. You get bonus points if your letter gets published.
2. Do some research to find someone in your community who has expert knowledge in your discipline. Write a letter inviting this person to make a presentation to your class. Include some details about your program and some ideas or suggestions that might be helpful.
3. Assume you are the person who was invited to speak to your class in exercise 2. Write a polite letter refusing the invitation. You can invent any suitable explanation.
   a. Use the indirect approach.
   b. Assume you have already refused the invitation by telephone. Write a follow-up refusal letter using the direct refusal approach.
4. Write a letter to your provincial or federal Member of Parliament asking for information about an issue of current interest. Prepare a fax cover page that could be used with your letter.
5. A group of students from your program toured Mexico (or some other country of your choice) recently. Encouraged by your program coordinator, your class has raised enough money to sponsor one Mexican student for an exchange term at your college. Several students have applied to be sponsored.
   a. Write a letter of congratulations to the winning student, explaining why she or he was chosen and giving details the student will need to plan for the term.
   b. Write an indirect refusal letter to a student who was not chosen.

For further assignments dealing with the content of this chapter, see case studies 3, 6, 8, 11, 17, 18, and 19 starting on page 277.

Complaint and Adjustment Letters chapter ten

complain

Looking for a great cocktail-party word? How about *plangiferous*? It means "accompanied by the sound of beating or pounding," and it comes from the Latin *plango, plangere.* The word *complain* comes from the same root. Although "complain" seems to denote whining or grumbling, its root *complangere* actually suggests a forceful eloquence and intensity.

Complaint or Claim Letters

The object of the complaint letter is not to insult or harangue the reader or to destroy the reader's morale, but rather to bring a problem to the attention of the reader in a clear and effective way. This task requires thought and care. You may feel like writing, "You idiots didn't send the right size. Your whole company is totally incompetent." But think of how *you* react to accusations, blame, and name-calling:

- You become defensive, even angry.
- You protest and come back fighting.
- You discount and ignore the complainer.
- You pass on your annoyance to those around you.

Errors occur for many reasons. When you think about it, what reputable company would deliberately make a mistake just to annoy a customer? Yet customers often react as though that's exactly what happened.

A well-written complaint letter explains the problem clearly but does not resort to melodrama. It also indicates precisely what sort of correction or amendment the writer requires. Unreasonable demands and insulting language tend to continue the problem rather than correct it. Here are some steps for writing an effective complaint letter:

1. Open with a *brief* statement of background.
2. Describe the situation, indicating how you have been inconvenienced.
3. State what correction you expect.
4. Use a neutral closing.

Along with these steps, keep the following dos and don'ts in mind whether you are making a complaint in writing or verbally:

- *Don't* make threats or accusations. They are not helpful and could land you in legal trouble.

- *Don't* go on and on or try to give a verbatim account of your experience.
- *Don't* exaggerate the problem. Your reader may assume you have invented the entire situation.
- *Do* be courteous and reasonable.

Open with a Brief Statement of Background

Begin your letter by acquainting the reader with the context. Explain the nature of your relationship to the company and any specific details that may apply. Limit your information; you do not need to write a long narrative.

> Your company has provided our lawn-care services for the past five years. ✓
>
> On March 12, my family and I visited your restaurant for the first time. We arrived at about noon, without a reservation. ✓
>
> I'm a third-semester student in the Accounting Program. During this past term I took the Business Ethics course from Professor Von Flingabout. ✓

Describe the Situation and Inconvenience

Once again, the key is brevity. When you have experienced poor service or some kind of problem, outrage will probably be your first reaction. There's no question that putting your emotions aside and describing the situation coolly can be difficult. For appropriate business communication, however, you must discipline yourself to do exactly that. When you have a legitimate complaint, make it eloquent by thinking carefully about the steps that led to the difficulty.

Use some rough notes if doing so helps you to keep your information in chronological order. You may want to use a numbered list for clarity, or list your experiences in point form. Remember that specifics such as dates and times are important. Look over your list, and if possible, remove from it items that refer only to feelings or assumptions. Stick to actions, facts, and results.

> The server was impatient and unfriendly and obviously didn't like his job. ✗ *(assumptions)*
>
> The server came to take our orders about two minutes after leaving the menus. When we were not ready to order, he left and did not return for more than 15 minutes. ✓ *(actions)*
>
> The warranty states that the HEPA filter should last for two years. We purchased our filter six months ago, but it has almost completely disintegrated. A copy of our invoice is attached, along with a Polaroid snapshot of the filter. ✓ *(facts)*

In addition to explaining the problem, be clear about how you have been inconvenienced. If your dining experience was unpleasant and you don't plan to return, say so. If you have had to pay another company to correct a problem, attach a copy of the invoice. If you were (merely?) angered by rude treatment, don't think that such feelings are not important: Companies want to know when their customers are not happy.

State What Correction You Expect

Annoyance can cause writers either to forget to say what they want or to ask for something completely unreasonable. Keeping in mind that most companies do want to fix problems that occur, indicate clearly what would make you a more satisfied customer. Provide the information that's needed, such as a part number or a specific date. You may not get what you ask for, but your request at least gives the receiver a clue about your expectations.

> We must have the film replaced before June 12. ✓ *(clear request)*
>
> I want you to fire that salesperson and her manager. ✗ *(request based on emotion)*
>
> Since the shops in the colonnade are such a visible part of the hotel, you might consider using professional shoppers to check the attitude of the salespeople once in a while. ✓ *(probably a reasonable request)*
>
> The filter is part no. RT-4003T. Please let me know by telephone or e-mail how I can get this item replaced quickly. The air filter is a necessary health device in my home. ✓ *(clear request)*

If you are making a claim based on a warranty or guarantee, you may find it helpful to enclose a photocopy of the relevant document and to use wording from it in your letter:

> Although we have owned the pump for only six months and have had no reason to remove the outer casing, the sparking problem seems to indicate a defect in the interior wiring assembly that is covered by your warranty. I've attached a photocopy of the warranty information from your Service Guide.

Use a Neutral Closing

Here is one final challenge: You may have no desire to add a goodwill closing, but a neutral comment will provide an effective closing. It should relate in some way to the letter's content. For example,

> I appreciate your attention to this request.

Sample Document 10.1 is an example of a complaint letter.

Sample Document 10.1 *Complaint Letter*

E A S T

M E T R O

Minor Hockey Association

Box 12, Station A
Toronto, ON M2R 4R6
(416) 503-5336

February 8, 2003

Mr. John Halliwell
Banquet Manager
The Ultimate Resort and Spa
Highway 60, R.R. 2
Mirror Falls, ON L3R 4R4

Dear Mr. Halliwell

RE: <u>Hockey Banquet May 29, 2003</u>

For 12 years the East Metro Minor Hockey Association has held its season-end banquet in the Westview Room. You have always provided satisfactory, friendly, and competent service. This year, however, we have run into a number of problems, and I want to get the situation cleared up as soon as possible.

- Despite our several telephone calls to your office, you have not yet sent a confirmation of our planned date.
- You have also not provided information about costs and room layout.
- This morning when I called, the person I spoke to in Catering was abrupt (rude actually) and simply said someone would call me back. It's now 3:30 and no one has called.

If we cannot get confirmation details settled <u>by the end of business hours tomorrow afternoon</u> (Friday February 9), we will have to go elsewhere to make our arrangements. This would be a disappointment and a great inconvenience to us, and I'm sure it would prove embarrassing to your restaurant. Obviously there have been some communication problems among your staff.

I would appreciate a telephone call and a written response to this letter.

Yours truly

Alicia Dunmore

Alicia Dunmore (Mrs.)
Secretary

c: Eldon Winhauser, Team Manager

Adjustment Letters

adjust

The derivation of the word *adjust* is complex. According to the *Oxford English Dictionary*, even though it does not actually arise from the Latin *ad* (toward) *justis* (justice), it looked like it did and was used in that sense (to place justly) from about the 12th century.

Customers with complaints or claims fall into various categories, so different types of letters are appropriate in different circumstances, as shown in Table 10.1.

Table 10.1 ***Letters for Different Types of Customers***

Type of Customer	Situation	Type of Letter
The customer has a problem that you can't fix, but you can offer some form of compensation.	The customer is in the right. Your company has made the error or caused the problem.	Adjustment letter
The customer has a problem that you can fix.	The customer is in the right. Your company has made the error or caused the problem.	Adjustment letter or direct letter
The customer has a request that you cannot grant.	Your company has a clear reason for refusing. No one has actually made an error.	Indirect refusal letter

If your customers are not happy, your business will suffer. Successful companies know that even if customers aren't always right, they are always important and their concerns need to be addressed with care and speed. An adjustment letter responds to or anticipates a complaint letter. Its purpose is to correct an error or make amends for a problem caused by the writer or the writer's organization. The best kind of adjustment letter is one that handles the problem and brings the situation to an end, not the one that exacerbates the problem or raises new issues.

Keep in mind that customers who write complaint letters don't always follow the guidelines outlined in a writing textbook. You may well receive letters that are insulting, abusive, and very angry. When you write an adjustment letter, your task is to sift through the information you have received and focus on facts rather than emotions.

The guidelines here focus chiefly on situations that involve problems with service, products, and general customer relations. If you encounter issues such as personal injury, theft, discrimination, or legal problems, you should obtain legal advice before writing.

Use the following formula when writing an adjustment letter:

1. Acknowledge the problem.
2. Deal with the problem.
3. Move away from the problem.
4. Use a goodwill closing.

Along with these steps, keep the following dos and don'ts in mind:

- *Do* treat the customer with respect.
- *Don't* contradict or argue with the customer.
- *Don't* use language that makes the problem worse.
- *Don't* blame individuals, departments, or company policies.
- *Don't* write a sales pitch.
- *Don't* overcompensate the customer.

Acknowledge the Problem

To acknowledge the problem effectively, you need to sift through the customer's complaint and summarize it in as few words as possible. Avoid extremes here: Don't minimize the situation, and don't exaggerate it. Focus on the customer's perceptions and refer to any contact you have had with the customer.

> I have reviewed the letter you sent regarding your unsatisfactory meal in the dining room last weekend. ✓
>
> I was extremely upset to learn about the terrible meal you had in our dining room. ✗
>
> We have received your letter along with the broken filter. ✓

Deal with the Problem

This task sounds simple enough, but often "the problem" has two parts: the customer's problem and your company's problem. Each needs to be handled in the right context. What can you offer this customer to correct the situation? Sometimes the answer is clear, and sometimes it's not. Avoid making excuses, throwing company policies at your customer, and, above all, dealing with the company's problem in front of the customer. Do not, for example, disclose confidential information about employees to your customer.

> I will personally be reviewing customer service procedures with all of our wait staff. ✓
>
> The server assigned to your table has caused problems before and he has been fired. ✗
>
> A new filter is being shipped to you today by courier. ✓
>
> Our trucks will be in your neighbourhood next week to replace the sod at the side of your house. ✓

You may want to use a standard sentence commenting on the level of service you and your company aspire to. This may be the appropriate place to add an apology.

> We apologize that you did not experience the efficient, friendly service that has made The Ultimate Resort and Spa famous. ✓
>
> Our company is proud of the service we have provided for over 30 years. We regret that this equipment has not lived up to our promise. ✓
>
> We appreciate the opportunity to assist you. I apologize for your trouble, and I assure you it is our hope that you always have a positive experience with our company. ✓

Move Away from the Problem

At this point in the adjustment letter, you should assume that you have handled the situation appropriately. Your aim now is to keep this person as a customer if at all possible. This step is similar to the forward-looking helpful comment you have used in refusal letters (see Chapter 9), except that this time an offer of compensation is more appropriate. Make sure that any offer you make is appropriate to the situation—don't go overboard, or the customer may think you are trying to distract her or him from a much more serious issue. Use your skills with positive language, avoiding any kind of heavy-handed sales pitch.

> You'll find two vouchers for free dessert enclosed in this letter so that you can return and experience the level of service you deserve. ✓
>
> We look forward to your next visit to The Ultimate Resort and Spa. Remember that this year's Bierfest runs October 6–8. I've enclosed a brochure with details about this exciting fall weekend. ✓

Use a Goodwill Closing

The goodwill closing may form part of the previous step (as in the examples above), or you may want to add one more brief comment. However, avoid referring to the original problem again or apologizing a second time. Also think twice about inviting further personal contact concerning the problem. If you suggest that more discussion is needed, your customer may assume that the issue is not yet closed. Say "thank you" if it is specific to something you are writing, but avoid using it as a generic ending to your letter.

> Once again, we are sorry for the delay. ✗ *(Don't repeat the apology or the problem.)*
>
> Feel free to contact me personally if you have more questions. ✗ *(Try to anticipate questions in your letter. Don't look for more.)*
>
> We look forward to serving you in the future. ✓
>
> Thank you. ✗ *(Too generic.)*

Sample Document 10.2 is an example of an adjustment letter.

Sample Document 10.2 *Adjustment Letter*

Highway 60, R.R. 2
Mirror Falls, Ontario L3R 4R4

Tel.: (705) 777-4000 Fax: (705) 777-4001
ultaspa@playground.on.ca

September 25, 2002

Mrs. Flossie Hall
P.O. Box 503
Fenelon Falls, ON
K0M IN0

Dear Mrs. Hall

RE: Your Letter of June 30, 2002

I am writing in regard to your recent visit to the Waterfall Room at The Ultimate Resort and Spa. Thank you for bringing your experience to our attention.

You are absolutely correct in saying that a certain level of service should be expected at The Ultimate. I pride myself on working in such a luxurious resort, as you do in staying here. The situations you speak of in your letter are not acceptable, and the management team will be targeting these areas immediately. The service you received comes nowhere near the service standards you should expect from our resort.

I would like to invite you to come again for lunch (on me) so that you can see the proper level of service we provide. Please call me at (705) 368-2511, extension 2313, and I will make the arrangements.

Sincerely

Abby Lindow

Abby Lindow
Manager, Arcade Level Restaurants

Activities and Exercises

1. Here is a problem that occurs occasionally in many communities. One home on your block is an eyesore. The grass is rarely cut; two rusted, unlicensed cars have been sitting on the driveway for months; garbage put out for pickup has been spilled and never cleaned up; and beer and pop cans litter the driveway.
   a. Research the bylaws in your area that might deal with this problem. Find out who would actually be responsible for dealing with this issue. Then write a letter of complaint describing the property and asking for help.
   b. In real life, this task would probably take more insight and a bit of courage: Instead of writing to a community representative, write to the owners of the property described above. What might you say that would be effective without being insulting or hurtful?
2. You accidentally broke a window in someone's house while tossing a ball with a friend. No one was home, so you notified the police and arranged to pay for the damage. Write a letter to the homeowners explaining the event and apologizing.
3. Parking is always a problem at a busy downtown hospital. Hospital employees have a few parking lots available, but the cost can be as much as $14 a day. As an alternative, some hospital employees have been using the lots reserved for customers of small businesses in the area.
   a. Assume you own one of the small businesses. Write a letter of complaint about the parking violations to the hospital's Human Resources department.
   b. As Director of Human Resources, write a response letter assuring the business owner that you will handle the problem.
4. You have been thinking of hiring a group of local students to do some landscaping for you. (You may choose another type of work if you wish.) They have started the work, but you can already tell they are not going to do the kind of job you want.
   a. Write a letter to the group explaining the problems you see. Tell them that you will allow them another two weeks to improve their work or you will not employ them any longer. You can invent any reasonable details for this letter.
   b. As director of the students, write a letter of response. Assure your customer that the students will improve their work and correct any mistakes they have made.

For further assignments dealing with the content of this chapter, see case studies 4, 11, 12, and 17 starting on page 278.

Employment and Career Letters

Some of the most important letters you may write during your lifetime are letters applying for jobs or promotions. It would be helpful to have one generic letter to use in all these situations, but that, of course, is not possible. Quite the contrary: Often you may find yourself writing and rewriting these letters almost endlessly as you try to find exactly the right tone and wording. This chapter looks at job application letters as well as other correspondence related to employment, such as letters of recommendation and resignation.

cover letter

An older and now less common form of *cover letter* is *covering letter*—an expression that helps to clarify the function of this document. A covering letter was originally a letter that, when folded, acted as a holder for other documents, something like an envelope. The covering letter provided an explanation for the enclosures.

Cover Letters

What cover letters "cover," when you apply for a job, is your résumé. Primarily a persuasive document, the cover letter should convince a prospective employer to read your résumé, arrange an interview, and, ultimately, hire you. Notice, in Table 11.1, how the components of both the direct approach (discussed in Chapter 9) and the sales approach (will be discussed in Chapter 12) are interwoven.

Table 11.1 *Aspects of the Cover Letter*

Direct Approach	Cover Letter	Sales Approach
State the main point.	State clearly why you are writing.	Attract the reader's attention.
Provide any necessary details.	Introduce yourself and outline your background briefly.	Name the product, service, or organization.
	Indicate how the company will benefit by hiring you.	Show how the reader will benefit.
Provide a goodwill closing.	Ask for an interview. Use a goodwill closing.	Indicate what action the reader should take.

State Clearly Why You Are Writing

Begin your cover letter by naming the position you are applying for. In some cases, you may also want to indicate how you learned about the position or where you saw the job advertisement.

> At the meeting of the Alberta Veterinary Association in Calgary on March 12th, I spoke to your Director of Publications, Mr. Anton Galen, who suggested that I submit my résumé to you. I am interested in a position as a Veterinary Assistant with Pharmalog International.

Introduce Yourself

If possible, avoid using your opening sentence as an introduction. As soon as you have stated why you are writing, however, tell the reader who you are and provide a brief, selective overview of your education and experience.

> My name is Anton Lumière and I am applying for the position of Computer Programmer. ✗

> I am applying for the position of Computer Programmer advertised in the *Vancouver Sun* on October 1st. As you will see in my résumé, I have more than six years' experience in programming and a diploma in Computer Design. ✓ *(State the purpose for writing, and then introduce yourself. Keep in mind that the reader will see your name at the end of the letter.)*

Indicate the Benefits of Hiring You

Tailor this section carefully. You don't want to repeat everything that the reader will see in your résumé. As much as possible, explain to the reader the benefits of hiring you and use reader-based language. At the same time, remember that this is a kind of sales letter, so don't try to eliminate every reference to "I." If you are applying for a job that has been advertised, use the ad to see what particular skills and characteristics you want to mention.

How the cover letter is organized into paragraphs will depend on the amount of information you have to present. Following your main point, in the opening paragraph, you may want to use two or even three middle paragraphs to expand on your qualifications, especially if you have a lot of education and experience. Follow a logical order by putting what's most relevant to the job first. You might even use a bulleted list, as in the following example, to display a series of points clearly and succinctly:

> A few of the qualifications I can offer your company are
> - excellent communication and customer relation skills acquired through my four years of Help Desk experience
> - extensive knowledge of DataFax
> - proficient knowledge of all Corel and Microsoft software, as well as Visual Basic, HTML, and various web design programs that I have both used and taught

Ask for an Interview

Provide clear details about how you can be reached, including any limits to your availability that may apply. The goodwill closing may refer to your anticipation of an interview, and it should certainly request action.

> You can reach me by e-mail or telephone. The numbers are both in the letterhead at the top of this page. I can be available for an interview at your convenience.
>
> My cell phone number is (891) 443-5547. I have voice mail in case I am not immediately available to answer. I look forward to meeting with you to discuss further your requirements and my qualifications.

Sample Document 11.1 is an example of a cover letter.

T-Letters

The *T-letter* is a new design for a letter of application developed by Tom Murrell.[1] This letter is designed specifically to get an interview by focusing on the qualifications listed in the job advertisement. The unique design arises from the T-letter's use of the ad as the basis for the letter's content. The first step, then, is to review the ad carefully, note the requirements, and compare them with your own qualifications. As an example, here is a job ad:

> **OPERATIONS MANAGER**
> This position offers an opportunity to join a progressive, well-established manufacturing company with an excellent reputation as a leader in its industry.
>
> **Desired Qualifications:**
>
> - Minimum of three years' general management experience
> - Strong sales and marketing experience
> - Strong people and communication skills
> - Able to read CAD drawings
> - Good understanding of AP, AR, and inventory control
> - Ability to speak French as well as English is an asset
> - College degree preferred
>
> **Location:** St. Hyacinthe, QC
> Salary commensurate with experience
> Direct inquiries to:
> Ms A. Marney
> 2001 Lane Highway East
> St. Laurent, QC H4T 6U1

---

[1]Murrell, T. (n.d.). Get more interviews with a T-letter. Retrieved May 8, 2002, from http://www.raycomm.com/techwhirl/employmentarticles/tletter.html.

Sample Document 11.1 *Cover Letter*

Francis Dreyfield

12 Depalma Ave.
Mactier, NB B2B 4N4
fdreyfield@monctoninfo.com
(506) 515-5679

March 28, 2003

Ms Anya Kudar
Manager, Clinical Data Management
Creiff Pharmaceuticals
1200 Yonge Street
Toronto, ON M2C 5L9

Dear Ms Kudar

Please accept my résumé in application for a Clinical Data Management Assistant position.

My educational background revolves primarily around human physiology. I have taken courses in metabolism, physiology, bioethics, psychopharmacology, neuropsychology, immunology, and bacteriology. These particular courses provide a broad spectrum of knowledge in all areas of human structure and function. Experience in the laboratory has enhanced the analytical skills that I can bring to Creiff Pharmaceuticals.

During the past year I have gained the specialized skills required to monitor the administration and progress of clinical trials. I am familiar with the research process and associated regulatory requirements for pharmaceuticals, biologics, and medical devices.

Many years of involvement in athletics have taught me the value of teamwork and loyalty as well as the obligations and responsibilities associated with commitment to a common goal. I am confident that my skills and abilities will be the assets your company is seeking.

You can reach me at the telephone number or e-mail address provided at the top of this letter. On alternate weekends I am on 24-hour call, so I use voice mail to keep track of messages. I look forward to arranging an interview at your convenience.

Sincerely

Francis Dreyfield

Francis Dreyfield

enc. 1

The next step is to create a two-column table that matches the company's requirements on the left with your qualifications on the right. You do not necessarily have to follow the order specified in the ad. Instead, arrange the points to emphasize the personal strengths you want to highlight. This chart will form the centre of your letter. See Table 11.2.

Table 11.2 *Comparing Requirements with Qualifications*

Requirements	Qualifications
• Strong sales and marketing experience	• Three years as Assistant Marketing Manager with Jenco Corporation
• Minimum of three years' general management experience	• Moved to Assistant Director of Marketing
• Able to read CAD drawings • College degree	• Diploma in Computer-Assisted Design from Capilano College
• Good understanding of AP, AR, and inventory control	• Used AP and AR for four years at Jenco • Supervised all inventory control systems
• Ability to speak French as well as English	• Bilingual French and English, and fluent in Italian and Portuguese
• Strong people and communication skills	• Received Highest Sales Award two consecutive years (1999, 2000) • Head of De Palma Chamber of Commerce since 1997 • Volunteer firefighter • Certified coach for local peewee soccer

The final step is to compose short opening and closing paragraphs. If an advertisement has specifically asked for a résumé, you may want to include it, but this style of letter may be used effectively even without a résumé. Sample Document 11.2 is an example of a T-letter.

Recommendation Letters

Recommendation letters can involve some challenging situations:

- You may be the person asking for the letter of recommendation.
- You may be asked to write the letter to a recipient you do not know.
- You may be asked to write a letter for someone you cannot honestly recommend.

The following guidelines refer to letters, but they can also apply to situations where you are responding verbally to any of the above situations.

Sample Document 11.2 *T-Letter*

R.J. Bradshaw
227 1st Avenue
Halifax, Nova Scotia S2T 5R5
rjbrjb@interlock.ca (902) 975-9263

27 May 2002

Ms A. Marney
2001 Lane Highway East
St. Laurent, QC H4T 6U1

Dear Ms Marney

I am responding to your advertisement in *The Globe and Mail* for an Operations Manager in your St. Hyacinthe, QC, location. As you will see from the chart below, I meet or exceed most of the qualifications you have specified. I look forward to meeting with you in person to discuss further the skills and abilities that I can bring to your organization. You can reach me anytime by e-mail or through my cell phone number, printed above.

Your Requirements

- Strong sales and marketing experience
- Minimum of three years' general management experience
- Able to read CAD drawings
- College degree
- Good understanding of AP, AR, and inventory control
- Ability to speak French as well as English
- Strong people and communication skills

My Qualifications

- Three years as Assistant Marketing Manager with Jenco Corporation
- Moved to Assistant Director of Marketing
- Diploma in Computer-Assisted Design from Capilano College
- Used AP and AR for four years at Jenco
- Supervised all inventory control systems
- Bilingual French and English, and fluent in Italian and Portuguese
- Received Highest Sales Award two consecutive years (1999, 2000)
- Head of De Palma Chamber of Commerce since 1997
- Volunteer firefighter
- Certified coach for local peewee soccer

Yours truly

Rhonda J. Bradshaw

Rhonda June Bradshaw

Asking for a Recommendation Letter

To request a letter of recommendation, use the direct approach and the following guidelines:

For the main point, clearly make your request. If necessary, remind your reader of who you are, as in the following example:

> I was a student in your Technical Drawing class during the Winter 2002 term at Campana College. I would appreciate it if you would write a letter of recommendation for me to use in an upcoming job interview.

In the details section, provide the context, and if possible, add some information that will help your reader prepare the letter for you. For example,

> The position I am applying for involves using QuarkXPress and Adobe Photoshop. Perhaps you could mention the special projects I completed using QuarkXPress during the term.

As always, give any further details, use a goodwill closing, and say thank you. For example,

> The letter can be faxed directly to Ellis Siper at (622) 476-9176. Thank you so much for helping me in this way. If you have any further questions, please call me at (452) 347-5232.

Writing a Recommendation Letter

The direct approach also works for writing letters of recommendation. The main point should provide the context. For example,

> A former student of mine, Aaron Gold, asked me to prepare this letter of recommendation for him, and I am happy to do so. I was Aaron's Technical Drawing instructor during his final term at Campana College, January to April 2002.

Add what you can in the way of relevant details, with examples if possible, as shown here. Avoid gushing generalities—focus instead on specifics.

> Aaron excelled in all aspects of the computer graphics course. His final grade of 99 almost speaks for itself. Aaron involved himself in far more than just the coursework, however. Together with another student, he developed a compendium of photographic design programs for the Rim Heslop Company. The resulting files have been incorporated into Heslop's international guidebook for office design.
>
> In addition, Aaron gave his time freely to tutor other students in the college despite his heavy course load. His people skills were reflected not only in his ability to work as part of a team, but also—and more importantly—in his skill in encouraging other students to work in teams.

Your goodwill closing may contain a brief summary statement, such as

> Aaron's skill at problem solving, his patience, and his ability to teach made him an inspiration to all of us who watched him work.

What if You Cannot Recommend Someone?

Occasionally you may be asked to write a letter for someone you cannot recommend. If you are asked by the person who wants the recommendation, you can use an indirect refusal letter to decline tactfully. Here is an example:

> I've received your request for a letter of recommendation.
>
> As you recall, I'm sure, your work in the maintenance department here was not particularly satisfactory to me on several occasions. I do not feel that I could write a positive letter about your employment at The Ultimate Resort. Perhaps you could ask the instructor who helped you to complete your apprenticeship placement.
>
> I wish you success in your future.

An even more difficult situation is to be asked by another company to recommend an employee you would not want to hire. This circumstance can involve potential legal problems: What if you give a poor recommendation and the employee tries to sue you? On the other hand, if you give a positive recommendation, you are not only being dishonest—you are also encouraging another company to hire a potentially inferior employee. This is one place where intentionally vague language and absence of detail may be your only recourse. For example,

> I am replying to your request for information on Jeanette Winkler. Jeanette worked in our maintenance department from August 1, 2000 until January 9, 2002. During that period, Jeanette experienced several bouts of illness and other personal difficulties that prevented her from becoming a strong contributor to our maintenance team. I hope that her situation has improved so that she can experience a successful future.

Resignation Letters

Normally you will use the direct approach for a resignation letter unless the circumstances are negative. Sample Document 11.3 is an example of a simple, straightforward letter of resignation.

Sample Document 11.3 *Resignation Letter*

Ibrahim Sol

9 - 934 Regent Avenue
Sutherland, SK
S2R 3T1

March 9, 2003

Allan Nyfield
Promotions Manager
The Ultimate Resort and Spa
Highway 60, R.R. 2
Mirror Falls, ON L3R 4R4

Dear Mr. Nyfield

This letter is formal notice that I will be resigning from The Ultimate at the end of April. My last day will be April 29, 2003.

I will be returning to school to continue graduate studies in Management and Human Resources.

All of the current projects I am working on should be complete by the middle of April.

Thank you for your direction and encouragement over the past two years.

Sincerely

Ibrahim Sol

Ibrahim Sol

Activities and Exercises

1. Locate and bring to class a job advertisement for a position in your field. Write a cover letter to apply for the job.
2. Write a second letter applying for the same position. This time, use the T-letter format. Compare your two letters. Which one seems more suitable? Why?
3. Write a letter of recommendation for yourself. This is actually a good exercise to try so that you can honestly assess your own strengths. Sometimes, if you ask teachers or employers for a letter of recommendation, they will ask you to prepare the letter and then they will sign it.

For further assignments dealing with the content of this chapter, see Case Study 18 starting on page 307.

Persuasive Letters and Form Letters

The formulas outlined in chapters 9–11 should help you compose most of the letters you will need to write. This chapter looks briefly at persuasive letters and form letters. Since the material here can only skim the surface of the larger topics of sales, fundraising, and bulk mailings, you should consult more specialized texts if you will be working predominantly in these areas.

Persuasive Letters

persuade

Suada (also known as *Pitho*) was the Roman goddess of persuasion and daughter of Venus. The Latin verbs *suadere* and *persuadere* mean "to induce" or "to draw in." The word *suave*—a word that originally meant "agreeable to the senses"—comes from the same root. Thus the term *persuasion* suggests the use of something agreeable to move a person from one place (physical or emotional) to another.

The study of the art of persuasion (*rhetorica*) comprises many disciplines from logic to politics to psychology, history, and ethics. This chapter can only skim the surface of such a dense and fascinating subject by looking at a few ways to write an effective persuasive document. Jay A. Conger has succinctly stated that these days most people no longer just ask, "What should I do? but Why should I do it? To answer this why question effectively is to persuade."[1] In the workplace, persuasion fuels sales, fundraising, job interviews, career advancement, and customer satisfaction in general.

In his work entitled *Ars Rhetorica*, Aristotle, the Greek philosopher, described the three classic forms of effective persuasion: *logos, pathos, ethos.*

logos

Logos, or the use of reason, underlies the study of formal logic: the use of premises and conclusions that can be affirmed or denied.

[1]Conger, J.A. (1998). The necessary art of persuasion. *Harvard Business Review* (May–June), 86.

Arguments based on logic are not that common, although they do occur in debates, law courts, and Parliament. The use of formal logic works much like chess—a game requiring intense mental effort. Unfortunately, most of the sales pitches that bombard us daily are founded on faulty or incomplete arguments. As for day-to-day communication, logic is supposed to be what takes place in that interval when we "count to 10" before allowing emotions to fuel our arguments.

pathos

Pathos is a term that originally denoted suffering or intense feeling—the passions, "the great springs of human action."[2]

One of the most common pitches for fundraisers is the emotional appeal. The Humane Society, for example, uses photographs of sad puppies in cages; Foster Parents Plan describes and illustrates the plight of children living in poverty. While these organizations may also add logical reasoning to their appeals, the emotional details are often the most convincing. The use of fear and our innate desire for love are also highly effective motivators. Many advertisements—whether for tires, vitamins, insurance, or toothpaste—work on the basis of thinly veiled threats to our comfort and well-being or by offering the promise of popularity. Patriotism and religious fervour are other highly effective emotional springboards.

ethos

Ethos is a Greek word referring to the character and credibility of a person or organization. It is, of course, the root from which we get the term *ethics*.

While the appeal to reason tries to present information logically and the appeal to emotions may prompt receivers to open and read a letter, the appeal of ethos is probably the most powerful. *Ethos* is not so much a technique as a quality—the quality of believability or moral strength. This quality arises from elements such as integrity, long service, a recognized brand name or label; it is the hard-earned essence of a good reputation, a quality passed by word of mouth from customer to customer. Needless to say, companies protect this quality fiercely.

The irony is that credibility can, at first, spring from surface features. Why else does the lawyer tell a scruffy client to wear a suit and tie to court? Why do you take time to make your résumé look clean and orderly on fine-quality stationery? Why do some com-

---

[2]Blair, H. (1990). Lecture 32 from *Lectures on rhetoric and belles lettres.* Quoted in P. Bizzell and B. Herzberg (Eds.), *The rhetorical tradition: Readings from classical times to the present* (p. 824). Boston: Bedford Books. (Original work published 1783.)

panies spend as much on packaging as they do on the product inside? In the end, however, *ethos* is difficult to fake over the long term. A document that looks good soon loses its credibility if the content is poorly written, illogical, inaccurate, or dishonest.

Sales and Fundraising

These days, computer software has made it easier to produce a seemingly endless stream of documents (both print and e-mail) that ask you to part with your money. The effectiveness of these communications can usually be traced to at least one of the persuasive techniques described by Aristotle. The following formula will help you to recognize these techniques and apply them effectively:

1. Attract the reader's attention.
2. Name the product, service, or organization.
3. Show how the reader will benefit.
4. Indicate what action the reader should take.

Attract the Reader's Attention

To attract the reader's attention, you may want to use language, graphics, layout, or all three. Sometimes an organization begins the "attract attention" element right on the envelope:

You may have already won!

The choice of an attention-getting device obviously depends on the product, the audience, and the credibility of the sending organization. This is probably the one place in business communication where exclamation marks and eye-popping fonts appear routinely.

Wrap up a smile this Christmas!

YOU could be the next millionaire!!!

Would you like to save a life?

Your opening may appeal to the reader's curiosity, sympathy, or—quite frankly—greed. Whatever the appeal, the goal of the writer is to make sure the document gets read, not discarded.

Name the Product, Service, or Organization

Early in your letter, you should identify your product, service, or organization and provide background details to establish credibility. For example,

> You know our name and our history well. For over 30 years, The Dreams Come True Foundation has turned dreams into reality for hundreds of children.
>
> The Atlas Exercise Regime has been proven successful by hundreds of satisfied customers. Recently, our products were featured on the Regis and Kelly

Show. Visit our new website and see for yourself the difference that a regulated program of exercise and proper nutrition can make. You can discover how to **change your life** for the better!

This step often separates legitimate appeals from scams. If a sales flyer or a request for money does not clearly identify the sender, or if the information seems fuzzy or ambiguous, readers should beware.

Now available for only a limited time in your community, this new product brings the secrets of Madame Flingabout to your door. Only a few people will receive this amazing offer.

Show How the Reader Will Benefit

Benefits may be concrete and measurable (such as a lower rate of interest on a credit card), abstract (such as a feeling of pride or altruism), or tempting and elusive. Look at the following examples:

Maybe you have wondered how one person can make a difference. Now you can discover the joy of helping one child learn to read.

Apply for your card today and you'll pay no annual membership fees. When you compare our offer with the fees you pay for other credit cards, you'll see that we are actually putting money in your pocket.

You can be an amazing 20 pounds slimmer in just six easy weeks! No dieting! No pills!

Indicate What Action the Reader Should Take

The encounter with your readers is not complete without closing the transaction. Action is the evidence that persuasion has worked. Readers may be drawn into your document because of your effective opening, and they may read it because of its appeal to their needs or wants. But they demonstrate the effectiveness of your persuasive technique by acting. Your job is to provide clear directions so they know exactly what to do. Your letter may include a mail-in card, a toll-free number, or an e-mail address along with detailed information about when you are available.

HERE'S HOW YOU CAN HELP!
MAIL your cheque today in the enclosed, postage-paid envelope.
SAVE your grocery store tapes.
GIVE this newsletter to a friend.

Sample Document 12.1 is an example of how persuasive language works in a sales letter.

Sample Document 12.1 ***Persuasive Language in a Sales Letter***

7.9%

Limited Time Rate

Whether you're burning through the mogul fields or dining out in a mountaintop restaurant, let your new credit card speak for you. We've captured the exhilaration of skiing and matched it with the financial strength of SUPERCARD in our new Ski and Snowboard cards, featuring a credit limit up to $20 000. No other card will better convey your passion for this great sport or show the financial status you've earned. And, we've got four great card design choices for you. But the good news doesn't end there!

Avid skiers demand the most out of their skis, so why shouldn't their credit cards work just as hard? By becoming a SUPERCARD cardholder, you'll gain the advantage of an interest rate that is drastically lower than many other credit cards—just 7.9% until September 2003—if you respond by March 30, 2003.*

No Annual Fee

Apply today and you'll pay NO ANNUAL MEMBERSHIP FEES. When you compare that with the fees you may pay with other credit cards, you'll see that we're actually putting money in your pocket!

Win Whistler!

Every applicant will be entered automatically to win one of four trips for two to Whistler—a value of almost $3250.

Free Balance Transfer

Rates this low are hard to find. So start saving money NOW by transferring balances from other cards that charge you more.

It's Never Been Easier

Simply complete the enclosed Three-Minute Acceptance Form and mail it today. The postage is paid. Once your application is approved, we'll assign your initial credit limit and immediately send your new SUPERCARD so you can enjoy the low interest rates you deserve.

*After the introductory period, you will continue to save with our ongoing rate of just 17.9%.

Form Letters

Computer programs allow you to make a *form letter* out of any document you have written simply by merging it with an address list. This practice saves time and is an effective means of communication for companies that need to send out identical information to hundreds of clients. In fact, form letters have many uses: for sales and fundraising, for collecting survey data, and for distributing general information to members of a large group.

Making a form letter that sounds personal and reader-based takes practice. You've probably already experienced those annoying "Dear Subscriber" or "Dear Occupant" letters that are so easy to ignore. The opposite problem—and equally annoying—is the practice of using a computer program that "personalizes" form letters by inserting a person's name at frequent points throughout the letter, as in the following example:

> Dear T. Bonsworth
>
> Readers' Preference is delighted to bring you this one-time specially designed reader offer. We know that you, T. Bonsworth, are a busy person with discriminating taste in literature. That's why we are sure you will appreciate our latest collection of great literature bound in genuine leather. And just for sampling the first volume in this series, T. Bonsworth, you will receive a free six-month subscription to *The New York Times Review of Books.*

If you decide that a form letter will be useful to your company, keep the following guidelines in mind:

- Use the correct formula for whatever type of letter is required (e.g., adjustment, complaint, sales).
- Avoid referring to your reader in the third person (he, she, they). Instead, use second person: you. Use your customer's name in the salutation if possible, but avoid overusing his or her name.
- Keep your message simple. If you are selecting comments from a list of choices, follow the rules of good letter setup so your information is clear and understandable.
- Practise meticulous proofreading. In fact, since this document will be read by many people, make extra sure that it has no errors. Ask several people to read it to make sure the content is clear and accurate.

Sample Document 12.2 is an example of a form letter.

Sample Document 12.2 *Form Letter*

Recreational Equitation Collective of Canada
100 Bay Street Winnipeg, MB W2L 4R4
Tel.: (203) 654-7833 Fax: (203) 663-4532
recc@mn.ca

Ms Alma George
Box 225
Fort Ancaster, NB
T2R 4W6

CLAIM NO.: 44612

Claims must be submitted within twelve (12) days of injury

Dear Ms Alma George

Your claim has been received and will be processed during the next four to six weeks. Please make sure you submit all reports issued by your veterinarian. You should also submit a certified copy of any personal injury claim that may have been submitted to other insuring agencies.

PLEASE NOTE If any subsequent injury or disablement occurs, you must include the above file number on the information you submit. Otherwise a new claim may be initiated and you will be assessed a penalty.

Yours sincerely

J. Surenta

J. SURENTA
Claims Representative
(203) 654-1236

c: D. Hardwick, DVM

Further documents required:

Personal Injury Claim Forms ☑
Patient's RECC Identity Card ☐
Accident Report Form ☐

Activities and Exercises

1. A good place to see letters that contain arguments (logical or not) is the Letters to the Editor section of a newspaper. Read through some of these letters, and discuss whether the arguments are well made.
2. Advertising provides excellent examples of the use of persuasion. Bring several different advertisements to class and identify the appeals being used.
3. Working on your own or with a small group, identify an issue at your school or workplace that could use improvement or change. Using the formula presented in this chapter, write a persuasive letter to the person who could approve such a change.

For further assignments dealing with the content of this chapter, see case studies 3, 7, and 8 starting on page 277.

Part Three

Short Documents

Shortened Versions of Longer Documents

A document of almost any length can be rewritten in a shorter version—often called an abstract or summary—to save time and space. Whatever the document, whatever the reason, when you condense it you should incorporate the gist of the original. The guidelines provided in this chapter refer to the conventional uses of the terms "abstract" and "summary."[1]

gist

Gist probably has its root in the French *gésir*, meaning "to lie" or "to contain," and *gîte*, "a vein" or "seam" (as in mining). *Gisement* is a French geological term referring to a vein of ore or to bedrock. The gist, therefore, is the fundamental or underlying idea.

No matter what you call the finished product, when you set out to condense a document, keep in mind two key points:

- Audience: Who is going to be reading the abstract or summary?
- Purpose: How and why will it be used?

As well, since you will nearly always be writing this type of document on demand, you must meet the requirements of the particular situation. So a third point to consider is

- Context: What has your instructor/manager/workplace/editor asked you to do?

Abstracts

Abstracts may be written by the writer of the original document, but often they are written by people whose specific job is to prepare commercial abstracts.

[1] For an excellent overview of the form and function of different types of summaries and abstracts, see David K. Vaughan's 1991 article, Abstracts and summaries: Some clarifying distinctions. *The Technical Writing Teacher 18*(2), 132–40. It describes accurately the confusion that arises in the use of terms such as "summary," "executive summary," "abstract," "synopsis," and even "introduction."

abstract

The term *abstract* comes from the Latin *ab*, meaning "away from," and *trahere* (*tractus*) meaning "to draw." In chemistry, "abstract" is a verb meaning "to separate an essence by distillation." The English writer Samuel Johnson provided this succinct definition of the word: "a smaller quantity containing the virtue or power of the greater." [2]

Descriptive Abstracts

Reading a *descriptive abstract* might be compared with reading the blurb on the back cover of a novel or running your eye down a book's table of contents. The descriptive abstract tells you what you're going to be reading about in the actual article or report. It usually touches on the purpose and scope of the original document, and it may outline how that document is organized. The distinctive characteristic of a descriptive abstract is that it can rarely stand on its own. Instead, it acts like an appetizer, leading you to read the complete article. Sample documents 13.1 and 13.2 are examples of descriptive abstracts.

Sample Document 13.1 ***Descriptive Abstract***

Murray, J.P. (1999). Faculty development in a national sample of community colleges. *Community College Review, 27*(3), 47–64.

The author defines the activities that distinguish successful development programs and describes a survey administered in 1998 to faculty development officers at 250 randomly selected community colleges. Based on responses from 130 colleges, the author profiles those responsible for faculty development, summarizes the extent that each development activity is used, and articulates the need for concerted faculty development efforts at community colleges.

Sample Document 13.2 ***Descriptive Abstract***

Veiga, N.E. (1989). Sexism, sex stereotyping, and the technical writer. *Journal of Technical Writing and Communication, 19*(3), 277–83.

This article discusses the impact of possible sex-based differences in communication styles on the technical writer's job. Linguistic research proposes a male and female style of communication. While it is helpful to acknowledge possible differences in communication styles, technical writers must be concerned with the moral and legal implications of sex stereotyping. To explore these issues, the article discusses what it is technical writers do, and who they interact with on a daily basis. It then reviews linguistic research and linguistic folklore. Finally, the article determines that technical writers can choose to use both male and female traits to acknowledge multiple audiences and improve the quality of their documents.

[2]Johnson, S. (1755). *Dictionary of the English Language.* London: J. Knapton.

Form and Style

Depending on the amount of detail the writer of the abstract chooses to incorporate and, of course, on the length of the original document, a descriptive abstract may be only one or two sentences or as long as 500 words.

Notice some of the distinctive features of sample documents 13.1 and 13.2:

- They refer to the original article or the writer in the third person:
  - "The author defines...."
  - "This article discusses...."
- They use a narrative or sequential approach, touching on the subject of the articles and then mentioning the various directions the articles take, using transition words such as "then" and "finally."
- They introduce topics and important terms ("activities," "male," and "female"), but they do not give details. For example, they do not tell the reader "what it is technical writers do" or explain what male and female styles are like, and they do not reveal which "activities ... distinguish successful development programs."

Informative Abstracts

Informative abstracts can and do stand alone; in fact, they are usually designed to do exactly that. Professional journals, as well as commercial indexing and abstracting services, provide abstracts that are used by readers who want to

- Read just the abstract because they can get enough information from it.
- Read the abstract first, to see whether they should then obtain and read the entire article.
- Read many abstracts as an efficient way to keep current with the latest knowledge in their field.

Sample documents 13.3 and 13.4 are examples of informative abstracts.

Sample Document 13.3 ***Informative Abstract***

Diaz, P.E., & Krauss, J.L. (1996). A needs analysis of an expanding hospitality market—Asian students. *Hospitality Research Journal, 20*(1), 15–22.

A study of Asian hospitality students was undertaken to determine why they came for an American education, how they heard about the program, and what support services they needed. The study revealed that academic reputation of both the university and the program are important, as are academic facilities, course variety, and other variables. Services desired were tutors, scholarships, matched peer advisors, home newspapers, and helpful faculty advisors.

Sample Document 13.4 ***Informative Abstract of a 19-Page Proposal***[3]

Title of Research: Equipment and Methods to Plant Pines and to Reduce Fuel Loads on Small Land Tracts

Company: Florida Recycling and Composting Consulting Services Inc.

Rt. 4, Box 1297 H.

Starke, FL 32091

Principal Investigator: Dr. Paul Still

Topic Area: Forests and Related Resources

Grant Amount: $70 000/6 months

Increasing numbers of people in the Southeast are moving onto small 5 to 50 acre tracts of land that are forested or were farm land. This change in land use increases risk of property loss from wildfires, increases the percentage of timber resources in small tracts, and results in under-utilized land resources. Current equipment and methods used in forestry operations are based on large tracts of land using large high capital cost equipment. This project will test compact lower capital cost equipment including a flail mower and a tiller mounted on a bi-directional compact 75 HP Antonio Carrao tractor. The equipment will serve to mow understory woody plants, to reduce fuel loads, and to mow and till sites before planting trees. Spray and wiper methods will be used to apply herbicides. Two test sites in each of five Florida counties will be used to evaluate the equipment and methods. A business model will be developed to help individuals decide if they want to provide forestry services to owners of small forest tracts. Services would include mowing and herbicide treatment to reduce fuel loads, timberland maintenance to increase productivity of existing timberlands, and establishment of longleaf pines.

Form and Style

Informative abstracts usually run from 250 to 500 words and include the purpose of the article, report or proposal; the scope of the research; the method or procedures; the principal results; and the most important conclusions or recommendations.

Notice the following features in sample documents 13.3 and 13.4:

- They use no self-referential words. That is, unlike the descriptive abstracts, they do not include words such as "this article."
- The passive voice is predominant.
- They provide information about the actual results (or expected results) of the study. The abstract, therefore, could contain all the information some readers need.

[3]United States Department of Agriculture. (2001). *USDA/SBIR Phase I technical abstracts, fiscal year 2001.* Retrieved May 18, 2002, from http://www.reeusda.gov/crgam/sbir/01phase1.htm#equipment. Reprinted with permission.

Summaries

You will find that the term *summary* is often used interchangeably with abstract. Abstracts seem to be written most often for an academic or professional reader, and they are usually one paragraph long.

summary

Summary is derived from the Latin *summa*, meaning "the highest (or most important) thing."

In business and technical writing, the term "summary" has two common uses:

- the executive summary, which appears at the beginning of a document
- the concluding or intermittent summary, which appears throughout or at the end of a document

Executive Summary

An *executive summary* targets a specific audience, usually management. Although it tends to follow a pattern similar to the informative abstract, the executive summary may incorporate a particular "spin" on the data. So the context in which the summary appears affects its tone and content. For example, it may skim over technical information and emphasize administrative issues such as costs, feasibility, resource management, and decision making.

As with abstracts, executive summaries may be prepared by the writer of the original document. They may also be written by individuals within specific organizations, custom-designed for their managers. These latter writers may even add editorial or evaluative comments about the original article. Sample Document 13.5 is an example of an executive summary. This one appears at the beginning of the journal in which the full article appears. Notice the language, which shows that the summary was not written by the author of the article; this summary targets readers of the journal and refers to the writer of the article in terms of his workplace and business philosophy:

> Xerox's business is technology, but Brown argues that any company, no matter what the business, must eventually grapple with the issues he raises.

Sample Document 13.5 ***Executive Summary*[4]**

Brown, J.S. (1991, January–February). Research that reinvents the corporation. *Harvard Business Review*, 41–61.

The most important invention that will come out of the corporate research lab in the future will be the corporation itself. As companies try to keep pace with rapid changes in technology and cope with unstable business environments, the research department has to do more than simply innovate new products. It must design the new technological and organization "architectures" that make a continuously innovating company possible.

In this article John Seely Brown, director of the Xerox Palo Alto Research Center (PARC), describes the business logic behind this distinctive vision of research's role and the ways PARC has tried to realize that vision. PARC researchers are prototyping new work practices as well as new technologies and products. They are designing new uses of technology to support the naturally occurring "local innovation" that takes place at all levels of any big company. And they are experimenting with new techniques for "coproducing" technological and organizational innovations—not only with other departments at Xerox but with the company's customers as well.

Xerox's business is technology, but Brown argues that any company, no matter what the business, must eventually grapple with the issues he raises. The successful company of the future must understand how people really work and how technology can help them work more effectively. It must know how to create an environment for continual innovation on the part of all employees. It must rethink traditional business assumptions and tap needs that customers don't even know they have yet. It must use research to reinvent the corporation.

Form and Style

An executive summary is traditionally one page long (double-spaced). This format fits well with most workplace documents such as reports and proposals. In reality, however, an executive summary may well be much longer—as many as six or eight pages long—depending on the length of the original document and the publication in which the summary appears. Sample Document 13.6 is the executive summary for the *Report of the Westray Mine Public Inquiry* by Justice K. Peter Richard.[5] This summary, written by the author of the report, comprises not so much an informative summary of the report's contents as an emotional overview of the context in which it was written.

---

[4]Reprinted by permission of *Harvard Business Review*. From "Research that reinvents the corporation" by John Seely Brown, January/February 1991 issue.

[5]Province of Nova Scotia. (1997, November). *The Westray story: A predictable path to disaster.* Retrieved May 18, 2002, from http://www.gov.ns.ca/labr/westray/execsumm.htm.

Report of the Westray Mine Public Inquiry
Justice K. Peter Richard, Commissioner
November 1997

Executive Summary

"The most important thing to come out of a mine is the miner."
Frédéric Le Play (1806–1882)
French sociologist and inspector general of mines of France

At 5:20 a.m. on 9 May 1992 the Westray mine exploded
taking the lives of the following 26 miners.

John Thomas Bates, 56
Bennie Joseph Benoit, 42
Ferris Todd Dewan, 35
Robert Steven Doyle, 22
Roy Edward Feltmate, 33
Myles Daniel Gillis, 32
Randolph Brian House, 27
Laurence Elwyn James, 34
Stephen Paul Lilley, 40
Angus Joseph MacNeil, 39
Harry A. McCallum, 41
George S. James Munroe, 38
Romeo Andrew Short, 35
Larry Arthur Bell, 25
Wayne Michael Conway, 38
Adonis J. Dollimont, 36
Remi Joseph Drolet, 38
Charles Robert Fraser, 29
John Philip Halloran, 33
Trevor Martin Jahn, 36
Eugene W. Johnson, 33
Michael Frederick MacKay, 38
Glenn David Martin, 35
Eric Earl McIsaac, 38
Danny James Poplar, 39
Peter Francis Vickers, 38

This Report is dedicated to their memory.

In the early morning of 9 May 1992 a violent explosion rocked the tiny community of Plymouth, just east of Stellarton, in Pictou County, Nova Scotia. The explosion occurred in the depths of the Westray coal mine, instantly killing the 26 miners working there at the time. On 15 May 1992, I was appointed by Order in Council to inquire into and report on this disaster.

During the formative days of this Inquiry, as my understanding of the underground coal mining industry developed, I was struck by two notions that have persisted throughout. The industry is very close-knit with an interdependence, camaraderie, and fellowship that may be unique in modern-day business. And people in the industry, at all levels, regard what occurred at Westray as a personal matter affecting them as if it had happened in their own backyard. It is for them a family tragedy. I suspect that these attitudes have deep historic roots.

(continued)

Westray Mine Public Inquiry
November 1997
page 2 of 3

There are few industries in which one's safety, indeed one's very survival, is so inextricably linked to the attitudes, practices, concerns, and behaviour of fellow workers. Truly, in the underground coal mining environment, you are "your brother's keeper." The miner who sneaks a smoke while underground is risking the lives of his fellow miners. On 7 December 1992, the flick of a cigarette lighter underground caused the death of eight miners at the Southmountain Coal Company in Virginia.

The Westray tragedy is regarded in the industry as a black mark against coal mining in general rather than as a merely localized event. As a result, I received a remarkable degree of cooperation from the industry, which, while being most encouraging, underscored the solemn responsibility I had assumed. The coal industry—miners, managers, operators, and regulators—is most anxious to determine what can be learned as a result of this tragedy and what can be done to prevent another.

The 1981 Report of the Joint Federal–Provincial Inquiry Commission into Safety in Mines and Mining Plants in Ontario (the Burkett Report) is aptly entitled Towards Safe Production. As its title suggests, the entire thrust of the report is to increase and to promote safe practices in mines. The only completely safe mine is a closed mine. By the same token, the only completely safe aircraft is on the ground with the engines off. The only truly safe automobile is the one parked in the garage. Once a mine is open, there begins the constant process of trade-off between production and safety. From the chief executive officer to the miner at the working face, the objective must be to operate the mine in a manner that ensures the personal safety of the worker over the economic imperatives of increased production. The two seemingly competing concepts—safety and production—must be so harmonized that they can co-exist without doing harm to each other. It is here that the regulator must assume the role of monitor and aggressively ensure that the balance is understood and maintained. In this sense, the function of the regulator is both instructive and supervisory. As one provincial mine inspector in Ontario told me, "Ideally, if we perform our duties properly we will eventually work ourselves out of a job." As I read Towards Safe Production, I was impressed with the clarity and wisdom of this regulatory role.

The Order in Council that established this Inquiry gives me power to "inquire into … whether the occurrence was or was not preventable." Of course it was. For this Report we have chosen the title The Westray Story: A Predictable Path to Disaster to convey that message. The message is that the Westray tragedy was predictable and, therefore, preventable. The Report contains recommendations and suggestions aimed at avoiding a similar occurrence in the future. Anyone who hopes to find in this Report a simple and conclusive answer as to

(continued)

Westray Mine Public Inquiry
November 1997
page 3 of 3

how this tragedy happened will be disappointed. Anyone who expects that this Report will single out one or two persons and assess total blame for the tragedy will be similarly disappointed. The Westray Story is a complex mosaic of actions, omissions, mistakes, incompetence, apathy, cynicism, stupidity, and neglect. Some well-intentioned but misguided blunders were also added to the mix. It was clear from the outset that the loss of 26 lives at Plymouth, Pictou County, in the early morning hours of 9 May 1992 was not the result of a single definable event or misstep. Only the serenely uninformed (the wilfully blind) or the cynically self-serving could be satisfied with such an explanation.

This Report has been written with the benefit of hindsight, which, as the saying goes, provides 20/20 vision. Many of the incidents that now appear to fit into the mosaic might at the time, and of themselves, have seemed trivial. Viewed in context, these seemingly isolated incidents constitute a mind-set or operating philosophy that appears to favour expediency over intelligent planning and that trivializes safety concerns.

Indeed, management at Westray displayed a certain disdain for safety and appeared to regard safety-conscious workers as the wimps in the organization. To its discredit, the management at Westray, through either incompetence or ignorance, lost sight of the basic tenet of coal mining: that safe mining is good business. As one mining executive remarked to me in June 1996 during a mine visit to Alabama, "We could not afford to operate an unsafe mine, due to the high cost of accidents and downtime." Certainly, the validity of this concept was never more obvious than in the horrible aftermath of Westray.

The tale that unfolds in the ensuing narrative is the Westray Story. It is a story of incompetence, of mismanagement, of bureaucratic bungling, of deceit, of ruthlessness, of cover-up, of apathy, of expediency, and of cynical indifference. It is a tragic story, with the inevitable moments of pathos and heroism. The Westray Story concerns an event that, in all good common sense, ought not to have occurred. It did occur—and that is our unfortunate legacy.

Periodic Summary

The *periodic summary* performs a completely different function from the descriptive abstract, the informative abstract, or the executive summary. It may appear at the beginning of a document that is divided into chapters, intermittently throughout a document, or at the end of a document.

Depending on whether a periodic summary precedes or follows a piece of writing, it acts like a preview or review. In a textbook, for example, each chapter may open with a brief list of the main points to be covered in that chapter. Or, each chapter may end with a checklist of important points. Often a speaker will keep listeners on track by verbally summing up what has been said and what the next topic will be. In very long documents, a periodic summary gives the reader a chance to stop and catch up—a brief refresher of what has been covered. Whether you are studying for an exam or trying to get through a long textbook, "rehearsal" summaries make the task easier. Sample Document 13.7 is an example of this type of summary.

Sample Document 13.7 ***Periodic Summary at the Beginning of a Chapter***[6]

> This chapter examines a range of external memory devices and systems. We begin with the most important device, the magnetic disk. Magnetic disks are the foundation of external memory on virtually all computer systems. The next section examines the use of disk arrays to achieve greater performance, looking specifically at the family of systems known as RAID (redundant array of independent disks). An increasingly important component of many computer systems is external optical memory, and this is examined in the third section. Finally, magnetic tape is described.

Condensing a Document Effectively

No matter which type of abstract or summary you plan to write, you may find that the techniques are similar: You choose some material to keep, and omit the rest.

One technique that's often helpful, especially if you already have experience with writing essays, is to use essay-writing skills in reverse. Most essays, for example, contain a thesis statement and then a series of paragraphs that expand on the thesis. The paragraphs are normally structured with a topic sentence and then several more sentences to add support. If you are summarizing an article, therefore, look for the structure that lies within it: Locate the thesis statement, and try to identify the topic sentence of each paragraph. If you are working with a very long document, you will probably discover that every paragraph does not begin a new topic; instead, one topic is introduced and developed in a series of paragraphs before the next point is introduced. With a pen and sheet of paper, you can try to diagram the outline the writer of the article might have used.

If you are summarizing a report with headings and subheadings, these will often give you the key points you need to include in your abstract or summary. Summaries of reports usually focus on their purpose and the principal findings.

[6] This summary appears at the beginning of Chapter 5, "External Memory," in Stallings, W. (2000). *Computer organization and architecture* (5th ed.). Upper Saddle River, NJ: Prentice Hall.

Consider the Context

You should know clearly what type of abstract or summary you have to write, who your readers will be, and under what circumstances your readers will use your abstract or summary. These details will affect the length, tone, and content of your writing.

Use a written guideline as you read so you know what specific points to look for. Here are two examples:

Summary Requirements

- I need an informative abstract.
- It should be one paragraph of approximately 200 words.
- It should focus on purpose, findings, and principal recommendations.

Summary Requirements

- I need an executive summary.
- It can be one to two pages long, double-spaced.
- The main readers will be the Finance and IT departments.
- It needs to focus on short- and long-term costs as well as software and hardware recommendations.

Know the Material

You must understand the overall tone and purpose of the article to capture the gist accurately. Read the entire article several times, and make sure you understand key terminology. As you become familiar with the material, you can usually omit the following elements:

- quotations
- graphics
- anecdotes
- personal comments by or about the author
- detailed descriptions and explanations
- examples, unless a unique or unusual example provides support for one of the main points of the article

Prepare a Draft

When you read the original article for the second or third time, begin to choose and highlight the various points you will need to include in your abstract or summary. Using the points you have chosen, write a draft. Use your own words as much as possible; however, if the article contains specialized terms or definitions that are critical to a clear understanding, you should incorporate these in your writing.

Edit Your Work

Reread and review your work as you would any piece of writing. Compare it with the original article for accuracy, tone, and logic. Make sure you have followed the guidelines you listed at the beginning. Check your writing for clear sentence structure, logic, and grammatical correctness.

Document the Original Material

An abstract or summary should always clearly state the source of the original article. Provide the author, full title, and all publication data (see the sample documents in this chapter for examples).

Activities and Exercises

1. Assume you have been asked to write a 200-word executive summary of an article entitled "Counterfeit Credit Cards: How to Protect Hotel Guests."[7] Even without seeing the actual article, you can make some assumptions about how the focus of your summary would change for different audiences. What issues might you highlight if you were writing for
   - hotel security staff?
   - hotel front desk staff?
   - hotel administration?
2. Locate an article of four to six pages in your discipline. In a small group, try each of the following methods of preparing a condensed version of the article:
   - Select the topic sentences from each paragraph, and use these to write an informative abstract.
   - If the article uses headings, try using just the headings to write an informative abstract. Does this method work? Why or why not?
   - Write a descriptive abstract.
   - Identify and highlight all the elements that would normally be omitted from an abstract (quotations, graphics, anecdotes, examples, etc.). Do not write the actual summary.
   - Write two intermittent summaries, one about halfway through and one at the end of the article. These should deal only with the material that has preceded them.
   - Write a one-page executive summary for a suitable target audience, such as a human resources, finance, or health and safety department.
3. Students were asked to write a summary of 80–100 words of the article "Shattering the Myths of the Part-Time Worker" by Crist Inman and Cathy Enz.

---

[7]Hobson, J.S.P., & Ko, M. (1995). *Cornell Quarterly, 36*(4), 48–54.

Working with a small group, choose one of the following four examples and write a brief evaluation under the headings: Accuracy, Grammar, Length, Point of View.

Try writing your own summary of the article, which appears in Chapter 5.

Summary 1

Although part-time workers can help an employer by filling in during peak business periods, they are actually expensive to employ because they need to be replaced often. Managers say that they are lazy and irresponsible and don't care about the customers or the benefits of the job. Inman and Enz interviewed 125 full-time employees in a restaurant chain. Their findings were a surprise. They learned that all the assumptions about part-time workers were myths. They recommend that employers should treat their employees better by revising compensation, providing training, and opening up the possibilities.

Summary 2

Since most employees in the food service industry are part-time, managers should treat them better. Instead of assuming that their part-time employees are expendable, managers should treat them the same as full-time employees. A survey of employees in a restaurant chain showed that all the employees felt the same way about their jobs, not just the full-time employees. To improve the way employees are treated, managers should communicate better, pay better, and train them better.

Summary 3

Most managers in the food service industry ignore their part-time employees. As a result, part-time employees become dissatisfied with their jobs and leave to find a new job. The managers then have to hire and train new employees, which is expensive to do. A survey of part-time and full-time employees in a restaurant chain found that the part-timers and full-timers felt the same way about their job. Employers, therefore, would save money if they treated part-timers in a way that would encourage them to stay. Some suggestions would be to pay them better, give them proper training, communicate with them more, and above all, offer them benefits.

Summary 4

High employee turnover is expensive for any company. In the food service industry, most workers are part-timers and they tend to change jobs frequently because they are not well treated. Managers assume, incorrectly, that part-timers are not important; they think that part-timers have lower work standards and are generally inferior to full-timers. The study conducted by Inman and Enz shows that these beliefs are wrong. Part-time workers have the same work attitudes as full-timers. Employers would save money in the long run if they encouraged their part-timers to stay by offering them better training, higher salaries, and benefits.

For further assignments dealing with the content of this chapter, see case studies 12, 13, 15, and 19 starting on page 293.

Definitions and Descriptions

Definitions and descriptions in technical and business documents may seem similar, and, in fact, they often appear in combination. Each mode, however, does differ in content, purpose, and style.

A definition explains the precise meaning of a term or concept. Definitions may include information about use or function, and may name parts in order to distinguish one item from many others in its class. Here is an example of a definition:

> A vase is an open container used for holding flowers.

If you are writing for an audience within your discipline or profession, using jargon is a good idea; it often saves time and you can assume that your readers will understand you. See Box 14.1.

Box 14.1 *Examples of Jargon*

> Usually, glucose is the only substrate metabolized by the brain to supply its energy requirements, and most of the energy from oxidative breakdown of glucose is transferred to ATP.
>
> The contribution approach has some advantages over the absorption-costing approach, or the full-cost approach, because the latter often fails to highlight different cost-behaviour patterns.
>
> Thin, malleable veneers will sometimes conform to very shallow curves in two directions, and such double curvature can be assisted by premoistening and pressing between heated cauls or formers, but the amount of stretch must be within the elastic limits of the wood plies.

In a situation where you must use jargon for a nonprofessional audience, use some form of definition. Definitions are important because they make sure that readers all understand the meaning of a term in the same way. You have various choices, depending on the circumstance.

Glossaries

glossary

The word *glossary* comes from gloss, the Latin word for "tongue."

A *glossary* is a vertical list of terms arranged alphabetically along with brief definitions. It is especially useful when you don't know for sure who all your readers might be. Some may understand your terminology and some may not.

Put a glossary either at the beginning or at the end of your document. In a multi-chapter report or an instructional manual, you may want to put a brief glossary at the beginning of each chapter or section to explain the new terms that will appear in that chapter. You should also indicate which words in the document are defined in the glossary by highlighting them in some way. Avoid making your definitions as difficult to understand as the original term, as in the following example:

> Infiltration: Permeation of something by penetration of its pores or interstices.

This definition will not be helpful to the average reader. Instead, help the reader understand the term in the context of the original document, as in the following example:

> Infiltration: The air leaking into a building from cracks around doors and windows.

This second definition, from an employee handbook, is much more useful because it addresses the context of the term. Notice also that this definition is a sentence fragment, which helps to limit the amount of writing. If more explanation is needed, you can add a complete sentence, as in the following example:

> Infiltration: The air leaking into a building from cracks around doors and windows. It is a major cause of dry air in homes during the winter.

Glossaries can include acronyms, abbreviations, foreign language terms, and symbols as well as technical jargon. Box 14.2 is an example of a glossary. Most of the definitions use the "fragment plus complete sentence" form.

Box 14.2 *Glossary of Forestry Terms*

Marginal Land	Land that does not consistently produce a profitable crop because of infertility, drought, or other physical limitations, such as shallow soils.
Marketing	The selling of timber or other forest resources. Successful sellers seek a satisfactory price through competition, skillful negotiation, knowledge of timber markets, and the aid of a competent broker or consultant.
Marking	The physical process of selecting trees to be cut or left during a harvest.
Mast	Fruits or nuts used as food sources by wildlife. Soft mast includes most fruits with fleshy coverings, such as dogwood seed. Hard mast refers to nuts, such as acorns and hickory nuts.
Mature Tree	A tree that has reached a desired size or age for its intended use. Size, age, or economic maturity varies depending on the species and intended use.
MBF	Abbreviation denoting 1000 board feet. MBF is a typical unit of trade for dimension lumber and sawtimber stumpage.

Sentence Definitions

When you have only a few terms to define, you will probably not need a glossary. Instead, you might choose to define your terms in the body of the text using *sentence definitions.* Often you will find sentence definitions in the opening lines of paragraphs or articles. They help to introduce new topics and establish the meaning that a writer will imply throughout the document.

A formal sentence definition consists of three elements: the term, the class to which it belongs, and its specific features. See Box 14.3 for an example. You can incorporate this definition as part of the sentence, as a parenthetical item, or as a footnote.

Box 14.3 ***Elements of a Sentence Definition***

1. The term	• high-grading
2. The class or *genus* to which the item belongs	• a harvesting technique
3. The *differentia*, or specific features that distinguish this item from the other items in its class	• removes only the biggest and most valuable trees from a stand • provides high returns at the expense of future growth potential

High-grading is a harvesting technique that removes only the biggest and most valuable trees from a stand. It provides high returns at the expense of future growth potential.

Although formal sentence definitions are interesting to learn, most technical and business documents do not necessarily follow such a structured format. The most important guideline is to keep your audience in mind whenever you write definitions. Box 14.4 lists definitions from a variety of documents. Notice how each has a clear audience in mind.

Box 14.4 ***Definitions Aimed at Various Audiences***

Galvanic corrosion, the insidious eating away of hull fittings caused by the immersion of different metals in an electrolyte such as seawater, is a complex problem. *(audience with basic knowledge of boat building or refurbishing)*

Dry flies are designed to float, representing adult insects on the water's surface, whereas wet flies are fished below the surface. *(audience with basic knowledge of fly fishing)*

A feasibility report essentially says whether a proposed line of research or technical innovation is worthwhile to undertake. *(audience that is new to technical research)*

The heart is a muscular organ enclosed in a fibrous sac, the pericardium, and located in the thorax. By means of rhythmic contractions, it drives blood through the pulmonary and systemic vascular systems and back again to the heart. *(audience with some knowledge of medical terminology)*

The heart is one of your organs, located in the left side of your chest. It pumps blood through your arteries and veins. *(audience with no knowledge of medical terminology)*

Descriptions

In contrast to a definition, a *description* provides a clear picture of a specific object by using words and sometimes graphics as well. Descriptions give accurate details about features such as size, weight, colour, and material. A complete description of an object may include a definition. The most useful descriptions include graphics. Sample Document 14.1 is an example of a simple description. Compare it with the sentence definition on the first page of this chapter.

Sample Document 14.1 *Simple Description*

The vase is 29 cm tall from base to rim.

The diameter of the rim is 11 cm. The vase tapers gradually toward the bottom. Its narrowest diameter, just before the foot, is 3.5 cm. Below this point, the circular base, or foot, of the vase is 5.5 cm.

The vase is made entirely of brass. The foot is yellow brass. The lip at the rim of the vase curls outward 4 mm; this outer rim is yellow brass. The remainder of the vase is finished in greyish-green enamel. Two thin lines have been etched in the enamel so the yellow brass shows through. The stripes are 2 mm wide and appear 3 cm and 3.5 cm from the lip of the vase.

The vase weighs 480 g.

Source: Steve Cole/PhotoDisc

By convention, a complete *technical description* follows a specific order that moves from the whole object to its individual parts. Sample Document 14.2 is an example of a complete technical description.

Description forms the basis of much business, technical, and scientific writing—whenever a writer wants to describe to a reader what is known, what has been accomplished, or what has occurred. Isolated technical descriptions rarely appear except perhaps as entries in an encyclopedia or a product catalogue. Richard Young calls these "static descriptions—the thing itself, unchanging, static, and unrelated to its surroundings."[1] See sample documents 14.3 and 14.4 for examples.

[1] Young, R.E., Becker, A.L., & Pike, K.L. (1970). *Rhetoric: Discovery and change* (p. 121). New York: Harcourt, Brace and World.

The Portrait Finch Feeder

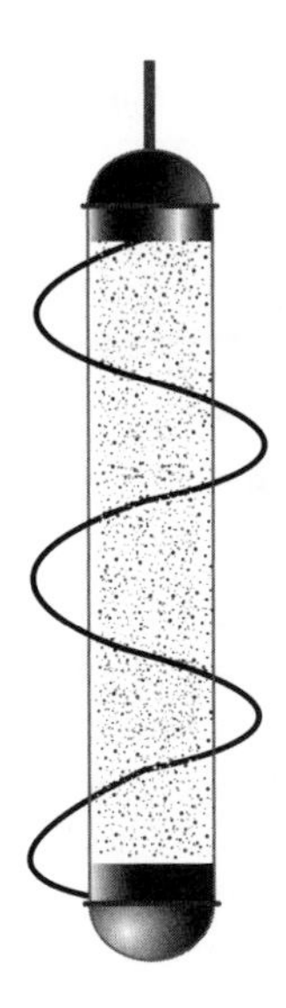

The Portrait Finch Feeder is a cylindrical container designed to hold niger seed for feeding wild finches. It is light and easy to handle, yet strong enough to withstand the cold and damp of Ontario winters.

The simple construction is composed of five parts: the cylinder, the base, the cap, the hanger, and the spiral perch.

Cylinder
The cylinder is made of clear hardened plastic. It is 18" long and $3\frac{1}{2}$" in diameter. The sides of the cylinder contain

- two holes of $\frac{3}{8}$" diameter for insertion of the spiral perch at top and bottom
- sixteen $\frac{1}{16}$" holes at various intervals for dispersal of niger seed

Base
The base is made of plastic-coated aluminum. It is dome-shaped, approximately $3\frac{5}{8}$" in diameter. The base is attached permanently to the bottom of the cylinder.

Cap
The cap is made of plastic-coated aluminum. It has a $\frac{1}{2}$" edge that slides down onto the top of the cylinder. It can be removed easily to permit the cylinder to be filled with seeds. The centre of the cap has a $\frac{1}{16}$" hole for the hanger wire.

Hanger
The hanger is made of $\frac{1}{16}$" plastic-coated aluminum wire. It feeds through the hole in the centre of the cap and is held in place by a welded metal ball on the underside. The hanger can be bent at any point to form a loop for hanging.

Spiral Perch
The perch is made of rigid plastic-coated aluminum wire. It is attached to the cylinder at the top and bottom by small holes through which the wire is fed. The wire curves around the cylinder in a double spiral approximately $1\frac{1}{2}$" from the tube.

Sample Document 14.3 *Technical Description from a Product Catalogue*

> The chair is manufactured using select kiln-dried solid wood with a tilt/tension mechanism that uses a self-lubricating nylon bearing to prevent squeaking. The seat measures 20" between the arms, is $17\frac{1}{2}$" deep, and adjusts between $16\frac{1}{2}$"and 21" above the floor. The finish is in dark cherry or natural oak.

Sample Document 14.4 *Technical Description from a Reference Booklet*

> When accuracy is a critical factor in temperature measurement, Platinum Resistance Thermometers (RTDs) are unequalled in performance. They operate on the principle of change in electrical resistance of platinum (Pt) wires as a function of temperature. The RTD consists of a small platinum wire wound around a ceramic or glass core and hermetically sealed within a glass or ceramic capsule. This sensing element is immobilized within a stainless steel sheath. Standard nickel-plated copper leads are insulated with a Teflon resin and Teflon tape.

More often, technical descriptions form part of larger documents such as tenders, advertising, building plans, inspection reports, lab reports, or instructions. These documents place the described item in a context where it relates to other items.

Any document that provides a technical description usually includes a list of specifications that gives details about all the parts of the whole item and enumerates particulars such as size, weight, quality, performance, and so on. Preparing specifications requires careful attention to accuracy, careful proofreading, and appropriate use of abbreviations, numerals, and punctuation marks. See Sample Document 14.5.

Sample Document 14.5 *Specifications*

SPECIFICATIONS
(Microwave Oven)

Power Source:	120 V, 60 Hz, AC only
Output:	600 watts full power
Outside Dimensions:	34.0 cm × 53.0 cm × 42.5 cm [$13\frac{3}{8}$" (H) × $20\frac{7}{8}$" (W) × $16\frac{3}{4}$" (D)]
Interior Oven Dimensions:	23.5 cm × 33.0 cm × 36.5 cm [$9\frac{1}{4}$" (H) × 13" (W) × $14\frac{3}{8}$" (D)]
Oven Capacity:	0.3 m^3 (1.0 cu. ft)
Uncrated Weight:	Approx. 18.9 kg (42 lbs)
Shipping Weight:	Approx. 21.1 kg (46 lbs)
Power Consumption:	10.8 amps, 1240 watts
Operating Frequency:	2450 MHz
Digital Timer:	99 minutes 99 seconds

Activities and Exercises

1. Choose three of the following terms and write clear sentence definitions that would be suitable for an average adult reader:

tectonics	volcano	heart attack	bouillabaisse
orienteering	emu	miso	justice of the peace
horsefly	bucksaw	spam	galvanize

You may use the Internet or reference books to help you. Remember, you are trying to find wording that will fit into the three sections of the sentence definition. You may want to add or change some of the wording you find. Arrange your definitions in a chart like the one below. If the term has more than one distinct meaning, choose one.

term	
class or genus	
differentia	

2. Write a definition of your major field of study. Try to take an approach that highlights some interesting or unusual features of the discipline—something that readers wouldn't already know about. Use two or three paragraphs for this definition.
3. Choose a topic or field of study that you don't know anything about. Find five terms that are unfamiliar to you. Do some research that will allow you to write clear definitions for each of the terms. Use the "fragment plus complete sentence" form commonly found in glossaries.
4. Following the example of the finch feeder in Sample Document 14.2, write a simple technical description of a common object that has four to six distinguishable parts. Use whatever you need to make your description accurate (e.g., scales, measuring tape, calipers, etc.).
5. Find articles, books (other than textbooks), or pamphlets that incorporate written definitions, descriptions, or specifications. Compare the documents and discuss their format, content, and writing style.

For further assignments dealing with the content of this chapter, see case studies 5 and 13 starting on page 280.

Instructions

Instructions are written explanations of how to use a piece of equipment or how to carry out a task by following a series of steps.

instruction

In Latin, the verb *struo* (*struere*) means "to place together," "to arrange"; with military troops, it means "to draw up in order." *Structio* means "a joining together"; *instruo* means "to build in," "to insert."

Most often, the complaint people make when they are having trouble with instructions (programming my VCR?) is "I'm lost." If you apply the derivation clues above, you see that "instruction" should involve an orderly arrangement of ideas within which readers can easily find their way around without getting lost. Good instructions should work like a clear map. The guidelines in this chapter will help you to produce instructions that are easy to read and follow.

Preparing to Write Instructions

Planning does not have to be a lengthy process, and it may not all be completed before you begin to write; it might be an ongoing process. Before you write, think about the following:

Know the Context

- Know your audience, if possible. Are you writing for ten-year-olds? Or postgraduate students? The focus of the instructions may help you to know who your readers will be. Will this be a list of instructions posted for someone replacing you in your job, or a booklet enclosed with a new electrical appliance?
- Know how your instructions will be used. Preparing instructions for a specific format—a label, a handbook, an insert card, a memo to be posted—will present some limitations that challenge your design skills.
- Know the implications of your instructions. Since instructions tell readers what to do, they may carry legal implications. A writing defect in product support literature carries liability just like a defect in the product itself.

Know How to Do the Task Yourself

- Do you know how to use the photocopier?
- Do you know the process for reporting an injury at work?
- Do you know the most efficient way to get to the downtown Vancouver office from Burnaby?

The idea of knowing how to do the task yourself should be obvious, but you might be surprised how often people try to give or write instructions when they themselves are not completely familiar with the task or equipment.

The opposite problem, of course, can be just as troublesome. If you know how to complete a task or use equipment without even thinking about it, you may make incorrect assumptions about your reader's knowledge, and as a result, you may overlook an important step.

Organizing the Instructions

To organize your instructions, follow the rules for appropriate use of headings and subheadings. Use a balanced layout to improve readability. See Sample Document 15.1 for an example.

Sample Document 15.1 *Instructions*

Using Rigid Styrofoam to Insulate a Crawlspace

Insulating the inside of the concrete blocks that form the crawlspace will help to prevent the pipes from freezing and minimize the formation of condensation under the building. Although the actual task is not difficult, the working space is likely to be somewhat cramped depending on the height of the crawlspace.

To complete the job correctly, you will have to perform four steps:

1. Clear the surface of debris.
2. Measure and cut the rigid insulation to fit.
3. Glue the insulation in place.
4. Fill cracks and spaces with fibreglass insulation.

You should be able to insulate a 50 ft × 30 ft area in about four hours.

Equipment and Materials

Sufficient rigid Styrofoam insulation $2\frac{1}{2}$"–3" thick
Styrofoam glue—check the container for advice about how much to purchase
Utility knife for scoring insulation
Straightedge, such as a yardstick or carpenter's square

(continued)

Scraper (and possibly a hammer) for clearing surface of concrete debris
Small amount of pink fibreglass insulation for filling cracks
Construction-grade facemask
Heavy gloves

1. Clear the surface of debris.

The insulation will adhere better if the surface of the concrete is relatively smooth.
Use a scraper or hammer to chip away any protrusions or dirt that may prevent the Styrofoam from lying flat.

2. Measure and cut the insulation.

Rigid Styrofoam insulation comes in 8-ft lengths and a variety of widths.
Use a utility knife and straightedge to score the insulation and then snap the pieces.
If you have uneven edges or small pieces left over, they can still be used.

3. Glue the insulation in place.

WARNING! WEAR PROTECTIVE GLOVES TO AVOID GETTING GLUE ON YOUR SKIN.

NOTE: Follow any specific directions on the glue you have purchased.

Apply a bead of glue in an "S" pattern down the full length of the Styrofoam.
Make sure the glue goes right to the edges on each side.
Press the insulation against the concrete blocks and hold in place for about one minute.
Continue around the entire perimeter of the building. Cut pieces to fit around pipes, corners, windows, etc.

4. Fill cracks and spaces with pink fibreglass insulation.

WARNING! WEAR PROTECTIVE FACEMASK AND GLOVES WHEN WORKING WITH FIBREGLASS INSULATION.

Work again around the whole perimeter of the crawlspace.
Stuff any cracks or places where concrete is visible using chunks of pink fibreglass insulation.

Begin by writing a brief overview statement describing exactly what task will be explained. This statement will help you, the writer, organize your work and will help the reader grasp the main steps quickly. You may also want to include a note about the skill level and the time required to complete the task successfully.

List all equipment and supplies that will be required. Don't let your readers get halfway through a project only to discover that they have to run out and buy something else.

Explain clearly each step mentioned in the overview. If individual steps are complex, divide them also into separate steps. Finish all the necessary instructions for each individual step before returning to the main list.

Include a brief explanation of why the steps are necessary. Doing so gives your reader useful information and often prevents important steps from being skipped.

Put any safety precautions before the relevant step.

Writing the Instructions

Write any necessary background or introductory notes that give an overview of what you are going to explain. You may, for example, distinguish between two different models of a product, define some terms to be used, or give a brief description of what the product is intended to do. For example,

> Your utility pump is ideal for many domestic water-out applications, including draining flat rooftops, flooded garages and storm cellars, flooded boats, and more. The pump body is made of tough noncorrosive polypropylene.

Use imperative verbs so that the action required is the first word in the sentence.

1. Unplug the electrical cord.
2. Remove the four screws from the bottom of the pump.
3. Remove the slotted intake screen and suction plate.
4. Remove debris and make sure the impeller turns freely.
5. Replace suction plates and screen.
6. Replace screws in bottom of pump.
7. Test pumping operation by placing in shallow water.

NEVER RUN PUMP DRY.

An exception to the above rule does occur whenever a step requires a specific context for safety or accuracy. For example,

1. Turn the main switch to OFF.
2. Open the upper valve approximately $\frac{1}{4}$ turn.
3. **If steam begins to escape,** close the valve immediately.

Choose your words according to the audience you expect to read the instructions. If in doubt, write for a general reader. Provide definitions for any specialized terms.

Use consistent terminology for parts and actions throughout the instructions—in the written steps and in any accompanying graphics. For example, if something is called a *toggle switch* in step 1, it should be called a *toggle switch* everywhere.

Incorporate safety information. Manuals use a number of different icons and terms to highlight safety information. Box 15.1 lists some standard ones. Some documents use different terms, such as HAZARD or STOP; some may use icons or a combination of both. See Box 15.2. Whichever terms or icons you use, your main task is to make sure your readers see and understand them.

Box 15.1 ***Safety Information***

NOTE	Directs readers to additional information that may be important or useful
CAUTION	Draws attention to an action or situation that may cause equipment failure or damage
WARNING! or DANGER!	Draws attention to an action or situation that may cause personal injury or may be fatal

Box 15.2 ***Safety Icons***

Use appropriate graphics and layout. Whenever possible, use illustrations to show parts of an item and to demonstrate correct and safe use of tools. Make the instructions clear and readable by applying layout cues, such as different levels of headings, indenting, numbered lists, colour, and white space. Sample Document 15.2 is another example of instructions that incorporates layout cues.

Sample Document 15.2 *Instructions Incorporating Layout Cues*

Closing the Drop-In Centre

The last person to leave the Centre should go through the CLOSING CHECKLIST and initial each step as it is completed. Obtain a copy of the CLOSING CHECKLIST from the office. When you have completed all the steps, drop the CLOSING CHECKLIST into the mailbox as you leave.

CLOSING CHECKLIST

1. TURN OFF the sound system at the main switch in the kitchen.	
2. CHECK the following areas to make sure that no one is still using equipment. As you check each area, turn off all lights and lock the doors. • weight room • counselling office • snack area	
3. TURN the furnace thermostat to 62°. 4. LOWER the blinds on the windows across the back of the main room.	
5. LOCK the back door and TURN ON the outside back light.	
6. CHECK to make sure no food has been left on the counters. If there is food remaining, put it in one of the refrigerators.	
7. REMOVE all change from the cash drawer in the file cabinet. Put it in the cash bag. Put the cash bag in the top file drawer in the main office. Lock the file cabinet.	
8. LOCK the main office.	
9. TURN OUT all remaining lights except for L1 and L3 (outside front and side).	
10. KEY IN the security code.	
11. CLOSE AND LOCK the front door. Check the handle by pushing gently.	

PLEASE REMEMBER to put the checklist through the mailbox.

Explaining a Process

Instead of explaining how to do something, a *process* explains how something happens. For example, a set of instructions tells a reader how to use the CD burner. A process explanation tells the reader how the CD burner actually works. Process explanations are common in scientific and technical writing. In the workplace, they may form part of sales documents and product catalogues. Normally they will be written by technical personnel who are familiar with the product or by operators who work with the equipment on a regular basis.

A process explanation may be written in paragraph form, or it may be handled in much the same way as written instructions: an overview and a chronological series of detailed steps. The actual grammatical format used in process explanations varies depending on the type of document. Most use a combination of active and passive voice as well as the indicative rather than the imperative mood (see Part Five: Roundup).

An excellent website to find examples of process explanations is http://www.howstuffworks.com. The example in Sample Document 15.3 comes from this site. Notice that it combines passive and active voice. The explanation is divided into short paragraphs, one for each step in the process. It does not use numbered steps.

Sample Document 15.3 *A Process Explanation*[1]

The Cable System

The most popular elevator design is the cable elevator. In cable elevators, the car is pulled from above rather than pushed from below.

The elevator car is connected to a series of metal cables, which are looped over a sheave at the top of the elevator shaft. A sheave is just a pulley with a grooved rim surface. The grooves grip the steel cables, so when you rotate the sheave, the cables move too.

The sheave is attached to a variable-speed electric motor. When the motor turns one way, the sheave raises the elevator; when the motor turns the other way, the sheave lowers the elevator. In gearless elevators, the motor rotates the sheaves directly. In geared elevators, the motor turns a gear train that rotates the sheave (this reduces the speed of the rotary motion). The sheave, the motor, and the control system are all housed in a machine room above the elevator shaft.

Activities and Exercises

1. Bring various examples of instructions to class from labels, handbooks, manuals, package inserts, and so on. Compare and evaluate them for clarity, audience-appropriate language, readability, layout, and completeness.
2. For this exercise, work with a partner in the same discipline as you. Decide on a task or a piece of equipment that you both know well. Each of you should write a complete set of instructions for performing the task or using the equipment. When you have finished, exchange your work and compare your instructions. Using both versions, produce one complete and accurate document.

[1] "The Cable System" retrieved from http://howstuffworks.com/elevator3.htm on 6 March 2002. Reprinted with permission.

3. Write a process explanation that explains how a piece of equipment works. Use graphics to clarify your explanation.
4. Find a book or article at your reading level that describes a process that interests you—for example, how a volcano works, how to invest in the stock market, and so on. Rewrite the process for a reader of about 12 years old. For help with this exercise, visit the children's section of the public library.

For further assignments dealing with the content of this chapter, see case studies 10, 16, 18, and 19 starting on page 287.

Documents That Work for You

The *résumé* is the document most commonly connected with the employment process. This chapter also looks briefly at job descriptions and documents related to meetings.

Résumés

Of all the documents you may ever write, your résumé may be the one you value the most. A good résumé can be the key that opens the door to employment and a secure future. You will find many sources of help when you want to prepare a résumé—from friends to full-time résumé-writing services. You will actually use many different résumés throughout your working life. Those sent in response to specific job ads should clearly address the requirements identified in the ad. At the same time, you may want to prepare a more general résumé to send unsolicited to many companies. In addition, you will be continually updating your résumé as you acquire new experience and skills.

Issues such as choice of paper and font, use of colour, and layout styles should follow the basic guidelines covered elsewhere in this textbook. This section will provide a series of guidelines you might want to consider. See Sample Document 16.1 to see these guidelines applied.

Sample Document 16.1 ***Résumé***

ELIZABETH EPLETT

16 Codrington Blvd.
Wenton, SK S4T 1Y1

(306) 765-4321
eeplett@midland.com

Special Qualifications

- Fluent in English, French, Italian.
- Supervised all Front Desk operations in an international hotel chain for six years.

(continued)

Elizabeth Eplett
16 Codrington Blvd.
Wenton, SK
S4T 1Y1
(306) 765-4321
eeplett@midland.com
page 2 of 2

Education
B.A. – Hospitality Management from Cornell University, 1992
Graduated 5th in a class of 120.
Diploma – Personnel and Payroll Administration from Branchton College, 1993

Related Work Experience
Front Desk Manager, The Ultimate Resort and Spa, Mirror Falls, ON, November 1994–April 2000

- Supervised a department of 22 people. Interviewed and hired all new staff; handled performance evaluations and termination interviews.
- Increased performance indicator 22% based on the standard Cornell-Price measurements.
- Prepared and submitted tenders for lobby renovations; oversaw all lobby reconstruction.
- Received 1997 HACA award for design and innovation.

Reservations Assistant, Seashore Inn, Fantasy Lake, BC, August 1992–October 1994

- Managed all aspects of reservations at this 400-room hotel under the supervision of the Front Desk Manager.
- Trained 21 new Front Desk employees on the Resercom Data System.

Other Experience
Choral Conductor, Stanmore Children's Chorus 1995–present

- Directed a 26-member youth choir (8–12 years old). Took second place in the 1997 Kiwanis Youth Choir Festival. Coordinated all travel, lodging, and chaperone arrangements for this group during an eight-day Ontario tour.

Interests

- Taught piano and voice to six pupils for the past four years.
- Participated as a music advisor in local high-school drama festivals.
- Fluent in ASL (American Sign Language).
- Avid hot-air balloon enthusiast.

Put your name and contact information at the beginning of the résumé. Use a slightly larger font for your name. Hint: Put your telephone number in bold print. If a company likes the sound of you, they'll call. If your résumé runs to more than one page, this information should appear at the top of every page. Indicate the page number and total number of pages.

Whatever appears at the beginning of your résumé will likely be read. Accordingly, tell your readers everything they need to know right up front in the first section. You will usually know from the job advertisement what specific characteristics they are looking for.

Omit skills and qualifications that everyone will bring to the job, such as answering the telephone, using a word processor, or possessing a driver's licence—unless these have actually been specified in the ad. Avoid anything that qualifies simply as "filler" in a résumé.

Think twice before putting one of those "Future Goals" statements at the beginning. They tend to be more self-serving than helpful, especially when you are at the start of your career. At this stage, you're simply going to tell a prospective employer, "I'm going to use this job as a steppingstone." Once you have several years of solid experience, you may want to use a "Goals" statement to help an employer decide whether you are the best fit for long-term employment.

Don't be a slave to chronology—you don't have to list your experience in date order. If a particular job you've had is not relevant, omit it or place it closer to the end. You will, of course, want to arrange your information in the most appropriate order depending on your background and skills and the job requirements. Sometimes your work experience may come first, sometimes your education.

Quantify—don't use vague terminology like "I supervised many employees." Prove it by using figures, percentages, and dates. The corollary is, "If you can't prove it, don't say it."

Always use action verbs: selected, wrote, supervised, completed, designed, trained, purchased, travelled. You may find it helpful to keep a list of appropriate verbs in front of you to refer to as you write your résumé.

Find value in every experience you list, or don't include it. Did you organize a summer picnic for employees when you worked part-time as a cashier? Perhaps that experience enhanced your ability to communicate in a multicultural environment or taught you to innovate.

Communicate balance in your life, if possible: Include sports, arts, and community and family activities. Knowing how to play the guitar, in itself, may not be a skill that's required for the job you want, but participating in an important recital demonstrates that you can commit to a task and persevere.

Be honest. It seems strange to include this advice, but more than one person has regretted fudging information on a résumé. Be real. Have depth, and communicate it.

Finally, but perhaps most importantly, preparing a polished and persuasive résumé cannot begin when you sit down to write the résumé. All the elegant stationery and fine printing in the world will not substitute for the picture of a well-rounded, interesting, and self-motivated person. You must create that over the long term. And the picture will change as your career, skills, and experiences change.

Job Descriptions

A *job description,* as the term suggests, lists and describes the responsibilities involved in a particular position. Job descriptions are useful for two groups:

- Managers and others who may be hiring new employees use job descriptions to create recruitment advertisements and to assess whether work is being appropriately distributed among various departments and employees.
- Employees use them to determine exactly what their job entails, especially if the company has given only general verbal directions.

For both groups, a clear job description provides a point of reference for performance evaluations and salary discussions.

Writing a Job Description

Writing a description of your own or someone else's job may seem like a straightforward task until you actually sit down to do it. It may take several attempts over a few weeks to actually itemize the tasks that the position involves. Inevitably, this process reveals problems with duplication of responsibility or confusion about who actually does what. You may need to talk to and observe many employees, and even contact other, similar workplaces to get a clear idea about how the work is, or should be, distributed. Feedback from customers and clients can also provide helpful information.

Job descriptions normally include the following information:

- the actual position title
- the context of the position—that is, where it fits on the organization chart
- a brief, summary description of the position
- an itemized list of the responsibilities
- hiring requirements, including education, skills, aptitudes, background, specific knowledge or training, previous job experience
- other relevant information, such as safety or health issues

Sample Document 16.2 is an example of a job description.

The level of detail you include may vary, but usually a job description focuses on generalities rather than specifics. For example, you would write

sorts all incoming mail

Sample Document 16.2 *Job Description*

<u>Job Title: Expediter</u> <u>Reports to: Purchasing Manager</u>

Summary Description:

The Expediter maintains an appropriate level of parts required by the production line by contacting suppliers, tracing shipments, preparing customs documents, and assigning release sheets as required.

Specific Duties

- Checks parts database daily to ascertain parts count
- Enters data into supplier documents accurately according to information supplied by Purchasing
- Faxes release sheets as necessary to suppliers to confirm future orders
- Contacts suppliers by telephone and/or e-mail to confirm shipments
- Traces shipments online or by telephone
- Prepares and delivers all customs documents as soon as possible after shipments arrive
- Keeps parts binders in good, up-to-date order
- Notifies Production Department immediately in the event of shipment delay

Incidental Duties

- May be asked to cover the responsibilities of an absent expediter on a short-term basis

Qualifications and Experience

- 2-year college diploma in business is preferred
- At least 1 year office experience
- Experience with database software

Other Skills or Aptitudes

- Ability to work under pressure and keep to deadlines
- Excellent verbal communication skills

Working Conditions

This position demands almost continual use of the telephone and the computer in a busy and occasionally noisy office environment.

Safety Issue

No special or protective clothing or training is required for this position.

rather than breaking this task down into its minor components:

picks up mail from front desk

classifies mail according to each department

places department mail in appropriate mail slots

The more detailed information, however, would be useful as instructions for training new staff. Salary details are usually not part of a job description, since this information may change according to qualifications and length of employment.

A job description should include some language that describes the level of expertise or efficiency that is appropriate for a position. In Box 16.1, the statement on the left names a task; the one on the right describes the desired performance level as well as the task.

Box 16.1 ***Job Description with and without Performance Details***

Sorts all incoming mail	Sorts all incoming mail accurately before the morning editorial meeting
Makes travel arrangements for convention speakers	Contacts all convention speakers at least three months prior to meetings and arranges appropriate and convenient travel plans in a timely manner
Prepares monthly department reports	Prepares clear and detailed department reports by the end of the third week of each month

Documents for Meetings

Someone once said, "But for the date of the next meeting, a meeting might have less relevance." Sometimes the workplace seems to function solely as a place to hold meetings. No one seems to want to go to meetings, yet everyone seems to think that having a meeting might be a good idea. The word *meeting* does not have an interesting etymology; however, the noun *meet* is described in the *Oxford English Dictionary* as the gathering of "hounds and men in preparation for a hunt." This definition may explain a lot.

Two types of documents are associated with meetings in the workplace: agendas and minutes.

Agendas

agenda

The origin of agenda is the Latin *agendum*, meaning "something to be done." The term "agenda" is actually plural, but it is now used as a singular English word. The agenda, then, is the list of things to be done at a meeting.

Without a printed agenda, a meeting can meander aimlessly and fail to accomplish any clear objective. The purpose of an *agenda* is to let everyone know in advance the goals of the meeting and the route it will take to meet those goals. Although preparing an agenda is not a difficult task, it does take some thought and planning. Keep the following guidelines in mind:

- Indicate the committee or group name at the beginning, along with the date, time, location, and, if possible, the expected time the meeting will end.
- Provide a clear indication of the purpose for the meeting. Besides helping everyone to know what the meeting is about, this statement will help to limit the length of the meeting by preventing unrelated topics from taking over.
- List all topics, activities, and speakers that need to be included. If time permits, consider giving some participants a draft of this list in case additional points need to be added.
- Put housekeeping items first, such as reviewing the previous meeting's minutes and the results of questions raised in an earlier meeting.
- List the remaining items on the agenda in the order in which they will take place. Usually the list will begin with the most current or important topics. If the list is long, you may find it helpful to give a time frame for all or some items.
- Distribute the agenda ahead of time whenever possible.

Sample Document 16.3 is an example of an agenda.

Minutes

If meetings provide a major forum for conducting business in most companies, no matter how large or small, well-written *minutes* provide a permanent and vital record of the information discussed and the decisions made at those meetings. The ability to record accurate and readable minutes is a welcome skill in any workplace.

Sample Document 16.3 *Agenda*

Highway 60, R.R. 2
Mirror Falls, Ontario L3R 4R4

Tel.: (705) 777-4000 Fax: (705) 777-4001
ultaspa@playground.on.ca

Health and Safety Committee
August 9, 2002 1:30 p.m.
Boardroom

AGENDA

1. Approval of Minutes of July 2nd meeting of the Health and Safety Committee (5 minutes)
2. Business arising from July 2nd meeting:
   - Contact with Wellspring Inc.—Bob Jeffries (10 minutes)
   - Expected date for completion of third-floor repairs—Fatima Leone (15 minutes)
3. Presentation of safety report—Bob Jeffries (20 minutes)
4. School tours—Anika Selma, Community Relations (5 minutes)
5. Hiring committee for Assistant Manager of Maintenance Department (10 minutes)
6. Date for safety inspections (10 minutes)
7. Other business (5 minutes)
8. Next meeting
9. Adjournment 2:50 p.m.

All minutes should record the context of the meeting: date, time, place, and names of all participants. If the meeting has a printed agenda, the minutes will usually follow that order, recording briefly what topics were raised and what decisions were made.

Minutes are actually a kind of summary; they are not a verbatim record. The primary skill involved in taking good minutes is distilling the essence of a discussion, an argument, or a long speech. If you are taking minutes and you miss part of a discussion or have difficulty understanding an issue, ask for clarification right then rather than later.

The amount of detail in the minutes usually depends on the type of meeting and how the minutes will be used. For example, minutes may be recorded only so that one copy can be filed for future reference. They may be distributed to everyone who attended the meeting as a reminder for future activities. They may be circulated or posted for many people to read—even those who were not at the meeting. This latter practice has become commonplace; many communities, for example, post minutes of council meetings on the Internet.

Minutes of routine meetings held on a regular schedule may record only the main discussion topics and decisions about future actions. The meetings of ad hoc committees (committees formed as they're needed for a specific purpose) or special projects may require much more detail. Sometimes minutes follow scrupulously the rules of formal meeting procedure, including details about motions, seconders, and voting.[1] For this type of meeting, a tape recorder allows the person recording the minutes to check details at a later time.

Impartiality is vital. Minutes should be an objective record of what takes place at a meeting. Problems arise if the person recording minutes uses biased language or subjective opinions or, even worse, fails to record some important information. Sometimes using impersonal passive constructions can help—but only if the actual speaker does not need to be identified. Compare the following examples:

> Luca Santani suggested that the parking lot needed to be resurfaced.
>
> It was suggested that the parking lot needed to be resurfaced.

> We circulated the Chrighton Report.
>
> The Chrighton Report was circulated.
>
> Each committee member received a copy of the Chrighton Report.

Finally, Action entries indicate clearly decisions that have been made and people who have committed to complete a task. Sample Document 16.4 is an example of minutes.

[1] See *Robert's Rules of Order*, http://www.robertsrules.com.

Sample Document 16.4 *Minutes*

Highway 60, R.R. 2
Mirror Falls, Ontario L3R 4R4

Tel.: (705) 777-4000 Fax: (705) 777-4001
ultaspa@playground.on.ca

Health and Safety Committee
August 9, 2002 1:30 p.m.

MINUTES

Present:

Lorimer Delanye
Anna Marie Gardner
Jack Horner
Bob Jeffries
Art Kyle
Fatima Leone
Judy Sedna
Anika Selma
Navinder Singh
Sabrina Wells-DeJung
Jasmine Wu

1. The Minutes of the July 2nd meeting had been circulated previous to the meeting. Approved by Singh. Seconded Horner.
2. Business arising from July 2nd meeting:
   - Bob Jeffries reported that he had contacted Wellspring Inc. regarding humidity problems in the men's locker room. Wellspring has suggested tentatively that the problem may be due to incorrect insulation between the locker room and the men's sauna. A representative of Wellspring will be coming on August 10.

   Action: Bob Jeffries will meet with the Wellspring rep and report back concerning his findings. Rather than wait for next month's meeting, Bob will circulate a memo to all committee members.

   - Fatima Leone has received a completion date of September 1 for repairs on the 3rd floor. Navinder suggested that we ask for a signed note to this effect. Fatima will speak to the contractor about this. Fatima submitted a letter from Howell Contracting expressing apologies for delays in this work. There was some discussion about whether we should use Howell for further work.

(continued)

Health and Safety Committee
August 9, 2002
page 2 of 2

Action: Fatima and Navinder will review the issues that have arisen in the past two months with Howell and investigate other possible contractors. Report at next meeting.

3. Presentation of Safety Report. Bob Jeffries brought safety reports from every department. He expressed appreciation that everyone cooperated to get these reports completed on time. No lost time due to work-related incidents in the past three months.
   Action: Bob suggested that a note about this excellent work record be posted in the main staff lounge and *Ultimatum*, the staff newsletter.
4. School Tours. Anika Selma reported that requests for class tours still arrive every month. During June, four tours took place. Most schools are interested in recreation and cooking areas. Already three requests are in for the coming fall. It was agreed that as long as tours do not coincide with other major events, they will be welcome.
5. Hiring committee for Assistant Manager of Maintenance Department. A new assistant manager will be required for October 1. Job postings are being prepared and will be published at the beginning of September. Jack suggested and the committee agreed that we wait until late August to strike a hiring committee.
6. Date for Safety Inspections. The following dates have been submitted to the Board:
   Pool and Sauna: July 19, August 22, September 22, October 30, November 30
   No other dates have been received at present.
7. Jasmine Wu asked about lifeguards. Sabrina reported that 12 students have been hired for the summer. They are putting together a schedule that will see the beachfront and indoor pool covered from 7:30 a.m. to 10:00 p.m. for the next two months.
8. Next meeting. September 8, 2002. Boardroom. 1:30 p.m.
9. The meeting adjourned at 2:35.

Activities and Exercises

1. If you currently have a part-time or full-time job, write a job description for it.
2. Prepare a résumé that you can use to apply for a position in your field. Combine this exercise with a cover letter based on the guidelines in Part Two of this text.

For further assignments dealing with the content of this chapter, see Case Study 5 starting on page 280.

1 2 3 4 5

Part Four

Reports and Proposals

The Nature of Reports and Proposals

chapter **seventeen**

17

report

There is some interesting change-about in the English and Latin terms for *report.* For example, in Latin, the noun *fama* means "report" or "rumour." The word *report* originally, then, meant one's reputation or fame, not a message. (In fact, a person who was decent and trustworthy used to be referred to as someone "of good report.")

As for the verb *to report,* the Latin word is *nuntio* (*nuntiare*), from which, of course, we get the verb "to announce." Most likely, the scarcity of written materials accounts for the fact that Latin has terms for "message" and "announcement" rather than the kind of document we think of as a report.

The Latin verb *porto* (*portare*) means "to bring" or "to carry"—to physically pick up and move something. A word we derive directly from *portare,* for example, is *portage.* The Latin prefix *re* adds the connotation of bringing something "back" to where it belongs.

The *Oxford English Dictionary* places the earliest use of the term "report" in the 17th century, where for the first time the word implied that a person had been given a task and was carrying back a document with the results of that task.

Nearly all reports and proposals have three distinctive characteristics:

- They are written as a result of a question or problem.
- They share a unique relationship between the sender and receiver.
- They demonstrate a similar approach to content, layout, and writing style.

The Question or Problem

Here are some examples of titles of long and short reports and proposals, along with the question or problem that initiated them.

Title of report: *Report of the Dubin Inquiry*
This report was prepared by Justice Charles Dubin in the wake of the 1988 Olympics. Justice Dubin collected information from individuals and organizations across the country, analyzed all the data, and reached a conclusion.
Question: How widespread is the use of drugs by our Olympic athletes?

Title of report: ***Report of the Royal Commission of Inquiry on the Blood System in Canada***
This massive document, comprising more than 1000 pages, was prepared by Justice Horace Krever. The preceding investigation, which took four years, produced more than 48 000 pages of testimony and half a million pages of exhibit evidence.
Problem: The need to learn about the system of controlling and maintaining Canada's blood supply system.

Title of proposal: ***Baycity Revival: West Hamilton Harbourfront Redevelopment Plan***
This proposal was prepared by Paul Shaker in August 2000 (see http://hamiltonwaterfront.8m.com).
Problem: The need to come up with a plan to revitalize the harbourfront of this large Ontario city.

Title of report: ***Report of the Walkerton Inquiry: The Events of May 2000 and Related Issues***
This 700-page report was prepared by The Honourable Dennis O'Connor after a lengthy public investigation (see http://www.walkertoninquiry.com).
Problem: *E coli* contamination of water had resulted in deaths and illness in the town of Walkerton, Ontario.

Although these particular reports and proposals are massive, they demonstrate the features that would be found even in brief documents in any workplace. For example,

Report: Sales Report, November 2003
Situation: The annual document is prepared by the Vice President of Sales, who collects and analyzes data for the preceding 12 months from all sales personnel.

Proposal: New Transport Service Recommendation
Problem: Recently the number of late deliveries has increased, and customers have been complaining. The Shipping Department investigates several different trucking companies and suggests signing a contract with a new company.

Report: Student Participation in Extracurricular Activities
Problem: For a class assignment, a student surveyed the grades 9 and 10 students in her area high school to find out what percentage of students were involved in school clubs and sports.

Notice that every report or proposal follows the process shown in Figure 17.1. The middle steps in the flow chart (collection and analysis) are not necessarily linear. They may take place simultaneously, or the investigator may go back and forth between the two steps.

Figure 17.1 ***The Process of Producing a Report or Proposal***

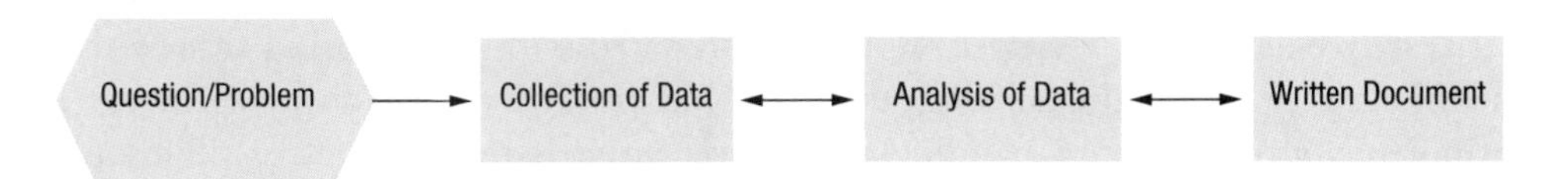

In each case, the writer (an individual or a group)

- identifies the main problem or question
- determines what information is required to supply a useful response or solution
- determines the best way to collect the necessary data
- collects the data
- analyzes the data
- organizes the data in a useful manner
- writes the document

The Sender/Receiver Relationship

The receivers of a report or proposal—whether they are managers, shareholders, customers, or even the general public—have the decision-making power, the power to act on recommendations made in the report or proposal. As a general rule, therefore, report writers are communicating upward. Managers do not send reports to their employees. In fact, we use the phrase "report to" to designate a position that is higher on a company's organization chart.

The question or problem that the report or proposal addresses may originate with the receiver, who then assigns the investigation into that question or problem to an employee or a group of employees. Or, the sender may come up with the question or problem, which means that the resulting document is unsolicited.

Whether a report is solicited or not, the person (or group) who becomes the most knowledgeable about its subject is the sender. The sender must collect and carefully analyze the data in order to present the significant findings in a way that is most accessible to the receiver.

Content, Layout, and Writing Style

While personal essays do use research and documented data, their theses arise principally from the writer's personal opinion or from the desire to add new information to an already established knowledge base. Essay writers use their skill with argument and language to convince, protest, describe, muse, and even amuse. Similarly, research papers, sometimes called research reports, pull together ideas and facts from many sources. This material may be analyzed, reviewed, refuted, or restated with the addition of new data. Conclusions may be exciting or disappointing, but research nearly always provides its own impetus, growing and expanding to discover answers to scientific or philosophic questions. Workplace reports, on the other hand, must simply be more practical, based on data that can be measured or clearly identified; they are produced to improve the bottom line and to facilitate the day-to-day activity of business.

Report writers focus on what might be called *hard data.* In other words, these writers emphasize information that can be named or measured, avoiding *soft data*—beliefs, hunches, feelings, conjectures—unless these are soundly based on other measurable data. Typically, business and technical documents are objective. While objectivity is highly desirable, the perspectives of writers and readers always act as filters for the "facts." For example, look at the following three statements:

> Sales are 22 percent higher this month than in the same month last year.
>
> Water is dripping from the ceiling in the photocopy room.
>
> The Fundraising Committee did not meet yesterday.

Each of these statements contains a fact, yet each requires interpretation and a clear context in order to convey useful information in the workplace. Facts can be used in different ways by writers with different perspectives; facts are also understood differently by readers at different cognitive levels.

Reports look different from essays, the differences arising from the way readers use them. Essay reading is usually *linear* reading—that is, essays, like novels or short stories, are designed to be read from the first word through to the last. They are usually read for interest as much as for information. Technical or business reading, on the other hand, is normally installment or piecemeal reading—reports are read primarily for specific pieces of information. Readers seldom want or need to read whole documents from cover to cover. A skillful writer must incorporate cues such as font changes, headings, graphics, summaries, lists, a table of contents, and an index to help busy readers locate the needed information quickly and efficiently.

Writers of essays and fiction may use figures of speech such as similes, metaphors, personification, hyperbole, and the like to enhance language and intensify meaning. Long and intricately structured sentences may weave around short, powerful fragments, so that a story is, quite literally, spun for the reader. Moreover, most narrative writing relates events sequentially, without commentary or input from the writer. Such writing may also include dialogue and flights of description for the pure joy of using language. So, for example, a creative writer might choose to write

> Overflowing into the neighbouring fields, cascading down the roadways in shining rivulets, the dancing sunlight marking its path with glistening streaks of silver, singing and chuckling with its freedom, the snow-fed creek burst from its wintry prison.

Workplace writers must use more conventional syntax and language. Reports are not the place to manipulate language merely for effect, and they are not mystery stories. They should rely not on narrative but on expository writing. Expository writing is not necessarily sequential; it tends to replace description with explanation, and it is more likely to use the third person. Box 17.1 gives examples of narrative and expository writing for comparison.

expose

The *Oxford English Dictionary* defines *expose* as "depriving something of shelter." Expository writing, then, should lay out information in clear view—not hidden by excessive language or difficult syntax.

Box 17.1 *Narrative and Expository Writing*

Narrative Paragraph

Rhonda described to her visitors the plans she had developed for a perennial border on the southeast side of her house. The gradual curve of the flowerbeds followed the driveway and led through an arched trellis of cedar boughs. "I thought I'd focus mostly on yellow and blue flowers with just a few white for accents," she commented. "They'll stand out well against the house. It has so much pink already in the bricks and the trim. I also want to find some evergreen shrubs that will look interesting during the winter—maybe even some that will have berries for the birds." As they strolled under the trellis, they could see the vegetable garden, already showing the beginnings of tomatoes, onions, and beans. Along one side, the raspberry canes were leafing out vigorously, and at the back, a huge rhubarb patch looked very inviting.

(continued)

Box 17.1 *Narrative and Expository Writing* (continued)

Expository Paragraph

A perennial garden that features just one or two colours provides an interesting focal point. Pastel shades of blue and pink, for example, will create a cottage garden effect. Larkspur (*delphinium*), bluebells (*mertensia*), forget-me-nots (*myosotis*), along with Jacob's ladder (*polemonium*), meadow rue (*thalictrum*), and several varieties of stonecrop (*sedum*) are just a few of the varieties that will give you a good start. These combine plants of various heights as well as blossoms that will appear throughout the season. In addition, they have an effective array of foliage—from greyish and feathery to crisp, almost lime green.

Activities and Exercises

1. Below is a list of common types of reports. Discuss how each is written as a result of a question or problem—what question or problem does each address? Identify the sender(s) and receiver(s). If possible, obtain samples of these documents and examine their content, layout, and writing style.
   - coroner's report after an unexplained death
   - incident report after a workplace injury
   - student's report card at the end of term
   - annual report of a business or organization
   - proposal to make a presentation at a workshop or conference
   - request for government funding for research
   - job application letter
2. This chapter refers to several recent reports that have made the national news. Look through a current issue of any newspaper to find examples of reports in progress or completed. Discuss how they demonstrate the characteristics of reports described in this chapter.

For further assignments dealing with the content of this chapter, see case studies 10, 12, 13, 14, 15, 16, 17, and 19 starting on page 287.

Primary Research

Primary research refers to investigation done in person by the researcher. Primary sources include direct observation (counting, weighing, measuring, etc.) experimentation, diaries, letters, speeches, photographs, minutes of meetings, personal interviews, surveys, and statistics. This chapter will look at two types of primary research that relate to business and technical reports: surveys and personal interviews.

Surveys

survey

The word *survey* comes from the Latin *super*, meaning "above" or "over," and *videre*, meaning "to see." The researcher who uses a questionnaire takes a broad overview, collecting and analyzing data from many sources.

We can hardly get through a day without participating in a *survey* of some sort. Many businesses have "how was our service?" cards for us to fill out. Professional pollsters telephone (usually during dinnertime) to ask how well we think politicians are doing their job. We duck into a store in the mall to avoid the person with the clipboard approaching us. Our favourite magazines want to know about our relationships, entertainment choices, and best vacations. We drive over counters on the road that are placed there to determine traffic density. All of these are methods of collecting data by counting.

Designing an effective survey is a complex and painstaking task that involves a thorough knowledge of sampling, marketing, and statistics. For a thorough study of questionnaires, you should consult a textbook on research methods. This chapter can only skim the surface of such a large topic; it provides some general guidelines to help you produce a short, effective survey.

Clarify Your Purpose

Before preparing any survey, be clear about your goals. Exactly what do you want to find out? Remember, if you cannot use the data you collect, everyone's time has been wasted. Write out a brief purpose statement to keep yourself on track and to avoid asking questions that do not relate directly to your purpose. Whenever possible, include your purpose statement at the top of your survey as a courtesy to your reader. For example,

> We are doing a study on the usefulness of the vending machines at Branchton College. Please help us by completing this short survey.

Make the Survey Accessible

If you want to design a survey that doesn't scare people away, make it readable and give it a professional appearance.

- Don't crowd your questions.
- Use a clear font.
- Leave enough space for readable answers.
- Write questions that are simple and clear and won't confuse your respondents.
- Check and double-check your spelling and grammar.
- Have several people proofread your survey before you distribute it.

Create Questions That Have Short, Countable Answers

Don't make the mistake of confusing a survey with a test. The whole purpose of a survey is to collect many responses that can be totalled and analyzed statistically. Accordingly, you want to elicit answers that are short and countable.

Give your respondents a choice of possible answers for each question. This is important because it gives you control over the types of answers you will receive. Open-ended questions, by contrast, allow unlimited responses. Here are three different types of questions:

> What brand of potato chips do you usually buy?
> *(This question could receive dozens of answers.)*
>
> Which of the following brands of potato chips have you bought in the past three months?
> ____ Hostess ____ Miss Vicki's ____President's Choice
>
> ____ Other ______________________________
> *(This question allows the surveyor to limit the number of answers.)*
>
> What do you think about potato chips as a snack?
> *(The answer to this question would be long and unfocused.)*

The first question is too broad. The second question allows the researcher to focus on three brands only (the "other" category allows respondents to add their own answer). The third, open-ended, question might be useful during a personal interview, but it would drastically reduce the effectiveness of a widely distributed survey. Sample Document 18.1 is an example of a survey that uses questions with short, countable answers.

Sample Document 18.1 *Questions with Short, Countable Answers*

Communication Questionnaire for Executives

1. Using two or three words, describe your type of company (manufacturing, high-tech, banking, education, etc.)

   ____

2. How many people do you employ? (Please check one.)

   _____ 5–25 _____ 100–150
   _____ 25–50 _____ 150–300
   _____ 50–100 _____ 300–450

3. How do you usually communicate with employees? (Check all that apply.)

   _____ memo _____ e-mail
   _____ in person _____ through supervisors, managers
   _____ bulletin boards _____ telephone
   _____ other (please specify) ______________________

4. Which types of writing are done in your company? (Please label each one by frequency: **N**ever, **R**arely, **S**ometimes, **O**ften.)

   _____ office memos _____ catalogues
   _____ manuals _____ advertisements
   _____ procedures _____ newsletters
   _____ letters _____ reports
   _____ other (please specify) ______________________

5. Does your company have writing guidelines? _____ yes _____ no

6. Does your company hire outside writers for specific projects?

   _____ yes _____ no

Choose Your Respondents Carefully

The topic of choosing a sample of people cannot be covered in detail in this text. However, even inexperienced researchers can apply some common sense when choosing respondents so that the resulting data is useful. The people who fill out a questionnaire should fit the subject of the survey, and they should represent, as nearly as possible, the larger population of people who fit the subject of the survey. The survey in Sample Document 18.2, for example, was distributed to students at Branchton College while they were using vending machines. Thus, the students doing the research were able to avoid giving the survey to people who might never have used the machines. Notice also that the survey meets the other criteria described above: It provides a brief introduction, it is concise and easy to read, it gives readers specific answers to choose from, and the answers will be easy to tabulate.

Sample Document 18.2 *Choosing Appropriate Respondents*

Vending Machines at Branchton College

We are doing a study on the usefulness of the vending machines at Branchton. Please help us by completing this short survey.

1. Approximately, how often do you use the vending machines at Branchton College?
   _____ once a day _____ once a week _____ once a month
   _____ hardly ever

2. Which of the following two brands of chips do you choose more often?
   _____ Hostess _____ Miss Vicki's

3. In the past four weeks, have you bought any of the following items from the vending machines? Check any that you have bought.
   _____ Bounty _____ Mexitos _____ Maxi Krisp
   _____ Bar None _____ Blue Diamond Almonds
   _____ Premier Peanuts _____ Hostess Ketchup Chips

4. What problems have you experienced with the vending machines?
   _____ no change _____ took money but gave no product
   _____ empty _____ items stale
   _____ other (please specify) ____________________________

Avoid Bias

This is often a difficult rule to follow, but a survey will not provide useful information if your wording points the respondent to the answers you want. For example, if the short survey in Sample Document 18.2 was introduced with this statement,

> We are doing a study on the problems being experienced with the vending machines at Branchton. Please help us by completing this short survey.

respondents would have been alerted to the negative answers anticipated by the surveyor. Compare the different versions of questions in Box 18.1.

Box 18.1 *Biased and Objective Questions*

How difficult was it for you to reach one of our technical support people? ✗

____ extremely difficult ____ a bit difficult ____ not too difficult

How long did you wait for technical support to answer your call? ✓

____ up to 1 minute ____ about 2–5 minutes ____ more than 5 minutes

Use Different Types of Questions

If you keep the above guidelines in mind, you should have a clear idea of the type of information you need. Here is a brief overview of the common types of questions used in surveys.

Yes/No Questions

Avoid the temptation to create an entire survey using only yes/no questions. Reserve these for questions of fact only. For example,

Have you bought potato chips in the past 30 days?
[ ] Yes [ ] No

Do you own a video camera?
[ ] Yes [ ] No

Does your company have printed guidelines for writing reports?
[ ] Yes [ ] No

Do not ask for yes/no answers to questions about opinions or for questions where a much wider range of answers exists. For example,

Do you like potato chips?
[ ] Yes [ ] No

This information would be collected more accurately with a ranking question.

Ranking Questions

If you are using ranking questions, tell your reader clearly how the ranking system works (for example, on a scale from 1 to 3, is an answer of "3" the highest or the lowest? the best or the worst?). If you use more than one ranking question, the ranking system should work the same way for each question.

Avoid asking your reader to rank too many choices. Most people, for example, would not know their sixth-favourite snack food. Here is an example of a ranking question:

If you were offered the following snacks, rank in order (1 = 1st choice, 2 = 2nd choice, 3 = 3rd choice) the three that you would choose:

____ popcorn
____ cheese snacks
____ pretzels
____ peanuts in the shell
____ pizza
____ potato chips

Continuum Questions

Continuum questions are similar to ranking questions in that they allow a range of responses. If you use an even number of choices, you force your respondents to move to one side or the other of a continuum. If you use an odd number, you will find that your answers tend to fall in the middle. Here are some examples of ranking questions:

In my household, I am responsible for grocery shopping.
[ ] always [ ] often [ ] occasionally [ ] never

Employees should be allowed to use their sick leave if their children are ill.
[ ] strongly agree [ ] somewhat agree [ ] somewhat disagree [ ] strongly disagree

How often do you buy snacks at the same store where you rent a video?
[ ] never [ ] rarely [ ] sometimes [ ] usually [ ] always

Multiple-Choice Questions

When you are using a multiple-choice question, tell your respondents how many items to choose and how to indicate their choice. Here are two examples:

Check the ONE potato chip brand you have purchased in the past week. If you have not purchased potato chips, leave this question blank. If you have purchased more than one brand, check the last box only.
[ ] Hostess [ ] Fritos [ ] Old Dutch [ ] Jack's
[ ] Miss Vicki's [ ] No Name [ ] More than one

If you have *ever* used the computer lab on a Saturday or a Sunday, indicate what time you were there. Circle *all* answers that apply.
8:00 a.m.–12:00 noon
12:00 noon–4:00 p.m.
4:00 p.m.–8:00 p.m.
8:00 p.m.–12:00 midnight
12:00 midnight–8:00 a.m.

Demographic Questions

demographics

Demographics is derived from two Greek words: *demos*, "people," and *graphia*, "description." Thus, demographics denotes a "picture of the people."

Demographic information includes data about age, gender, income, education, and other "people" factors that describe your respondents. You should ask for such information only if it is relevant in some way to the purpose of your survey.

For example, if you want to know which movie is the most popular, you do not need demographic information. However, if you want to know which movie is most popular among people of various ages, you would ask about age to divide the results accordingly. Sample Document 18.3 shows how you might tabulate data from a question that includes demographic data.

Sample Document 18.3 ***Tabulating Demographic Data***

How often do you eat breakfast? Please check the appropriate box below.

	Always	Sometimes	Never
I am under 25.	❏	❏	❏
I am 26 or older.	❏	❏	❏

Do you own a car?

	Yes		No	
	Male	Female	Male	Female
Under 25	❏	❏	❏	❏
25 and over	❏	❏	❏	❏

Personal Interviews

interview

The word *interview* uses the same Latin verb as "survey" for its root: *videre*, meaning "to see." The preposition *inter*, however, means "between" and implies much closer contact than a survey.

Interviews and surveys collect different kinds of data in different ways. Instead of surveying a large sample of people to provide short answers, a researcher conducting a *personal interview* focuses on just a few people or even on one individual with specialized, relevant information. Interviewers can use open-ended answers, so the respondents can say as much as they want. Interviewers also don't have to use the same questions in every interview; they can adjust their questions depending on the situation and the answers received.

Select the Interviewee Carefully

The person to be interviewed should be someone who will make a useful contribution to your work, not just a friend who happens to be nearby. Choose someone who has at least one of the following qualifications:

- expert knowledge of the subject area
- extensive education in a relevant field
- specialized experience in the discipline

You should be able to name or justify your choice of interviewee in your report so that the information you collect has the ring of authority.

Plan the Interview

Do not go into an interview "cold," or you will waste everyone's time. Make an appointment, and explain to the interviewee ahead of time why you want the interview and what type of information you are looking for. Set a definite time limit so your interviewee knows how much time to set aside.

Prepare your questions ahead of time. If you arrange for a 30-minute interview, you may have time for only three or four questions. Time moves much faster than you might expect. Write down your questions in order of importance, and plan a couple of extra questions in case you do have time. If you have questions that might require the interviewee to look up data, let the person know a few days earlier so he or she can prepare.

Be Professional

Arrive early for the interview. Dress and act professionally. This is not the time to get shy and giggly. Limit small talk; get down to your questions as quickly as possible. Take responsibility for watching the clock, and stop when your time is up. Even if you have not finished your questions, you should thank the person and leave. If the interviewee gives permission for more time, don't prolong the session unduly.

Tape-recording the interview eliminates the need to take notes and allows you to listen more carefully to the whole answer. Ask permission ahead of time to record, and take a tape recorder with working batteries so you don't waste time trying to find a plug.

Follow Up

Send a brief thank-you letter to the interviewee. As soon as possible after the interview, go through your notes and write up a careful summary of the points you want to use in your report. Double-check details such as figures, dates, and spelling so your report will be accurate.

Summarize the Interview

Unless it has been specifically requested, using the "question and answer" format for a report on the interview is not the best choice. Your readers likely do not want a verbatim account. Instead, using your notes, write a summary of the information you received that's most important and most relevant to your subject. Be careful to avoid distorting the information in any way. For example, don't omit answers that you disagree with or you may, by implication, change the overall impact of the interview. You may find that you use only a few short quotations from a half-hour interview.

Activities and Exercises

1. Edit and improve the following smoking survey using the guidelines provided in this chapter. You may want to begin with a clear statement of purpose so that you can make the questions more appropriate.

Questionnaire Investigating Smoking

This questionnaire will be asking questions to college student related to quitting smoking. If your answer to this question (Have you ever tried to quit smoking?) is NO, please return this questionnaire to the people who handed it to you.

(Where blank spaces are provided please specify number, method, etc.)

1. What made you want to quit? (Please check off your choice.)

--- Health reasons --- too much money spent --- New Year's Resolution --- bad habit
--- Other ____

2. Who wanted or told you to quit? (check off reason)

--- you did --- friends --- family --- girl/boy friend --- physician
Other ____

3. When you tried to quit, how did you go about doing it? (Check off your methods)

--- nicotine gum --- cold turkey --- got group help -- your physician
--- the patch --- moved to a lighter brand
mechanical devices (specify) ____________________________________
other method____

4. How many times per year have you tried to quit smoking? (check one)

--- twice a year --- every month --- during holidays --- more

5. What has been the longest time span you have been able to stop smoking? (check one)

— less than a day — one day — one week — one month — one year a
— longer than a year other ______________

6. If you ever succeeded in quitting, what made your return to smoking? (check one)

--- nerves --- lit a cigarette out of habit --- stress --- don't know
other ____

7. What do you think smoking is? (check one)

--- a bad habit --- a past time --- sometehing that helps calm nerves
--- an addiction to nicotine

If possible, can you please fill in some questions regarding your babit?

8. How old are you? ____________________
9. At what age did you start smoking?____________________
10. How long have you been smoking? ____________________

2. A student prepared the draft of a survey on shark awareness for a class report. Provide some advice about revising this effort.

QUESTIONNAIRE

This investigation is to determine the public's awareness of sharks and the reason for shark attacks on humans.

1. Have you ever seen a live shark?
2. Have you or anyone you know ever been attacked by a shark?
3. How many different species of shark can you name?
4. Has the idea of a shark ever kep you from going into the water (swimming, diving, surfing, etc.)?
5. How often are you concerned aobut shark attacks when swimming, diving, surfing etc. in the ocean?
6. Why do you think sharks attack people?
   a. food
   b. mistake them for food
   c. protecting themselves
   d. protecting territory or their young
   e. natural instinct of a killer
7. Where did you get most of your knowledge on sharks?
8. Do you consider sharks to be a major threat to swimmers, divers, fishermen, surfers, etc.?
9. Who do you think is most inclined to be attacked by a shark?
   a. diver
   b. swimmer
   c. surfer
   d. fisherman
10. Where do you think most shark attacks occur?

3. Develop a short survey (no more than five questions) to collect information from your classmates or other students in your college. Here are some suggestions for topics. Pick

one or come up with your own. Compare your survey with those of others in the class. Evaluate your questions and edit where appropriate.

- how students get to school (bus, walk, car, carpool, dropped off by a friend, etc.)
- who plays a musical instrument (type of instrument, for how long, level of expertise)
- pet ownership (type of pet, how many)
- financial or political knowledge (e.g., familiarity with RRSPs or stock markets; awareness of local, provincial, or federal government issues)

4. Conduct the survey you prepared for question 3 with 50–100 students. Include demographic information.
5. Prepare and carry out an interview with a professional in your field. Here are some suggestions for topics, or your instructor may suggest a topic.
   - How important are writing skills in this field?
   - Apart from formal educational requirements, what aptitudes are important in this field?
   - Is mandatory retirement a good or a bad idea? Why?
   - What sort of continuing education or training for employees does the person's organization offer?
6. As a class, collect samples of survey cards used to assess customer satisfaction from a variety of businesses in your area. Analyze and evaluate the cards using the guidelines in this chapter.
7. Aweo is a student who is preparing a report on the effectiveness of flu shots. She surveyed 100 students at her college to find out who got a flu shot. Three months later, she tried to find as many of these same students as possible and questioned them about whether they had had the flu. She also wanted to conduct an in-depth interview for her report. Below is the write-up on her interview. Discuss its effectiveness. What advice can you give Aweo?

> I decide to interview my grandmother because she had a flu shot last year for the first time in her life (age 80) and had never been sicker. She feels her shot contributed to her illnesses throughout the entire winter. She lost approximately 15 pounds and had to be hospitalized twice. Her symptoms were flu-related, such as fever, muscle aches, nausea etc. The doctors could do nothing but run some blood tests and send her home. Apparently her test results came out normal, and her immune system seemed fine. The doctors had no explanation for the way she was feeling but to say that she probably had a virus. Her first symptoms occurred a couple of days after her vaccination and this is why she blames the shot on her illness and she is hesitant to ever get another one.

For further assignments dealing with the content of this chapter, see case studies 10 and 16 starting on page 287.

Secondary Research

secondary

Secondary may denote something of inferior or subordinate importance—as second place is to first place. However, it also can mean something arising from a derived authority, and that is the meaning in the expression "secondary sources." Secondary sources are vital, not subordinate, sources.

Why Use Secondary Sources?

Secondary sources act much like the persuasive technique of ethos: They add weight and credibility to your ideas. Support from authoritative outside sources is especially important for ideas that may be innovative, unorthodox, costly, or problematic in other ways. The more authoritative your source, the more it can benefit your writing.

Secondary sources provide a variety of opinions and viewpoints on a subject, thus allowing a writer to produce a balanced and well-reasoned document.

Secondary sources also save time by providing you with background data that has already been researched and written down.

Choosing Secondary Sources

Sources used for research do not neatly divide into categories of primary and secondary. The data you collect with a questionnaire constitutes a primary source. If someone else uses your data later on to support an idea, it becomes, for that person, a secondary source. A *secondary source* is actually any data that's written about a primary source. Secondary sources include books, periodicals, pamphlets, statistics, television shows, documentary films, websites, CD-ROMs, and other kinds of published material. They provide commentary, analysis, interpretation, evaluation, or even refutation of primary sources.

Using the Internet as a Secondary Source

As a source of information, the Internet goes far beyond what any researcher could have imagined even a few years ago. And just because of its extensive variety, the information on the Internet must also be carefully evaluated. This evaluation process requires skill, experience, and lots of common sense. Here are some questions to ask as you look at various websites.

Is the author reliable? Remember that anyone can put information on the web. Right now, you could prepare a page of completely bogus data on kickboxing and upload it onto the Internet. Check to see whether the author or source is clearly identified. If so, what can you learn about the author? Is this person well known in the discipline? Checking this information will likely require a completely separate search.

Is the website endorsed by any reputable organizations? Is there an e-mail link to organizations where you can obtain further information? Are telephone numbers and mailing addresses also provided? Legitimate writers should not hesitate to support their information.

When was the information last updated? If nothing has been added or changed for months or years, chances are the site is not being monitored for accuracy or current material.

Is the tone of the material sensational or unorthodox? If the opinions or ideas are unlike anything else you have come across, you need to exercise some healthy skepticism. This type of site is often based largely on unproven, first-person testimonials rather than documented sources.

Does the site have an obvious bias? Even reputable websites need to be evaluated critically for the bias of the writer. For example, a webpage published by a pro-life group will naturally express that organization's point of view. Make sure you balance this source with opposing ideas.

Is the material age- and audience-appropriate? Just as you would not use a children's picture book to support a research idea, you should not choose a website aimed at an inappropriate level of reader. Academic and scholarly sites approach topics differently from popular sites. An article on the moon in *Reader's Digest* approaches its topic in a completely different way from an article on the same topic in *Astronomy and Astrophysics Journal.*

Does the design of the site add to its credibility? Use the same criteria here that you might use for any written work—even your own. Look for a clear, readable layout, correct spelling and grammar, graphics that are relevant rather than merely decorative, and a logical flow of ideas.

Finally, remember that the Internet is not the only reliable source of information. Be careful not to rely solely on the Internet simply because that seems easiest. It has not replaced up-to-date, authoritative print publications.

Using Books and Periodicals

Apart from the Internet, the sources most writers rely on are books. Keep in mind that getting from the initial idea to the published book can take up to three years or even more. So, although you may find a book on a sensational subject (such as the O.J.

Simpson trial) that is rushed through publication, you will not likely find well-researched, authoritative books on current topics. Also keep in mind that books are not necessarily published on every subject—especially subjects that are new, ongoing, or quite specific. For example, three keyword searches of the Toronto Public Library online catalogue yielded the following results:

Enron	0
Bugatti	13
O.J. Simpson	68

Thus, depending on your subject, the search for a book may or may not prove useful. Don't make the mistake, however, of thinking that no sources on your subject are available.

Apart from monographs (books devoted to a single topic), you still have almost limitless resources. See Table 19.1 for just a few examples.

Table 19.1 *Types of Print Resources*

Resources	Types of Information
Reference books such as dictionaries, encyclopedias, atlases, directories, etc.	Definitions, history and background material, illustrations, names of relevant people, etc.
Government publications	Statistics, laws, public inquiries, research, political views, timely details that cannot be found anywhere else
Publications of associations and organizations	Booklets, pamphlets, newsletters, and brochures from local community groups to international associations
Periodical indexes and abstracts	Lead to articles and illustrations in hundreds of magazines and newspapers

A periodical is any type of publication that appears on a regular schedule. It might be a daily newspaper, a bi-weekly magazine, or an annual report, for example. Periodicals (sometimes called journals or magazines) tend to provide more up-to-date information than books simply because they are published more quickly. The articles they contain may also be much more focused. For example, on a given day, although no books were available with the keyword "Enron" in the title, a search of *Canadian Business and Current Affairs* periodical index on the same day yielded 200 hits.

To return, full circle, to web-based resources, you will find that the catalogues of hundreds of libraries are now available online, as are many searchable databases. You may even find the full text of articles in newspapers and magazines.

How to Use Secondary Sources

Choose relevant, authoritative information that is timely and appropriate for the audience.

Recognize secondary sources whether they agree or disagree with your own point of view. Those that disagree provide a balance of ideas; they will also force you to weigh and improve your arguments. On the other hand, sources that echo or agree with your ideas add valuable support to your writing. Look through any scientific or academic publication and you will see clearly the importance these writers attach to secondary sources.

Use only what you need—a name, a date, a statistic, or a strong quotation. Avoid the temptation to quote long passages just to fill up space or to look impressive. Remember to document all information you use, including graphics.

Activities and Exercises

1. For the past several years, The Ultimate Resort and Spa has been considering adding several new recreational activities, such as

   - riding stables
   - snowboarding
   - scuba diving
   - go-karts
   - hang gliding

   Conduct an Internet search to find three reliable websites that might provide useful information to the committees considering one of these activities or one suggested by your instructor. Look for information on issues such as construction costs, health and safety laws, land requirements, maintenance requirements, personnel requirements, and target audiences. For each site you find, provide the following information:

   - URL (website address)
   - type of site (commercial, government, etc.)
   - actual source of information (name of author or organization)
   - contact information (e-mail, address, telephone number, fax number)
   - date of last update
   - target audience
   - ease of use
   - presence of helpful links

   Based on this information, write a brief report that compares the sites and evaluates their usefulness.

2. Using the same list of subjects as those in exercise 1, conduct a search of other secondary sources such as books, pamphlets, periodicals, government publications, and reference books. Prepare an annotated bibliography of five sources.

3. Working in a small group, decide on a topic for a short report (some ideas are listed below). Try to locate a secondary source of information on the topic from each of the following categories:
   - pamphlet or brochure published by a relevant organization
   - current, authoritative website
   - recent article in a newspaper (within the past three months)
   - recent book (within the past two years)
   - article published in a popular magazine
   - article published in a professional or academic journal
   - film or television documentary

   Possible topics:
   - keeping exotic animals as pets
   - the V-chip in home computers
   - home schooling your children
   - investing money in antiques
   - ostrich farming
4. Using a topic from question 3 or one suggested by your instructor, compare the kinds of information you can gather using different search engines such as
   - http://www.lycos.com
   - http://www.google.com
   - http://www.excite.com
   - http://www.altavista.com

   and any others that you want to try out. Write up your findings in a short report.

For further assignments dealing with the content of this chapter, see case studies 10 and 16 starting on page 287.

Short, Informal Reports

Nearly every organization, regardless of its size, has some kind of report-writing system. The larger and more complex a company is, the more likely it will rely on written reports for its communication needs. Short, informal reports may be stand-alone documents, or they may form part of a memo or letter. Preprinted forms are used for accident reports or travel reports. This chapter looks at several specific types of short reports, focusing mainly on how they are organized. Keep in mind that some of these examples might be formal reports if they were long and complex.

The Short Investigative Report

investigate

The word *investigate* is derived from the Latin *vestigare*, meaning "to track" or "to trace." In Latin, *vestigium* means "footprint." Think of a detective tracking footprints to solve a mystery. An investigative report presents the results of a careful search.

Common investigative reports include coroners' reports, police reports, scientific research reports, and public inquiries. At work or in the classroom, they may be called problem/solution reports or recommendation reports.

Choosing an Appropriate Topic

Unless you have the time and funding to conduct a comprehensive investigation and write a massive report, be careful to keep your topic focused and narrow. If you choose a topic that's too general and huge, your report will be too vague to be useful. Here are some examples of good and poor topic choices:

Area of Interest: Hockey
Poor Topic: Violence in hockey
This topic is too broad and too vague. It has been overdone. There is no clear question to investigate.
Better Topic: How much does it cost to keep a child in a hockey league?
This topic is in the form of a clear question that can be answered. The writer has several possible groups to interview such as parents, coaches, and sports stores.

Area of Interest: Health and fitness

Poor Topic: How important is it to keep fit?

This question has already been asked and answered many times. It's difficult to answer a "how important" question. The expression "keep fit" is vague and undefined.

Better Topic: What percentage of college students eat breakfast at least five times a week?

This topic suggests a clear survey and a specific question that can be answered. Secondary sources about nutrition would provide good support.

Organizing the Report

Sample Document 20.1 is an example of a short investigative report prepared by a writer who had suddenly encountered a case of hepatitis C in her own family. She experienced considerable difficulty obtaining helpful advice and information about this condition, and as a result, she used the situation as a topic for a short memo report.

Notice the conventional headings used in Sample Document 20.1.

Background and Purpose

These two sections may be combined or separate, depending on the amount of material.

Background material is supplied to bring the reader up to speed on the topic in question. Depending on the length of the full report, this section may be as short as a sentence or two. It provides a context for everything that is to follow.

The Purpose statement presents the actual question or problem under investigation. Since objectivity is important, Josie does not use the word "prove" in her purpose statement. Investigations that begin this way tend to be biased, and their writers may make the mistake of ignoring data that conflicts with what they are trying to "prove."

Method

The Method section should describe precisely how the investigation was carried out. In scientific research, the method is vital since it allows other scientists to replicate an experiment or test. Since Josie used a questionnaire, she included a copy of it with her report (not shown in Sample Document 20.1) and described the people that she surveyed. She has clearly identified the person she interviewed, along with that person's particular qualifications. Josie's secondary sources are documented throughout the report and at the end.

Many writers confuse the information that appears under these three headings:

Method	*how* you found your data
Findings	*the actual data* that you found
Discussion	*the importance* or *meaning* of the data

Sample Document 20.1 *A Short Investigative Report in Memo Form*

Josie Luciani

Iqaluit, NT
X0A 0H0
(867) 979-8363

TO: Lainie Grupp, Health Services Administrator, Fraser College

FROM: Josie Luciani

DATE: April 1997

SUBJECT: Public Awareness of Hepatitis C

BACKGROUND AND PURPOSE

Hepatitis C is a relatively new disease that is a silent killer. It has been associated with HIV and haemophilia for the past 15 years. Gary Dusheiko (1995) has described clearly how the virus attacks the liver and leads to cirrhosis, skin disorders, muscle cramping, excessive exhaustion, and, eventually, death. Hepatitis C seems to have a cloud of mystery surrounding it. It does not discriminate in its choice of victims. Newborns and elderly patients alike are attacked (Gold, Melester, & Richardson, 1994). Unfortunately, few people have ever heard of the hepatitis C virus (HCV), and even those who have know very little about it. This investigation was carried out to determine the extent of awareness among college students and to evaluate what information about this disease is available.

METHOD

- I selected 140 adults at a community college and asked them to complete a questionnaire regarding their knowledge of HCV. All were aged 20 or above. The oldest was 56. Half the group was male; half was female.
- I interviewed Dr. E. Winestock, a family practitioner, regarding his views on HCV and his efforts to educate patients.
- I contacted the health services offices of three community colleges and asked for any information they had on HCV.
- I also contacted the following organizations:
    - the Canadian Red Cross
    - the Toronto Public Health Department
    - the Liver Study Program at Mount Sinai Hospital, Toronto
    - the People with AIDS Foundation
    - the Haemophilia Society

(continued)

Public Awareness of Hepatitis C
April 1997
page 2 of 3

FINDINGS

Survey

Fifty-two percent of those surveyed had never even heard of hepatitis C. This group was split almost evenly between males and females.

The group that "had heard of" hepatitis C will be the focus of the following statistics:

- 28 percent actually knew someone who had contracted HCV.
- 28 percent also knew that HCV was not hereditary.
- All respondents answered correctly that HCV affects both heterosexuals and homosexuals.
- Only 15 percent knew that HCV is a terminal disease.
- 65 percent did not know how HCV is contracted or spread. This figure, combined with the 50 percent who had never heard of HCV, indicates that 83 percent of the surveyed group had little or no knowledge about the nature of this disease.

Interviews

A spokesperson from the Public Health Department said the department does not want to alarm the public and so "we release very little information about HCV." He went on to add that a public information campaign, costly in itself, would also incur the following expenses:

- costs of testing blood supply
- costs of educating medical personal
- costs of examining past records to see who, if anyone, may have received tainted blood through transfusions
- costs of lawsuits

The three educational facilities I contacted had no information about HCV—none in brochure form, and none that they could provide me with verbally. I was told that students who inquired about HCV would be directed to their own physician or given the name of a physician in the area.

Although each of the organizations I contacted was willing to provide verbal information, I was surprised to learn that no printed information addressed to a general reader was readily available.

(continued)

Public Awareness of Hepatitis C
April 1997
page 3 of 3

DISCUSSION

Overall, the findings were discouraging. As with many "new" diseases, information about HCV changes constantly. As a result, the public can easily become confused. HCV is a disease that affects the liver and is spread by blood-to-blood contact, such as blood transfusion and intravenous drug use. Some recent work suggests that HCV may be spread by sexual contact or even transmitted from mother to infant (Blanchette, 1993).

Rather than resulting in an influx of educational material, this uncertainty seems to have resulted in a complete lack of information. Cold calls to the three colleges and two clinics drew a blank. Even the Canadian Liver Foundation had no information that they could mail to me, although they encouraged me to make an appointment to be tested. This call, in fact, veered off into a discussion of the costs involved in better educating the public.

Unfortunately, as Blanchette (1993) points out, lack of information usually results in misinformation. As a result, those who contract the disease become panicky and open to rumours and unsubstantiated advice (Alloway, 1995).

RECOMMENDATION

Ideally, testing and education should be widespread and thorough. Based on my own very limited research, I suggest that a clear, readable brochure should be made as widely available as information on HIV is, since these two diseases have similar consequences and similar means of control.

REFERENCES

Alloway, T. (1995, March). Memo to national and Ontario hepatitis C task forces. *Haemophilia Ontario*, 2.

Blanchette, V. (1993, Summer). Hepatitis C infection in patients with haemophilia: Results of a national survey. *Haemophilia Today*, 288–291.

Dusheiko, G.M. (1995, March 4). Genetic diversity of hepatitis C virus: Implications for pathogenesis, treatment, and prevention. *Lancet*, 562–566.

Gold, D., Melester, T., & Richardson, I. (1994). Liver disease and HIV. *GMHC: Treatment Issues*, *8*(5), 22–23.

Findings

In the Method section, Josie describes *how* she collected her data. In the Findings section, she presents the data itself. The Findings section of any report provides the results of a survey, a summary of an interview, and any other information that was learned through observation or experiment. It's important to filter out irrelevant material in order to help the reader see clearly what's most important. Although Josie has not used graphics, they can often make the Findings more reader-friendly.

Findings should be presented as objectively as possible; for example, do not omit data just because it disagrees with what you hoped to find.

Discussion

In the Discussion section, Josie interprets her findings. Information in the Discussion section might answer (but is not limited to) the following:

- If the findings are completely unexpected, what might be the reason?
- Assuming the findings are accurate, what group or activity might be affected? Should anyone's behaviour change?
- Can the results help anyone to save time? money?
- If a different group had been surveyed, would the results be quite different? Why?
- Do the findings relate to the purpose of the report?

Recommendation

Josie has made one recommendation that relates directly to the question that prompted her investigation. Not every investigative report will contain recommendations; however, often collecting and analyzing data will prompt the writer to think of suggestions that might affect future behaviour or decisions. Any recommendations you make must be based solidly on the findings of the report. They cannot be unsupported opinions.

Periodic Reports

Periodic reports can also be called interim reports, progress reports, or an even more precise name such as monthly or quarterly reports. Periodic reports provide data on a regular or predetermined schedule to keep the reader updated on ongoing work. A company's annual report is a type of progress report issued to shareholders. A student's report card is also a progress report. Depending on the reason for the report and the reader's knowledge, these documents may be organized by date or by topic.

A progress report is directed at the person or group that assigned the project or provided the funding. The time period covered by the report should be clearly indicated at the beginning or in the title.

A periodic report looks at three categories of data:

- what has been done
- what is currently being done
- what remains to be done

The information, however, can be further classified by project so that it focuses on tasks one at a time. Often a project report will include a Gantt chart so that the overall progress of the work is easy to visualize. See Figure 20.1.

Figure 20.1 ***Gantt Chart***

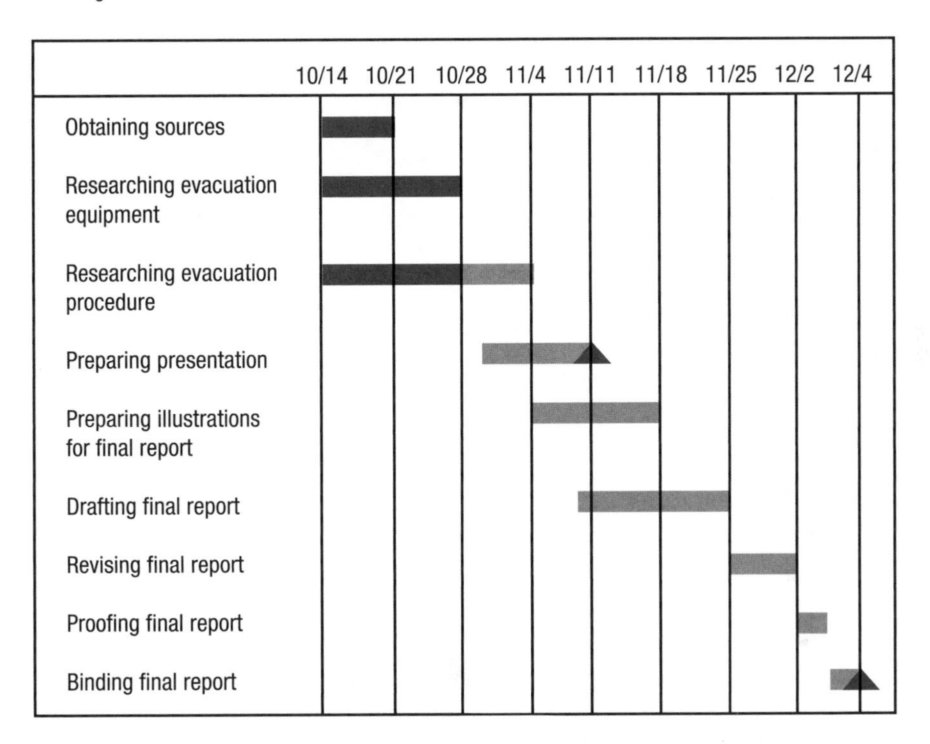

The filled bars indicate the work that has been completed. The open bars indicate the work that has yet to be done. The triangles indicate the key milestones: the formal presentation (November 11) and the formal report (December 4).

Source: Virginia Polytechnic Institute and State University. (n.d.). *Writing guidelines for engineering and science students.* Retrieved May 20, 2002, from http://filebox.vt.edu/eng/mech/writing.

In addition to updating the reader about ongoing work, a progress report should convey information about any problems, interruptions, or delays that have been experienced. The writer should end with an overview of how the work is progressing, answering questions such as

- Are objectives being met?
- Is the anticipated completion date still valid?
- Are budgetary commitments being met?

Any changes in the original project requirements should also be explained clearly in a progress report.

Some companies use preprinted forms for monthly reports or project updates. When you use these, your actual written information may be brief. See Sample Document 20.2 for an example.

Sample Document 20.2 *A Progress Report on a Preprinted Form*

The Ultimate Resort and Spa

Highway 60, R.R. 2
Mirror Falls, Ontario L3R 4R4

Tel.: (705) 777-4000 Fax: (705) 777-4001
ultaspa@playground.on.ca

SCHEDULED REPORT DATE

May 1, 2000

WORK ORDER 6000-110

PAGE 1 OF 2

PROJECT SUPERVISORS

Melissa Kaminsky
John Bancheri

COMPLETED WORK TO DATE

1. Ventilation openings have been completed in the elevator machine rooms.
2. A passageway has been completed through the West Annex door from Wing A.

SCHEDULED WORK

1. Provide 45 min labelled fire dampers on the ventilation openings in the east and west walls of the elevator machine room.
2. Provide a new 45 min labelled door and frame complete with self-closing and latching device.

(continued)

WORK ORDER 6000-110

PAGE 2 OF 2

PROJECT ASSESSMENT

1. New cable materials have been ordered to meet environmental qualification requirements (Ref. Contract 06-77). Expected delivery date is early June 2000.
2. Fire extinguishers in Wing A should be mounted on hangers or brackets so they are readily visible.

DISTRIBUTION TO:
James Persad, Maintenance Manager

Trip or Conference Reports

If your company pays for you to attend a conference or educational program, you will usually write this type of report as a follow-up. A *trip report* provides justification for expenses and it assures the reader that the time spent was beneficial to the company. Box 20.1 lists examples of headings that might be used for a trip or conference report.

Box 20.1 ***Suggested Headings for a Trip or Conference Report***

IDENTIFICATION OF CONFERENCE

- Name
- Purpose
- Location and dates

INTRODUCTION

- What the conference was about
- Who sponsored it
- What sessions or workshops you attended

EXPENSE RECORD
This may be part of the report or attached as a separate document.

ANTICIPATED BENEFITS FOR YOUR COMPANY
What new ideas, equipment, or techniques have you learned that can be applied in your workplace?

ACKNOWLEDGMENTS
Express appreciation for funding and time allowance.

CLOSING COMMENTS

Incident Reports

Incident reports are used in case of an accident, injury, or unexpected event. Most organizations have a standard form for this type of report. See Sample Document 20.3 for an example. If you have to write one on your own, you might use a plan such as the one in Box 20.2.

Box 20.2 ***Suggested Headings for an Incident Report***

IDENTIFICATION
Provide all information necessary to identify the context of the incident: names, dates, times, and specific locations.

DESCRIPTION OF INCIDENT
Most workplaces require a narrative summary of the event.

DETAILS OF INJURY OR DAMAGE
Again, a narrative description in the writer's own words is the best approach. Avoid trying to use medical or legal jargon.

WITNESS NAMES
List names and contact information for people who were actually present and saw the incident take place.

DESCRIPTION OF INCIDENT FROM WITNESS
If one or two people witnessed the entire incident, you might find it useful for them to attach their own narrative account of the incident.

ACTION TAKEN
Use list or point-form format to detail what events took place following the incident.

Sample Document 20.3 ***Incident Report***

Name:			Date/time of accident:		
Address:			Date/time reported:		
Phone:			Supervisor reported to:		
Dept./position:			Accident location:		
Employee #:			Modified work offered?	Yes	No
Was employee treated in the medical centre?	Yes	No	Employee responsibility form signed?	Yes	No
Will employee see doctor/hospital?	Yes	No	Security gave first aid?	Yes	No
If yes, name of doctor/hospital:					
Note: Supervisor must follow up if employee sees doctor. Doctor's visit must be reported to Benefits Specialist within 24 hours.					
Parts of body affected (be specific: right, left, ring finger, etc.):					
Nature/extent of injury:					
Describe cause of accident (be specific, include diagram or photos if necessary):					
Do you have reason to doubt the cause of the injury? (if yes, explain below)					
Witness(es) to the accident:			Department:		
Accident investigation notes (including witness statements, condition of equipment, area, etc.):					
Action to be taken:			Date to be followed up:		
Security called?			Officer attended (name):		
Form filled out by:					

Activities and Exercises

1. Review Sample Document 20.1.
   a. Can you identify any places in the report where the writer expresses her own point of view?
   b. Is her recommendation based on actual data contained in the report?
2. Read the article "Shattering the Myths of the Part-Time Worker" by Inman and Enz in Chapter 5, or other investigative reports, and discuss in a small group the following questions:
   - What organization strategy do the authors use? (e.g., chronological? problem/solution?)
   - What categories of information come from secondary sources?
   - What primary research did the authors do?
   - Can you decide what questions were asked on the survey?
   - Are definitions used? How and where?
   - Are graphics used appropriately?
3. Divide up the content of the Inman and Enz article using the standard set of headings recommended for a short investigative report:
   - Background and Purpose
   - Method
   - Findings
   - Discussion
   - Recommendations

   Try writing the material the way it might appear as a short memo report.

For further assignments dealing with the content of this chapter, see case studies 9, 10, 14, 16, and 17 starting on page 285.

Formal Reports

chapter twenty-one

The distinction between formal and informal reports is somewhat arbitrary. Some sources suggest that length is the deciding factor: that a formal report should be used any time the document will run to 2000 words or more than 10 pages. The choice of the appropriate form will often be made by the company, department, or writer producing the report. In the end, the quality and type of report you write will depend on your own experience and your writing skills.

Formal reports include a series of ancillary elements, each designed to facilitate access and increase the usefulness of a lengthy document. For a very short document, these elements are rarely necessary.

Front Elements

The ancillary elements in formal reports appear at the beginning and the end. The actual body of the report comes in between. Not surprisingly, the features at the beginning prepare the reader for the report's content.

Cover

The choice of a cover for a formal report depends on a number of factors. Companies that produce many reports usually have standardized, sometimes even preprinted, covers. If you have no standardized format to use, keep in mind the following points:

- The title of the report should be visible on the cover. You may choose to use a stick-on label, a cutout window, or a clear plastic cover that allows the title page to show through.
- The colour and weight of your cover material should have a professional feel and appearance. Avoid flamboyant covers unless, of course, that's your company's particular style.
- A report that lies flat on a desk when open is much easier to read than one that snaps shut every time it is put down.

Title Page

For the title of a report, use words that clearly identify the nature of its content, such as

Evaluation of Teaching Methods for Adult Learners

Recommendations for Improving Package Inserts for OTC Drugs

A **Comparison** of Hospital Admissions in St. Stevens: 1999 and 2000

Analysis of Tube Failure in the F/M Fuelling Machine Carriage

A **Description** of Eco-tourism Projects in Antarctica

Feasibility of Hemp Production in Southwestern Ontario

Avoid vague or generic wording. The following title gives little information about the report's contents:

Motor Vehicle Accidents 1997–2001

With more detail and a key term, "Frequency," the title prepares the reader by forecasting the contents:

Frequency of Motor Vehicle Accidents on the Morre Freeway

July 1, 1997–June 30, 2001

In addition, the title page of the report may contain all or some of the following:

- name of the writer(s)
- name of the intended audience
- date of completion
- relevant identification, such as grant number or series number
- name and logo of the writer's company

Letter or Memo of Transmittal

A *letter* or *memo of transmittal* acts as a kind of enclosure card or cover letter when you are sending a report to a receiver. You choose an external or internal letter or memo, and then follow the direct approach using the following information:

1. *Refer* to the title of your project and the reason why it was done.
2. *Comment* about the content of the project, especially findings that may particularly interest your receiver.
3. *Acknowledge* any help you received while working on the project.
4. *Close* by offering to provide further assistance.

As with all correspondence, your transmittal document should use a writing style that is appropriate to the receiver and the circumstances. Often it may be somewhat less formal than the project it accompanies. Sample Document 21.1 shows a memo of transmittal. You can see an example of a letter of transmittal in Sample Document 7.6.

Sample Document 21.1 *Memo of Transmittal*

Highway 60, R.R. 2
Mirror Falls, Ontario L3R 4R4

Tel.: (705) 777-4000 Fax: (705) 777-4001
ultaspa@playground.on.ca

TO: April McAllistair, Human Resources

C: Hans Greig

FROM: Angela McPhail, Co-op Student

DATE: August 23, 2001

SUBJECT: Vending Machine Survey

Attached is my work report entitled *Evaluation of Vending Machine Services at The Ultimate Resort.*

I found this report interesting to work on. A lot of the guests and staff I surveyed had really strong opinions about the vending machines. As you suggested, I have given a copy to Hans Greig in the Food Services department.

Thanks for helping me decide on a topic. If you have any more questions about my findings, please let me know.

AM

Table of Contents

The items in the table of contents should match the headings used in the report. Depending on the length of the document, you might choose to use only first-level headings. Only if the report is very long or detailed should you include more heading levels. A well-structured index (discussed later in this chapter) is a useful complement to the table of contents.

List of Illustrations

The list of illustrations or list of figures directs the reader to the various graphics used throughout a report. The list should appear on a separate page and should include each figure or table number, the title of the graphic, and the page number. See Box 21.1 for an example.

Box 21.1 *A List of Illustrations*

Executive Summary or Abstract

After all the investigation and analysis, all the preparation of graphics, and all the careful writing, the summary page is still likely to be the one section of any report that is read the most. The reasons for this have been discussed in Chapter 13: brevity and clarity. The summary should be written last, after the main body of the report is complete.

Introduction

The introduction to a formal report explains the reasons for the report's existence and helps the reader understand the context in which it was written. In essence, the introduction says, "Here is what you are going to be reading about, and why."

The introduction may include

- Background: What situation led up to this particular study or investigation?
- Purpose: What outcome does the writer have in mind?
- Significance: Why is this topic or subject matter important?
- Scope: How intense has the study been? What are its limits? What specific information has been included or excluded?
- Arrangement: How is the report put together—what information comes first, second, last?
- Acknowledgments: Who funded this report? Who contributed in other important ways?

Sample Document 21.2 is an example of an introduction from a report entitled "The Feasibility of Using Wood as a Source of Energy."

Sample Document 21.2 *Introduction to a Formal Report*

Introduction

The purpose of this report is to identify the areas where using wood as a source of energy would be feasible. Specifically, the report examines the possibility of supplementing the province's dependence on nuclear energy and fossil fuels with increased use of wood.

This report was written at the request of the Honourable Mrs. June Barry, Minister of Energy and Natural Resources. Wood is selected as the focus of the study because it is one of Canada's major natural resources. Unlike other resources (such as coal and oil), it is a renewable source of energy.

Government reports have provided the main sources of information since ample studies exist on the use of wood as an energy source. I have supplemented these sources with articles from trade magazines.

This report is not intended to be an in-depth study; rather, it surveys areas where the use of wood might reduce dependence on nonrenewable sources of energy.

The report opens with an examination of the energy content of wood as compared with other forms of fuel. The next two sections briefly examine the feasibility of using wood for energy in the home and in industry, respectively. A list of recommendations concludes the report. I am grateful to the staff at the Ministry of Energy and Natural Resources for their patience and help with my research. The Energy Council of Canada provided funding for this project.

Back Elements

Following the main body of the report, the elements at the end give readers information about further material that may be useful.

Appendix

appendix

The Latin word *appendere* means "to hang on to." Although the word seems to imply that the appendix just "hangs on to" the main document, it actually works the other way: The material in the appendix provides support for the main document.

Just like the appendix you may have had removed with surgery, the appendix in a book or report should be a component that is interesting or helpful, but not necessarily vital. The *appendix*, in fact, is a helpful feature since it allows you to incorporate data—sometimes a large quantity—that would simply be extraneous in the main body of the report. The appendix may include statistics, tables, lists, examples of surveys, and relevant correspondence.

Use one or more appendixes (or appendices) depending on the amount and nature of the subsidiary material. Mention each appendix in your table of contents, as well as in relevant places throughout the document.

Avoid hiding all of your graphics in an appendix unless they are all optional viewing. Any illustrative material that is vital to understanding the report should appear in the body of the report.

Bibliography

Documenting the sources you have used is, of course, essential. The method you choose for documentation will vary depending on the requirements of your instructor or your company. This feature might also be called References, Works Cited, or List of Sources.

In addition to listing the material you have used in your report, you might want to provide readers with a list of other related documents in a page called Further Reading.

Index

index

Here's another term with an interesting journey from its Latin origins. The verb *dico* (*dicere*) means "to say" or "to speak." With the addition of the prefix *in*, the verb *indicere* means "to point out" or "to make known." In Latin, the noun *index* refers to the forefinger—the one you still call your "index finger." Think of the way you use an index, and you'll probably see your forefinger running down a list of items until it stops at the one you are seeking.

An *index* works in conjunction with a table of contents to help readers find specific pieces of information. At the front of your document, the table of contents provides a linear or sequential list; at the back, the index uses a hierarchical (usually alphabetical) list. Most word-processing and desktop-publishing software allows the writer to put together an index while writing the report.

Activities and Exercises

1. Choose a topic for a report using the questions in the list below for ideas, or a topic suggested by your instructor. Prepare a formal report that includes all or most of the elements described in this chapter. (Your instructor may have asked you to prepare a proposal memo earlier.)
   - What is involved in starting a small art gallery or photographic studio?
   - Compare the advantages and disadvantages of hair colouring done at home and at a hair salon.
   - Estimate the costs of buying and raising a puppy.
   - Assess the wheelchair accessibility of various businesses in your area.
   - Investigate the involvement of high-school students in your area in extra-curricular activities such as chess clubs, band, etc.
   - Are students in your college interested in jazz? classical music?
   - Should parents be prosecuted when their children break the law?
2. Design and write a document entitled "How to Become a ___________________." (Fill in a profession related to your field of study.) You can decide who your target audience will be: high-school students, or people in mid-career who want to make a change. Think carefully about what features you want to include and the order in which they should appear. You might consider topics such as educational requirements, employment possibilities, salary expectations, aptitudes, special skills, and so on. Include one or two relevant graphics, but avoid using graphics just for decoration.
3. Find a problem in your community that needs solving and prepare a recommendation report. For this assignment you should try, as much as possible, to focus on a real issue and use real resources rather than just inventing information. Research the topic to see how other communities handle the problem. Find out who could be a potential reader for your report. It should include background information and a cost analysis, if possible.
4. Working in a small group, design a survey and carry out a mini-census of students in your college program or some other group of about 100 people. Plan the kind of information you want to record: age, gender, birthplace, siblings, car ownership, part-time employment, etc. Once you have collected your information, evaluate it and produce a formal report that describes the characteristics of the sample group you chose.

For further assignments dealing with the content of this chapter, see Case Study 19 starting on page 309.

Proposals

chapter twenty-two

proposal

The word *proposal* comes from the Latin *pro*, meaning "forward," and *ponere*, meaning "to put."

A *proposal* is a document that states something the writer would like to have or do and then backs up the statement with hard evidence and a strong argument. A proposal is a kind of sales pitch that seeks to meet a need by supplying a product or service. A proposal is a request, often for money, personnel, time, equipment—or possibly all of these. It offers a kind of exchange: I want to do ABC, but first I need you to do XYZ.

Everyone's most common understanding of this term probably involves a proposal of marriage and, perhaps, an acceptance of that proposal. When that happens, each party has specific goals and self-interests as well as something to offer as an advantage to the other party. These characteristics also apply to written proposals in the workplace.

Some proposals are short and informal, while others are hundreds of pages long. The successful proposal must convince the reader that the proposed activity will be a good investment, will produce beneficial results, and will do so better than any similar proposals submitted by others.

Job-Related Proposals

Many companies that work on a contract basis use proposals continually to acquire new projects. These firms may look for *requests for proposals* (RFPs; also called invitations to tender) in newspapers and trade magazines, or they may submit unsolicited proposals based on their assessment of work that needs to be done. Sample Document 22.1 is an example of a request for proposal.

Businesses and organizations that hold regular conferences or meetings will issue a *call for proposals*, inviting submissions from individuals or groups who want to make presentations or run workshops. All the proposals submitted are reviewed by a committee, which then selects the most relevant or innovative ones.

Sample Document 22.1 *A Request for Proposal*

Loraine County District School Board

2660 Tim Shaw Ave. W.
Port Delaney, NL T1A 4R4
(805) 234-8201

REQUEST FOR PROPOSAL

#01-LCC-06

Requests for Proposal for IN-CAR INSTRUCTION FOR DRIVER EDUCATION PROGRAM AT VARIOUS SCHOOL LOCATIONS will be received at the Loraine County District School Board, 2660 Tim Shaw Ave. W., Port Delaney, NL, T1A 4R4 until 2:30 Thursday, February 9th, 2002. For further details, contact the Purchasing Tenders Clerk at (805) 234-5465.

A.R. Ipton	G. Hall
Chairperson	Director

Community organizations, as well as new and expanding businesses, write proposals to obtain funding from a wide variety of foundations, charities, and government departments. This kind of proposal writing is big business: If you learn to write successful grant applications, you may be in demand.

Proposals may be solicited or unsolicited. A *solicited proposal* responds to an invitation to tender or an RFP. The RFP may list very detailed instructions about the information required—even to the extent of providing a checklist. Or it may be open-ended, providing only a general framework for the project and leaving the details up to the writer. An *unsolicited proposal* may be written to offer services or products to an organization as a result of the writer's own investigation and ideas. Sample Document 22.2 is an example of a brief, point-form proposal.

Sample Document 22.2 *A Point-Form Proposal*

Highway 60, R.R. 2
Mirror Falls, Ontario L3R 4R4

Tel.: (705) 777-4000 Fax: (705) 777-4001
ultaspa@playground.on.ca

TO: Anne Youngman, Assistant Manager, Food and Beverage
FROM: Eric Burton, Assistant Chief Steward
DATE: March 2, 2002
SUBJECT: Proposal for Relocation of the Silver Pantry to the Stewarding Office

The Project
To relocate the silver pantry to the current stewarding office, and just outside the stewarding office.

Abstract
We will relocate the existing pantry down to the area currently occupied by the stewarding office. Once this is moved, the pantry space will become the central small wares storeroom. Next, the stewarding office will be moved into the current small wares storeroom, and chemicals and PPEs[1] will be stored in the existing cart washstation.

Benefits
- increased labour productivity with more ergonomic storage
- improvement in EOS[2]—pantry attendant, C-floor stewards, stewarding management
- increased ware storage
- decreased clutter in kitchen and outside beverage office
- secure equipment storage
- increased office size in a more central location

Resource Support Required
- wiring to accommodate burnishing machines
- plumbing to accommodate a triple sink—the plumbing exists in this location
- eco-lab to move its equipment
- assistance in relocating the burnishing machine and the triple sink from the existing silver pantry

(continued)

[1] Personal protective equipment
[2] Employee opinion survey

- possible ventilation upgrade (if required)
- wiring the existing storeroom on C-floor for phones and computer service for the office

Background

Stewarding is consistently running short of storage space for small wares on the C-floor. As well, the management team currently consists of nine people working at only three desks in a very small office. This crowding has led to friction between the pantry attendant and the steward helpers on the C-floor, and it presents a working challenge for the management team.

Motivation and Need

This project will greatly increase storage space and proportionally decrease complaints from the beverage department, kitchen, banquets, and our own staff.

The management team will be able to work more effectively in a larger space, and will present a better air of professionalism. Additionally, the supervisors and office will be more centrally located for staff access.

Pantry Relocation

Required Resources	*Cost*
Removing side wall of Victor's office, removing interior wall of office, plumbing triple sink, wiring burnishing machine, floor	$3000

Office Relocation

Required Resources	
Flooring and painting	*Cost*
Doors with window	routine maint.
Wall for chief steward's office	$800
Wiring for phones (4), and fax	$800
Wiring for networked printer	$500
Computer	incl. in phones
Phone × 2[3]	$2000
Desk, cubicles, bookshelves	$1100
	$5000

[3]Jargon for "2 phones"

Writing an Effective Proposal

Whatever reasons you might have for writing a proposal, keep the following guidelines in mind:

- Make every effort to know your reader well, since in the end, the reader is the one with the money and the power to spend it. Background research will ensure that your proposal fits well with the needs and perspectives of the reader. If time allows, you may even want to interview the person who will read the proposal, or others who may have insight into what's needed.
- Follow to the letter any guidelines for preparing the proposal that have been provided. Companies spend time and effort preparing such guidelines, and they do so for a purpose. If you ignore their directions at this point, don't expect them to trust you with future contracts.
- Be meticulous. While your reader may not consciously base a decision on an effective layout or on good grammar, the absence of these features will almost always affect the response to your proposal.
- Understand that both you and the reader have similar goals: You both want to get some work done efficiently and effectively. Whether you are applying for a job, responding to an RFP, or proposing an idea that you yourself have initiated, your written proposal will speak for you first.

The design and features of formal and informal proposals are similar to those for reports. But, whereas a report looks back on what has occurred, a proposal looks ahead at what will occur. Accordingly, include many, if not all, of the following elements in your proposal:

- identification of the problem(s) to be solved or objective(s) to be met
- detailed description of the proposed solutions or products
- drawings and verbal descriptions of specific projects
- detailed schedule for completing each objective or for implementing a new process
- accurate account of what service or product you will *not* provide
- advantages of the proposed process or method or product
- comparison with competitors' products or rebuttal of anticipated disadvantages
- ranking of proposed solutions if you are offering more than one
- names and qualifications of all personnel who may be involved
- tabulated budget with justification for each item
- list of references who can support your proposal

Sample Document 22.3 is an example of a short proposal memo written by a co-op student at The Ultimate Resort and Spa.

Sample Document 22.3 *A Short Proposal Memo*

Highway 60, R.R. 2
Mirror Falls, Ontario L3R 4R4

Tel.: (705) 777-4000 Fax: (705) 777-4001
ultaspa@playground.on.ca

TO: Anika Scheim, Director of Human Resources

FROM: Louise Boulder, Co-op Student

DATE: January 16, 2002

SUBJECT: Work Report

Summary

Over the past four months, several staff members have complained of symptoms related to repetitive stress injuries (RSIs). RSIs are muscle-related problems caused by doing successive motions without rest or variation. The most common RSI is carpal tunnel syndrome, which affects 87 percent of computer users who repeatedly use their mouse. If we are not proactive, The Ultimate's medical claims and short-term and long-term disability costs will increase significantly. By taking preventive measures to decrease the rapid increase of RSIs, employees of The Ultimate can slow down and perhaps reverse some RSIs. The result will be happier, healthier employees and better customer service.

Purpose

I plan to outline the causes of repetitive stress injuries and locate areas at The Ultimate Resort where we are at high risk of these injuries. I will also propose solutions to reduce our risk areas.

Research Plan

Information for the report will be drawn from various sources, including the following:

- Through my contacts with an ergonomic consulting firm, I will gather information on the causes and risks and will develop a set of guidelines on how to prevent repetitive stress injuries.
- I will create a survey to be completed by employees to determine their knowledge of repetitive stress injuries. The survey will include questions that will help to detect areas of risk at the resort.

(continued)

- I will check with our employee assistance program provider to determine whether the company has literature or "lunch and learn" sessions that address RSIs.
- I will gather information from published articles on causes, risks, and prevention of RSIs.

Qualifications

My previous work experience involved doing task and workstation reviews. I was required to advise employees on the setup of their workstations to prevent RSIs. As the trainee in the Compensation and Benefits Department here at The Ultimate Resort, I want to ensure that we can reduce potential health premium and insurance costs. Employee wellness is important for The Ultimate Resort to be profitable.

Time and Budget Requirements

The initial report on RSIs will be complete by February 15, 2002. I estimate that it will take 30 hours of work to complete this report.

Excluding my own time, costs should be approximately $300. This figure includes printing, faxing, Internet time, telephone calls, and some possible outcalls to our insurance provider.

Potential Problems

I foresee two possible difficulties:

- poor rate of return of employee surveys
- difficulty determining actual cause of RSI (i.e., Is a problem work-related or recreation-related?)

Conclusion

Repetitive stress injuries take time to develop. As a result, once employees begin to feel pain, the injury has already occurred. Raising awareness of the causes, risks, and prevention can benefit employees and The Ultimate overall. We can reduce not only our health benefit costs, but also increase our customer service.

2

Activities and Exercises

1. Evaluate the two proposals included in this chapter. Comment on layout, content, persuasive tone, and writing style, including use of jargon. What changes, additions, or deletions do you suggest?
2. Write a proposal suggesting a reasonable change or improvement in some aspect of your workplace, college, or community. Choose something that fits your field of study. Write a short proposal memo, similar to the one in Sample Document 22.3, recommending the change and backing up your idea.
3. Assume you want to hire a new staff member for your department. Prepare a list of qualifications for the person you need and write an appropriate job advertisement. Exchange advertisements with a classmate. Write a letter of application for the ad you receive.
4. Write a proposal in response to the following posted announcement. When all of the class proposals are complete, set up a panel to review them anonymously and pick the best six.

Synopsis Techniques Incorporated • • • • • • • • • •

Request for Proposals

File #6008

We are a broad-based research company looking for young, innovative people who need an opportunity to bring their ideas to life.

We have six developmental awards of up to $4000 each for six people who can demonstrate that they have an idea worth trying out. These awards will cover an employment period of four months and may be considered by some students to comprise a co-op work term. Here are a few examples:

- You may have an idea for a new type of violin bow.
- You may have an idea for a public service brochure that you'd like to design and write.
- You may have developed a new computer game and you need the chance to refine it.

Prepare a proposal for us and tell us about your idea. You may be one of the people chosen.

Your proposal should be 2–4 pages long. Include a detailed description of your idea, including graphics if appropriate. Tell us how you envision your idea being useful as a commercial venture or how it will benefit your community.

Include information about your background and qualifications, although we do not require a complete résumé.

> You should include a cost breakdown—mainly for materials, travel, or other incidental expenses—or an overview of what you require to bring your idea to life.
>
> This proposal should not include salary expectations. Your salary for the four-month period will be negotiated separately with our Human Resources Department.

For further assignments dealing with the content of this chapter, see Case Study 5 starting on page 280.

Part Five

Roundup

Short Forms

Short forms can be abbreviations, acronyms, initializations, or even symbols. An abbreviation is a short form of a word or expression that is usually formed by using part of it. You can abbreviate almost anything as long as you ensure that the reader understands. Short forms are similar to jargon: Some audiences will know them better than others. Scientific, technical, and mathematical abbreviations follow specific rules for capitalization, punctuation, and plurals.

Unless the abbreviation is very common, spell out the entire word the first time you use it and put the short form in parentheses. After that, use only the short form.

parts per billion (ppb)

cathode-ray tube (crt)

deadweight ton (dwt)

Punctuation and Plurals

Omit the period when you are abbreviating most measurements unless, of course, the period is part of the sentence punctuation. Add the period if a reader might mistake the abbreviation for another word. Abbreviations of Latin words require a period, as do abbreviations of English words that are not units of measure. The plural of an abbreviation is the same as the singular.

6 in.
no. 5
400 gal.
400 mL
a.m.
Hon.
dept.
fwd.

When read aloud, an abbreviation is normally pronounced in full.

Sept.	read as	September
p.	read as	page
kg	read as	kilogram

Common Latin Abbreviations

Even experienced writers occasionally misuse or overuse the following three common abbreviations: *i.e.*, *e.g.*, and *etc.*

i.e.

i.e. is from the Latin *id est*, meaning "that is to say."

The abbreviation *i.e.* is usually written as two lowercase letters with a period after each. Use it to introduce an explanation or clarification of a word or phrase. It is usually followed by a comma.

> He wanted too many changes to the final agreement (i.e., the agreement reached after the part-time workers left).
>
> The zenith is the point in the sky that is overhead (i.e., straight up).
>
> Avoid over-watering plants that require little water in their natural habitat (i.e., cacti and succulents).

Some writers use *i.e.* incorrectly to mean "for example" or "such as."

> He wanted too many changes to the final agreement (i.e., no overtime; no salary concessions; no bonuses). ✗

e.g.

e.g. is from the Latin *exempli gratia*, meaning "for the sake of an example."

The abbreviation *e.g.* should also be written with a period after each letter. It tends to be overused, often with faulty grammar or sentence structure. Don't try to make it a substitute for a complete sentence. It can usually be used correctly within parentheses or in specialized layouts. The following two examples are both sentence fragments:

> For example, Holstein cows.
>
> e.g., Holstein cows.

Here are some further examples to show the correct and incorrect uses of *e.g.*:

> The agreement has too many problems. e.g. no discussion of raises and no time frame for further discussion. ✗ *(punctuation error)*

The agreement has too many problems: no discussion of raises; no time frame for further discussion. ✓ *(appropriate use of colon)*

The agreement has too many problems such as no discussion of raises and no time frame for further discussion. ✓

The agreement has too many problems (e.g., no discussion of raises). ✓

Do not use *e.g.* if the example comes first; instead, spell out the complete words.

Only a few members of the population would have been able to attend university: those who could read Latin, for example.

etc.

etc. is from the Latin *et cetera,* meaning "and the rest."

The abbreviation *etc.* ends with a period. It is frequently misspelled, mispronounced, misused, and overused. Notice that it does not mean "and others." Instead, it implies that the writer is referring not only to the items just mentioned but also to *the rest of the list*—that is, a list of other items *that are likely known by the reader.* Here are some examples:

(In a letter to an insurance adjuster)

You'll find the required forms enclosed: salary confirmation, physician's assessment, etc. *(In this example, the insurance adjuster would know all the required forms, so the writer doesn't list them all.)*

Avoid using *etc.* when you just can't bother to think up appropriate examples for the reader.

Our company deals in trophies, badges, etc. ✗ *(not helpful to a potential customer who might not be able to complete the list correctly)*

Our company deals in a wide variety of award items such as trophies, badges, cups, crests, and framed certificates. ✓

Acronyms

An *acronym* is an abbreviation usually formed from the first letters of a series of words. Acronyms are nearly always written in capital letters; a few, such as "laser" have become part of everyday speech. An acronym is pronounceable as a word.

Meaning	Acronym	Pronounced as
light amplification by stimulated emission of radiation	laser	lāzer
auto-immune deficiency syndrome	AIDS	āds
North Atlantic Treaty Organization	NATO	nātō
graphic user interface	GUI	gooey

Initializations

A less common term, *initialization*, refers to a group of letters, usually unpronounceable as a word, that stands in for a group of words. There are thousands of initializations. Treat them like jargon—that is, use them only if your reader will understand them. Otherwise, write them in full the first time you use them, as you would any abbreviation.

Here are some examples:

> Patients will be evaluated using the 17-item Hamilton Depression Scale (HAMD).
>
> Since responsibility varies from stage to stage, a project is not supervised by a single individual in the Information Systems Department (ISD), so the user must communicate with many different people during the development life cycle.
>
> The use of private branch exchanges (PBXs) and voice mail systems has been growing dramatically over the past ten years.
>
> The evolution of resistance really goes into fast-forward when patients with tuberculosis (TB) do not follow doctors' orders.
>
> System Classification List (SCL)
>
> Fire Safety Shutdown Analysis (FSSA)
>
> Technical writers may collect information by interviewing subject matter experts (SMEs).

Using Numbers

When you write workplace documents, you will often run into situations where you must refer to quantities, measurements, dates, or costs. Many publishers and businesses have their own style guides that you should follow, but sometimes the decision will simply be a judgment call.

The guidelines below represent the conventional rules to follow on those occasions when you have a few numerals in a document that is mainly text. These rules will not usually apply if you are writing a primarily narrative text, such as a novel. Furthermore, if your document is mainly numbers—such as accounting data, mathematical calculations, statistics, or laboratory experiments—different rules may apply. For a complete list, refer to a handbook in the relevant discipline. Notice that some rules override others.

Numbers That Begin a Sentence

Always spell out a number that begins a sentence.

> Twelve packages were delivered yesterday. ✓
>
> 1987 was a very good year. ✗

As a result of this rule, you might choose to revise a sentence in order to avoid awkward wording.

> Nine eighty-six was the year Herjolfsson arrived in Iceland.
>
> Herjolfsson arrived in Iceland in the year 986.

You may find that writing out a number that begins an independent clause, even when it appears mid-sentence, looks better.

> Since the conference begins so soon and no time for a lengthy selection program remains, fifteen students will be chosen at random.

Measurement and Quantity

Use numerals when you are writing about measurement or quantity (if a unit of measure is involved).

> 7 yards
> 8×12 m
> $\frac{1}{4}$ lb.
> 6 cm
> 60 W
> 400 horsepower

Time

Use numerals to express time (less than 24 hours) if you are using the abbreviation "a.m." or "p.m." In some documents, such as narratives, you will use words. Use numerals if you are expressing time using the 24-hour clock.

> 4:00 p.m.
> four o'clock
> 21:00 hours
> 3 min
> six years

Dates

Always use numerals to express dates.

October 1, 1912

1066 A.D.

On the 3rd of March, we will evaluate your performance.

Numbers Greater than Ten

Represent most numbers (not covered by the above rules) by numerals if they are greater than ten.[1] Note that this rule varies depending on the style manual you are using—follow the style used by your workplace, and be consistent.

The department now has a total of 25 employees.

The meeting attracted 400 students.

The three delinquent staff members were disciplined.

Large Numbers

If you are spelling out a large number, omit the "and" normally used in speaking.

456	four hundred fifty-six
12 902	twelve thousand nine hundred two

Use a combination of words and numerals for large, round numbers as in the following examples:

The ancient city of Antaka had nearly 1 million horses.

The earth's population is approaching 5 billion.

If you are referring to extremely large numbers in a business document, check to make sure you are using them correctly. For example, in Europe a billion is 10^{12} (1 000 000 000 000), whereas in North America a billion is 10^{9} (1 000 000 000).

Costs and Prices

Use numerals for costs and prices. Use a combination of numerals and words for very large amounts.

$4.98

Our most expensive tie is $168.

We expect sales to surpass $2 million.

---

[1]Rubens, Philip (Ed.). (2000). *Science and technical writing: A manual of style.* New York: Holt.

For amounts less than $1 in a document that is primarily text, you usually spell out the word "cents."

The shares actually rose 13 cents above the original forecast.

Repeating a Spelled-Out Number

Don't repeat a spelled-out number as a numeral unless you are working with legal documents.

You have seven (7) days from receipt of this notice.

More than One Number in a Sentence

Treat related numbers in the same sentence the same way, even if the rules vary. Normally, you should use the rule that applies to the first number.

The third team located 66 pottery fragments and 6 arrowheads.

If the two numbers are not related at all, or if using the same form will cause confusion, you may choose to ignore this rule and apply a rule to each number separately.

In 2002, three students were hired for the summer term.

Because the postage was more than $6, two of the letters were not sent.

Percentages

Use numerals to express percentages. Spell out the word "percent."

More than 12 percent of the employees were absent with the flu during December.

A markup of 22 percent seems excessive.

The stock fell by three percentage points last week.

Numbers and Hyphens

Compound numbers composed of two words always use a hyphen.

sixty-seven

forty-four

If you use a number and a word together to form a modifier, use a hyphen whether you are using a numeral or a word.

a three-man team

The principal clue was a 1-inch piece of thread.

The only tool we could find was a 6-m measuring tape.

When you use a number and unit as a modifier that requires an apostrophe, omit the hyphen. Be careful about where you place the apostrophe.

We paid Josh for only two weeks' work.

I received a pass for one day's leave.

I was exhausted even after eight hours of sleep.

Fractions

Use a hyphen when using words for a fraction unless the expression would already contain another hyphen.

Two-thirds of the employees are upset.

One one-hundredth of a second was all that separated the gold and silver medallists.

Symbols

Unless you are working specifically on scientific or mathematic material, you will rarely need to use symbols. If you do have to use symbols, double-check the correct font and format. If a formula or equation is part of a sentence, it should fit correctly with the grammatical structure. For example, treat the symbol "=" like the verb "equals." An actual equation or formula should be treated like a noun. Here are a few examples:

The floor joist spacing is either 16'' or 24''.

Place the hot container at least 6' from any flammable material.

We'll need at least six 2' × 4's to complete the job.

The temperature today hit a record high of 34°.

We all probably know that $e = mc^2$ even if we don't know what that means.

Water to cement ratio (w:c) is the weight of the water used divided by the weight of the cement used.

If $x = 0$ is the starting point, the result will be $x + 66$.

If a salt (such as Na_2Cl_4) is introduced, the reaction will not take place.

Parallel Structure

Parallel structure is a powerful technique used to organize two or more related items in a sentence (horizontal) or in a list (vertical). Parallel structure works well because it establishes a rhythm in a piece of writing.

> *veni; vidi; vici*
>
> I came; I saw; I conquered.

In addition, because the elements in a parallel construction are all so similar, they tend to be easy for a reader to remember. The various levels of headings you use in a document should use parallel structure.

Vertical lists are distinctive elements in business documents. They emphasize and highlight important material and provide a visual cue for readers. Any time you have three or more items, you should at least consider the value of using a list.

Similar Grammar

The items in a series should be grammatically similar whether written in a sentence or a vertical list: all nouns, all adjectives, all short sentences, all questions, and so on. Notice how the vertical list accentuates the information in the second example here.

> Lorne found that he could save the company money by billing each customer monthly, by decreasing overtime hours, and by assigning a code for long-distance calls.

> Lorne found three ways to save money:
>
> 1. Bill customers monthly.
> 2. Decrease overtime hours.
> 3. Assign a code for long-distance calls.

Introductory Line

Introduce a vertical list with a heading or a short sentence or phrase. Do not use a colon unless your introductory line is a complete independent clause. Headings that come before paragraphs do not require a colon or dash after them. The following example shows correct use of an introductory line:

> Upon completion of the course, you will be able to
>
> - Explain the different types of payroll processes.
> - Distinguish the advantages and disadvantages of computerized payroll systems.
> - Understand technical advance in computerized systems.
> - Select the most appropriate method of payroll processing.
> - Implement and maintain a new payroll package.

This next example uses the colon incorrectly:

Information can be collected from several sources. These include: ✗

- telephone book
- provincial tourist and travel offices
- chamber of commerce
- historical societies

Numbers and Bullets

Use numbers for items in a list only if priority or order is important. Otherwise, use bullets. Compare the following two examples: The first uses numbers because it lists a series of steps in order; the second lists items that are all of equal importance.

In the process of designing a document, follow these general steps:

1. Plan the whole document, considering purpose, reader, tools, and conventions.
2. Design individual pages, making them consistent with one another, yet designed as individual entities.
3. Choose type sizes, fonts, and styles for ease of reading and for focusing attention.
4. Review the design to ensure that it follows good design principles.

Elements of page design include

- margins
- line length
- line spacing
- justification
- white space
- colour

Repeated Terms

To make some parallel constructions clear, you may have to repeat the word used at the beginning of each phrase.

The rewards rest not *in* the task but *in* the pay.

I can fill in for her *because* she has been really ill and *because* I have the time.

Correlatives

Correlatives are connectives used in pairs. They require parallel constructions. Be careful to place the correlatives in the right spot. Here are some examples:

We judge our friends *both* by their words *and* their actions. ✗

We judge our friends by *both* their words *and* their actions. ✓

The team *not only* practises at 6 a.m. on weekdays *but also* meets on Sunday afternoons. ✓

Whether we revise the estimate *or* cancel the contract, we will owe them money. ✓

Neither Embro Industries *nor* Simco and Co. has responded to our request. ✓

Punctuation and Capital Letters

If each item in a list is a complete sentence, begin it with a capital letter and end it with a period. If each item is a fragment, phrase, or single word, begin it with a lowercase letter and use no end punctuation. Here are some examples:

Here are some guidelines to keep in mind regarding sentence length:

- Be cautious about exceeding 20 words per sentence.
- Include no more than two independent clauses in a sentence.
- Include no more than two subordinate clauses in a sentence.
- Focus on only one main item of information per sentence.
- Avoid sentences that you cannot read aloud without stopping for a breath.

A patient may withdraw from the study prematurely for the following reasons:

- adverse experience
- lack of efficacy
- deviation from protocol
- termination by sponsor

Technical writing is required for many different types of projects such as

- user's manuals
- catalogues
- annual reports
- webpages

Active and Passive Voice

We say a verb is in the *active voice* when the subject of the sentence is the "doer" of the action.

A blue delivery van *hit* a deer on the road last night.

At the managers' meeting last Tuesday, the Human Resources department *presented* a draft of the new Employee Handbook.

Send your completed application and a copy of your résumé to the address below.

When the wording of these sentences changes, so that the subject is receiving (not doing) the action, the verbs are in *passive voice.*

> Last night, a deer *was hit* by a blue delivery van.
>
> At the managers' meeting last Tuesday, a draft of the new Employee Handbook *was presented* by the Human Resources department.
>
> Your completed application and a copy of your résumé *should be sent* to the address below.

The Sound of Active and Passive Voice

The very names *active* and *passive* should give you an idea of how these styles will sound in your writing.

Sentences written in the active voice sound stronger, more active (naturally), and more personal (because they have a clear doer as the subject).

Sentences in the passive voice, on the other hand, make writing sound impersonal, and sometimes boring, especially if you use them frequently. Using the passive voice too much may be the reason so much business and technical writing has a reputation for being flat and dull.

The Uses of Active and Passive Voice

While the active voice is preferable in most business and technical documents, sometimes the passive voice is the better choice. For example, if the receiver of an action is more important than the doer, the passive voice is effective. The passive voice also has the advantage of concealing the doer of an action, so it is useful if you want to be discrete or you simply don't know who did something. Here are some examples:

> The gold medal winners were photographed as they left the arena.
> *(It doesn't matter here who did the photographing.)*
>
> Four applications were submitted late.
> *(You don't want to name the people involved.)*
>
> Several shots were fired into the crowded room.
> *(Perhaps you don't know who fired the shots.)*

Notice that when you use the passive voice, the doer of an action can be revealed in an agent phrase that begins with "by."

> Abraham Lincoln was assassinated *by John Wilkes Booth* shortly after the end of the war.

The Grammar of Active and Passive Voice

To recognize and use active and passive voice correctly, you may find it helpful to know the grammatical construction.

Understand the difference between the two helping verbs *to be* and *to have.*

To Be		To Have	
I am	we are	I have	we have
you are		you have	
she is	they are	he has	they have
I was		I had	
I will be		I will have	
I have been		I have had	
I will have been		I will have had	
Present participle: being		having	
Past participle: been		had	

Form the passive voice by combining the helping verb *to be* with any past participle.

Subject	Form of Verb "To Be"	Past Participle
I	am	given
you	were	seen
they	will have been	fed
it	can't be	decided

Don't confuse the passive voice with the past tense. Do you know the difference? Which verbs in the following table are passive voice?

I have been given	you had seen	I've been tricked
he might be giving	you were seen	they will have fed
they will be fed	they were fed	she has had

Avoid mixing active and passive voice in the same sentence, especially in the same grammatical construction.

Six men arrived and were briefed about the situation. ✗
(one subject with an active and a passive verb)

The six men who arrived were briefed about the situation. ✓

Here are some more examples so you can hear and see the difference between active and passive voice:

Active	Passive
If you specify the "automatic save" option, the operating system will create file names.	If the "automatic save" option is specified, file names will be created by the operating system.
The Soviets provided vehicle drawings and onboard photographs of the civilian version, and they allowed reporters access to training mockups.	Vehicle drawings and onboard photographs of the civilian version were provided by the Soviets and reporters were allowed access to training mockups.
Researchers weighed and interviewed participants in the training program after 6 days and 12 days.	Participants in the training program were weighed and interviewed after 6 days and 12 days.

Special Punctuation Marks

A wide variety of *punctuation marks* is available to writers; each helps to clarify meaning. Each also needs to follow rules of correct usage. Consult a grammar handbook for complete details on punctuation.

Ellipsis Points

Ellipsis points, or ellipses, are used to indicate that words have been omitted, usually to shorten quoted material. Depending on where they are used, ellipses might be three dots or four. In the first example below, three ellipsis points indicate that part of a sentence has been omitted. Usually, three ellipsis points are not inserted at the beginning of a quote; however, if for some reason the beginning of the quote might be mistaken for the beginning of a sentence, begin the quote with ellipses (see the second example). Use four dots to indicate that you have omitted at least one entire sentence (see the third example).

Original text

A complicated process takes place when the health professional attempts to communicate health care information to a patient or to that patient's family. Such communication might take any of several forms: family conferences, questions answered by a physician or nurse, patient-teaching programs, pamphlets read by a patient or family member. In each situation, the health professional or healthcare institution must anticipate patient needs, recognize patient limitations, and respond with useful, accurate, and understandable information. No small task. Unfortunately, face-to-face patient education is rapidly being replaced by information gleaned from the Internet. Many people don't realize (or they tend to forget) that any one can post information to the Internet. The report prepared by Mathews focuses on the development of web-based health information and the need for careful evaluation by both patient and physician.

Example 1 *Quoted material*

The writer emphasizes that when "the health professional ... communicate[s] ... to a patient or to that patient's family," many issues must be addressed.

Example 2 *Quoted material*

The reviewer acknowledges that "... Mathews focuses on ... web-based health information," which has been expanding at a remarkable rate.

Example 3 *Quoted material*

It's apparent that the writer knows about the prevalence of "information gleaned from the Internet.... and the need for careful evaluation by both patient and physician."

In a business document, avoid using ellipses to mean "and so on" or to indicate uncertainty.

He tried to explain his lateness, but.... ✗

Dash

The dash is sometimes called an "em dash" (from the days of metal type, when the piece of type for the dash was the width of a capital M). The correct form is two hyphens (--) with no space before or after. Most word-processing software will automatically convert two hyphens to one solid em dash (—).

The dash is not a common feature in formal business and technical writing. Its principal use is to indicate a sudden change in the thought or idea being expressed. For example,

He will—I can assure you of this—be at least an hour late.

A dash can be used instead of a colon if a series of items comes at the beginning of a sentence, indicating a somewhat emphatic pause before continuing.

Money, fame, looks—he had it all.

Note that the em dash is different from the shorter en dash (–), which is used in place of the word "to" in number ranges, such as "See pages 22–78."

Parentheses

Other parts of this text have indicated that parentheses are used to introduce abbreviations and to mention figures and references. In addition, you can use parentheses around part of a sentence to indicate that the information is useful, but not quite as important as the rest of the sentence. Here are some examples:

Jordan has a number of outstanding archaeological and historical sites, such as Jarash (a preserved Roman city), Madaba (extensive mosaics), and Petra (a temple carved out of a cliff wall).

In many instances, the client (a manager at the Allergy Clinic, for example) is responsible for several ongoing projects.

Notice the differences in the following usage. Parentheses tend to section off less important information; dashes emphasize information; commas indicate about equal importance of all information.

The telephone rang (14 times), but no one answered it.

The telephone rang—14 times—but no one answered it.

The telephone rang, 14 times, if I recall correctly, but no one answered it.

Brackets

The principal use of brackets is to indicate that material has been added or changed by a writer to make a quotation clearer or to interject comments about the quote.

"The [honours] students received framed certificates."

The chairman indicated that "[c]ertain board members" would likely be dismissed.

If you encounter a situation where a double set of parentheses is required, the usual form is to combine parentheses with brackets, as in the following example:

Preliminary research shows that the preparations were fairly straightforward. The supervisor of the construction (a Mr. Arnold Hamilton [no relation to Arnold Hamilton of Keswick]) presented the completed plans to the committee on January 9, 2002.

Activities and Exercises

1. Exercises can give you some practice in identifying and correcting errors; however, working with real documents can be much more useful. For each of the topics in Part Five, do a search of various letters, reports, proposals, brochures, etc. to evaluate how the various elements are handled. Discuss in class any deviations from the rules; suggest any changes you might recommend.
2. Correct errors in parallel structure in the following selections. Look for other errors to correct also.
   a. Some of the characteristics of a good writer are:
      - organized
      - team players
      - adaptable to change
      - curious about technology and interested in helping others understand it

    - excellent communicator
    - language
    - technical skills
    - creative
  b. Safety tips if you are thinking of installing a pool:
    - make sure your yard is fully fenced
    - It is also a good idea to fence in your pool and lock the gate.
    - Never leave children unattended. No matter how well they can swim
    - Never swim alone
    - Alcohol and water don't mix: be responsible
3. Identify each of the following as active or passive voice:
  a. Mr. Singh was paged on the hospital intercom 20 minutes ago.
  b. Marika has decided against joining the pension plan.
  c. The discussion was going on too long.
  d. A person is usually asked for two pieces of identification when writing a cheque.
  e. I was never consulted about the idea.
  f. Where have all the interoffice envelopes gone?
  g. They were taken by the Purchasing department.
  h. Many are called but few are chosen.
  i. I have met with the grievance committee three times this month.
  j. No decision has been made.
4. Change the following examples of active voice to passive voice:
  a. Children playing with matches started the fire.
  b. Three people who saw smoke and flames coming from a ground floor window sounded the alarm.
  c. A police officer who was driving by rescued the children.
  d. A dog bit Maxine.
  e. Over 500 people have signed the petition.
  f. Jacques won first prize for his tortellini.
  g. The investigator should obtain the subject's freely given informed consent before proceeding.
  h. Many people express their creativity through painting.
  i. You will find the "start" button on the bottom left-hand corner of your keyboard.
  j. First, identify the level of security in the current application.
5. Change the following examples of passive voice to active voice:
  a. A new tax on gasoline has been imposed by the federal government.
  b. The path was blocked by a large tree.
  c. The availability of low-cost housing has been reduced by the construction of luxury apartments in the downtown core.
  d. All the wiring must be checked by a qualified electrician.

e. The baseball tournament was ended by a violent rainstorm.
f. All searches for fingerprints would be conducted electronically if the new system was installed.
g. Students have been told many times to use report covers on their assignments.
h. Reduction in dose by one level is permitted at any time during the study.
i. The apprenticeship is offered on a part-time basis by most colleges.
j. After the pool has been filled, the sides of the liner should be scrubbed to remove any algae.

6. Review the following paragraphs for use of active and passive verbs. Discuss what changes you would make, and why. Then, rewrite the whole selection in an appropriate format, correcting all errors.

Pool Testing:

Testing your pool daily will keep your water in proper balance, and takes only 5 minutes. Water samples should be taken from at least one ft. below the surface, and away from the skimmer and return jets.

The instructions on the test kit should be followed; add appropriate test chemicals to sample. The test results should be compared by holding it up against something white, not the sunlight. You want to maintain a chlorine level of 1.5 to 3.0 ppms, and a pH level between 7.4 and 7.6 (7.5 is the ideal). This is done by either pouring the chemicals into the pool or, if you have a chlorinator, adding chemical pucks to the basket. Adjust the setting on your chlorinator to reflect the outside temperature. For example, setting the dial to 3 may be appropriate when temperatures are moderate, but as the temperature rises a higher setting will be necessary to release more chlorine into your water. Once a week, your pool will need to be shocked to keep the water clean. Your water chemistry will determine the amount of shock added to your water. If you are uncertain of your water, a sample can be taken to your local pool store for testing. It is a good idea for your water to be tested before winterizing, since high levels of alkalinity and calcium can damage liners, fibreglass, paint, and concrete finishes.

7. Review and revise the use of numbers in the following sentences. Avoid altering the meaning.
   a. 30 years ago, 17 high-school students and 30 professors went on a simple archaeological dig.
   b. They did not know that their 2 month expedition would change the course of history.
   c. Their camp, near the foothills of Mount Orn, housed 52 people.
   d. Each team was responsible for an area twelve metres by twelve metres.
   e. Working under the hot sun for sixty days and armed only with brushes that were no more than one cm wide, they dusted the rough ground and moved tiny twigs and plants by hand.
   f. Every three days they had a half day off.

g. There was little to do in this free time since they were more than 60 miles from the nearest town and had only 1 schoolbus and 1 jeep for transportation.
h. On the fifty-third (53rd) day, 1 of the students let out a yelp.
i. Her brush had uncovered a small piece of bone 2.5 centimetres thick and thirty-five centimetres long.
j. This apparently insignificant find was the 1st time that remains of an ancient people had been found in the Easter Islands.

Case Studies

Case Studies

case one
The Tardy Trays

As a management trainee in The Ultimate Resort and Spa, you have been assigned to spend a week at a time in each of the many food service areas. This week you are working as acting assistant manager for Room Service from 4 a.m. to 11 a.m.

You have noticed a serious shortage of staff during the hours from 6 a.m. to 8 a.m., when most breakfast orders come in. Often guests have to call two or three times for their orders; some end up cancelling. You have had several visits from angry guests, and even your staff is disgruntled. Because of your schedule, you don't get to speak personally to Dal Lewis, the Manager of Food and Beverage, but you must make sure he knows about the situation.

1. Identify all the components of the situation using the terminology of communication theory (sender, receiver, medium, message, anticipated feedback). List as many potential barriers to communication as you can.
2. Write a memo to Dal Lewis clearly explaining the extent of the problem and suggesting a solution. (Remember to use confident language: you don't want him to think you are just experiencing new staff jitters.)
3. Prepare a notice to post for your staff to let them know you are trying to improve the situation. Try to use motivating language.

case two
Particularly Pesky Parking

There are two different versions of this problem:

1. You work as a server in one of the restaurants of The Ultimate Resort and Spa. Yesterday, when you left to go home, you found your car blocked by a large transport truck that had been left while the driver waited to unload at the hotel's shipping dock. It took nearly an hour for you to find the driver and get the truck moved. This is the second time this problem has happened. You have been assigned a specific parking spot, so you have little choice about where to leave your car.

   Your boss says that you have to contact Mark Atakado, the chief receiver, who looks after all the parking and deliveries.

   a. Write a memo to Mr. Atakado explaining the situation. (Remember that he probably doesn't know who you are.)
   b. Instead of a written memo, send an e-mail to Mr. Atakado explaining the situation. Will your wording change? Why or why not?
   c. As a server, you don't have access all the time to the interoffice mail system. You decide to call Mr. Atakado about the problem. When you do, you hear the following voice mail message:

      > You've reached Mark Atakado. I'm out of the office for three days. I will return on October 5th. However, I will be picking up my voice mail daily, so please leave a message at the sound of the tone.

   Leave your message using voice mail.

2. You are the vice president of The Ultimate Resort and Spa. Yesterday, when you left to go home, you found your car blocked by a large transport truck that had been left while the driver waited to unload at the hotel's shipping dock. It took nearly an hour for you to find the driver. This happened once before about two weeks ago. You may, of course, park your car somewhere else, but you want to use this particular spot because it is convenient. Other hotel staff also park in the same area and may be running into the same problem.

   a. Write a memo to Mr. Atakado explaining the situation.
   b. Instead of a written memo, send an e-mail explaining the situation. Will your wording change? Why or why not?
   c. You decide to call Mr. Atakado about the problem. What voice mail message will you leave after hearing the above message?

case three
Pictures and Permission

You are working as the director of a summer day camp for children aged 7 to 12. During the annual camp carnival, a photographer from the local newspaper shows up and begins to take photographs of the staff and campers. You approach the photographer and introduce yourself.

You share your concern with him that, although photographs in the local paper would be good publicity, your priority is taking care of the children. You explain that for the photographer to publish pictures of the children, you need to have written permission from their parents.

You and the photographer agree that he may take the pictures but must then show you the proofs. In turn, you will notify the parents for their permission.

1. Create a clear form letter for the children to take home to their parents, asking them to sign if they will allow pictures of their children to be published in the newspaper.
2. Prepare a memo for all camp staff reminding them of the policy regarding picture taking.
3. To prevent such a problem in the future, send a letter to the three local newspapers to tell them they are welcome to attend the camp's special events as long as they notify you beforehand.

case four
Two-Car Tango

Read the following lengthy complaint letter sent to an apartment superintendent:

Dear Jack
My wife and I have two cars, one of which is a Pontiac registered as #47 and assigned spot #42. Our other car, a black '94 Dodge Shadow two-door, licence number 975 RTL, is not registered. Over the past month, two separate requests have been made to the superintendent for registry in your new parking system.

On 16th of August 2002 at 2:30 in the morning, we were informed that the black Shadow, described above, was going to be towed because it was not registered to be parked there. Apparently the superintendent assumed my wife wanted my car towed because it was in her spot. The funny thing is, my wife didn't mind; but if she did, and would have asked me to move it, I would have. Our unregistered vehicle was in spot #42 and our Pontiac was in a visitor's spot.

If instead of being overenergetic about punishing perceived violators of a poorly explained, shoddily implemented, and barely established parking system, the super had taken a moment to register my car (or at least checked her twice-given information and realized that both cars are registered to the same apartment), you would not be receiving this letter.

Please note that in my stay here over the last year, I have had no problem parking any vehicle in our lot, except for one time when my friend parked his pickup truck outside the superintendent's apartment for ten minutes instead of the five minutes we requested. There have never been any parking problems in our lot that have caused me any concern except when you have intervened.

(continued)

I am very upset at being disturbed, as I was between 12-hour shifts and the interruption deprived me of my sleep requirements. I am dismayed at the gross mismanagement of my requests, made in good time, to be registered properly in your parking system and request that no additional charge be made to register or park my car in your lot.

This is the fourth request to be registered and I hope it will not be overlooked. I realize that the landlord–tenant relationship is very much a two-way street, and I eagerly desire the resolution of this misunderstanding so as nothing would impede our intention to be,

Your model tenants

Ted and Anne Johannsen

Ted and Anne Johannsen
Apartment 601

1. Revise this complaint letter completely so that it is clear and brief. Use the appropriate complaint letter formula. Incorporate all the appropriate letter template elements, inventing any details you may need.
2. Write a polite and businesslike adjustment letter using any response you feel is appropriate.

case five
Recreational Roundup

Up to this point, the recreational opportunities at The Ultimate Resort and Spa have been

- swimming at the indoor pool and the beach
- sailing
- tennis on four outdoor courts
- gym and exercise room
- shuffleboard
- pickup basketball court
- 18-hole golf course
- skiing nearby in winter

Input has come from several of your staff, and also from guests over the past ten months, requesting additional sports and recreation possibilities. Some of the suggestions have been

- a riding stable
- a skateboard mountain
- snowboarding
- ice fishing
- walking/hiking tours of surrounding areas
- sports fishing
- squash and racquetball courts
- grass tennis court
- cross-country ski trails

1. Prepare an agenda for a meeting to discuss what sort of investigation needs to be carried out in order to make some good decisions about recreation offerings.
2. Hold the meeting as part of your class. Record the minutes of the meeting, and type them up.
3. Pick a sport or leisure activity from the above list or one that you are interested in and research it. Find out everything you can in the way of
   - construction costs
   - equipment required
   - maintenance
   - safety issues
   - additional personnel who would have to be hired
   - probable demand
4. Prepare a short memo report on what you have learned. Make a recommendation based on your findings.

5. Prepare a technical description of one of the following items. Include a clearly labelled graphic.
   - an ice-fishing hut
   - a shuffleboard court
   - a skateboard mountain
   - a squash or racquetball racquet

case six
The Regretful Refusal

(Choose any department of The Ultimate Resort and Spa to be the "facilities" for this case: food services, dining rooms, recreation areas, accounting, etc.)

You have received a letter from a nearby public school class asking whether the class can tour your facilities to see how they operate. The particular time the class has requested is not appropriate, however. (Invent a reasonable explanation for why the tour cannot occur at the time requested.)

1. Assume you are the class teacher. Write the original letter of request, giving appropriate details.
2. Write an indirect refusal letter and offer a helpful alternative. Keep in mind the importance of maintaining excellent public relations in your community. Direct a copy of your letter to the resort's general manager.
3. Write the same letter as a direct refusal. Assume that you have already telephoned someone at the school.

case seven
New Business Venture

The Ultimate Resort and Spa is adding three new boutiques to its shopping concourse. You have been successful in bidding for one of these shops, and you will be setting up in the next few months.

- Design and write a one-page direct letter aimed at guests of the spa. Your task is to provide as much information as possible about your product or service and your hours of operation. You may choose any type of business that seems suitable for such a location.

Remember to keep the letter reader-based and to use specific, concrete detail. Most guests of the spa come for at least a week, and many bring their children.

case eight
The Very Bad Headache

Aubrey Johnson, who is on vacation, decides to come to The Ultimate Resort and Spa to try some snowboarding. He has tried snowboarding before on his own, but this morning Aubrey spends two hours taking some lessons and reviewing the basic positions. He wants to figure out why he's wiping out on the flats so much. Marcel, the instructor, tells Aubrey the bindings on his board are not in good shape. "Good bindings on a beat-up board would be OK," he says, "but you've got scruffy bindings and they won't serve you well. You should be able to adjust the angle of the back to your board so you can tip the board safely."

After completing his lessons and buying his lift ticket, Aubrey is ready to hit the slopes.

During his very first descent he wipes out and hurts his ankle. When he is brought into the lodge, Aubrey says that the bright sun brought on a migraine and that he was unable to see clearly. Marcel inspects the snowboard and finds that the binding has slipped. If Aubrey had tried to edge the board into a curve, he would have had to lock his knees to stay balanced. This is probably what caused him to fall.

Even though he has quit 20 minutes after the money-back grace period, Aubrey gets a full refund on his lift ticket. After a short visit to the first aid office, he leaves satisfied, but still feeling grumpy about not getting a chance to snowboard for the full day.

1. Assume you are the manager of the shop that rents skis and snowboards and provides lessons. Write a short incident report about this situation.
2. Write a follow-up letter to Mr. Johnson encouraging him to come back to your resort to try snowboarding again once he is feeling better.
3. Write Mr. Johnson a sales letter recommending a new snowboard with the latest bindings.
4. Prepare a clearly labelled graphic to accompany your letter.

case nine
Telephone Tag

Beginning tonight, the Canadian Veterinary Association (CVA) will be holding a three-day conference at The Ultimate Resort and Spa. This will be one of the biggest events of the year at The Ultimate, and management has put out the word that everything must be meticulously handled. As special events coordinator, Emma Derrin-Smith's job is to make sure all details requested by clients are checked and double-checked. Emma has been communicating weekly and now daily with the banquets supervisor (Al Smart), the recreation supervisor (Krista De Jong), and the front desk to make sure all facilities are ready.

At about 10:00 a.m., Emma asks her assistant Lexa to call Dr. Wildfong, the person coordinating the event for the CVA, to check on a late request for a guest with special dietary requirements. After three rings, the phone at Dr. Wildfong's office picks up, and Lexa hears this message:

> Good morning. You've reached the Best Friends Animal Hospital. Our office is closed until noon today. If you wish to make an appointment, please call back after 1:00 p.m. If this is an emergency, please contact the Emergency Animal Clinic at 613 555 2345. If you wish to leave a message, please wait for the beep.

Lexa leaves the following message:

> I'm calling for Emma Derrin-Smith at The Ultimate Resort. We need some information about the special diet that has been requested. Please call us back, before 5:30 if possible. The number is 705 777 4000, extension 2814.

At about 4 p.m., Lexa hears this voice mail message on her office telephone:

> Hello. I'm calling from Dr. Wildfong's office. You had called asking about special diet information. We don't have a record of your visit here and need a bit more information. Can you tell us your pet's name and when your original appointment was? We'll be in the office tonight until 7:00 p.m. and Saturday from 8:30 until noon.

At first Lexa is confused about the message, and then she realizes the mistake that's been made. She calls Dr. Wildfong's office right away. The receptionist tells her that Dr. Wildfong will be busy with patients until 7 o'clock and asks her to make an appointment. Lexa explains that a pet is not involved, and that she needs to verify conference information with Dr. Wildfong. The receptionist asks Lexa to call back around 7:00 p.m. Lexa goes home at 5:00 p.m., but she leaves a message with Al Smart, a coworker, asking him to call Dr. Wildfong to verify the diet information. By the time Al is able to call, it's nearly 8:00 p.m. and he gets the following voice mail message:

> Hello. You've reached the Best Friends Animal Hospital. Our office is closed until 8:30 a.m. Saturday. To make an appointment, please call back then. If this is an emergency, please contact the Emergency Animal Clinic at 613 555 2345. If you wish to leave a message, please wait for the beep.

Al leaves a message that is almost the same as Lexa's original message asking for information on the special diet request.

At 8:00 a.m. on Saturday morning, Emma Derrin-Smith notices that no information has yet been obtained on the special diet. She calls Dr. Wildfong's office, but it is not yet open. She leaves a message asking Dr. Wildfong to call her back immediately. At 8:45 a.m., Emma receives a call from a Dr. Ebert. Dr. Ebert explains that he is in charge of Dr. Wildfong's practice for three days while Dr. Wildfong is at the Canadian Veterinary Association Conference. Apparently Dr. Wildfong is now onsite at The Ultimate.

Emma goes in search of the doctor. After a half-hour of hunting through the crowded registration rooms and lobby, she finally tracks down Dr. Wildfong at the breakfast buffet and is able to learn that one of the guests has a serious allergy to shellfish. Fortunately, the guest has been able to stay clear of the seafood offerings and a disaster has been avoided.

As you consider the following questions, keep in mind that both The Ultimate Resort and Dr. Wildfong's office are extremely busy places. The telephones ring almost constantly, and the same people do not always answer the telephones or take messages.

1. Discuss the problem that occurred here, and locate at least three places where communication could have been handled better.
2. Assess the original voice mail message left by Lexa. Suggest a better message.
3. After each conference and special event, Emma Derrin-Smith writes up brief summaries of any problems that occurred. These are filed in a binder, to be used as teaching and reference tools for both new and long-term staff. Devise a one-page form that could be used for such summaries, and write up the incident described above.

case ten
Ultimate Sex Spa

The following two memos have come across your desk in the past few weeks:

The Ultimate Resort and Spa

Highway 60, R.R. 2
Mirror Falls, Ontario L3R 4R4

Tel.: (705) 777-4000 Fax: (705) 777-4001
ultaspa@playground.on.ca

TO: Jack Horner

FROM: Lynda Liebnicht

DATE: April 11, 2002

SUBJECT: Website Problems in Reservations

We have been getting complaints from all over about our website. Apparently, The Ultimate Resort and Spa is linked to various triple-X-rated porn sites. When clients want to make reservations via the Internet, they get spammed with downloads of hardcore stuff.

As you know, when Judy Sedna of Ashimoff Robotics proposed that we set up a website to serve our clients and guests more quickly, we thought only of the benefits and profits it would bring. How could we have known that typing ULTIMATE could call up ULTIMA SEX, INTIMATE, and INTIMATEXX? Or that RESORT and SPA can conjure up sadomasochistic sites? It's disgusting.

Worse still is that once these sites pop up on the monitor, our clients cannot get rid of them. They have shut down their computer and restart.

We have a public relations nightmare in our hands, Jack. You are the promotions director. Do something before our reputation goes down the drain.

LL

[e-mail message]

To: Jack Horner, J Horner@UltimateResort.ca
From: Judy Sedna, Jsedna@AshimoffRobo.com
Date: May 1, 2002
Subject: The Ultimate Resort Linked To Porn Sites

Jack,
My team at Ashimoff Robotics and I have been working on your problem at The Ultimate Resort, and I regret to tell you very little can be done to screen out the porn sites.

I draw your attention to the conversation we had last May when I proposed The Ultimate Website. If you recall, I mentioned that you needed to buy out domains that approximate or are remotely connected in wording to The Ultimate Resort and Spa. At that time, I estimated a conservative number of 100 variants that you had to create, buy new, or buy out if they already existed. Needless to say, your budget for promotions and public relations couldn't allow for such an expense.

In addition, there is the ever-present danger of typos. A slip in spelling or keying of the significant words ULTIMATE, RESORT, or SPA may trigger another site. (Let's hope your clients can both spell and type! However, you cannot control that variable.)

I won't suggest that you change your business name from The Ultimate Resort and Spa to something else. After all, you have been established for quite a while, and such a drastic change may garner adverse publicity. Of course, you can cancel the website, but that would also put you at a disadvantage to other resorts who have websites.

However, you can do something to improve the situation. Your Internet service provider may be able to remove the offending links to your website. If the company can reduce e-mail spam, surely it can eliminate the connections.

If you find that some websites add you to their links, you can request that they remove the link. However, finding all or a percentage of them will be tedious, if not impossible. And you can only ask—you can't compel anyone to drop the link. Such is the freedom of the Internet.

If only this were a hardware or software problem, Jack, my team at Ashimoff Robotics could remedy the situation. Unfortunately, it is not.

Judy

1. Write a report in memo form on the dangers of the Internet for businesses.
2. Prepare a short survey that you can use to collect information from 20 to 30 small businesses in your area regarding their use of the Internet to promote their products or services. If possible, interview one or two business owners in more depth. Using the information you collect, prepare a set of useful guidelines.
3. Design a website for The Ultimate Resort and Spa. Or, what links would you add to The Ultimate Website and propose to Jack Horner?

case eleven
Of Viruses and Vices

Sergei Malik, manager and owner of CyberTel Computronics Limited, calls you into his office. You have been working for CyberTel for eight months now, after receiving your Computer Engineering Technician (CET) Certificate. As an assistant, you install hardware and software, schedule the maintenance of leased equipment, and troubleshoot problems that clients phone in about to a 1-800 number. The company is small, but Sergei treats everyone like family, and you feel there is potential for growth here.

"Got a job for you," Sergei says. "About a year ago, The Ultimate Resort and Spa leased a state-of-the-art computer mainframe from Ashimoff Robotics. Judy Sedna subcontracted us to do maintenance and troubleshooting. She just got a call from The Ultimate complaining about problems. Joe Tyler's their onsite technician, but he's on vacation. Practically had to order him to relax. So I want you to find out what's wrong and fix it, okay?"

You quickly realize this is a promotion of sorts. Moreover, you want to prove to Sergei that his trust is not misplaced and that you can handle anything he throws at you. You figure that the computers have picked up a few new viruses that some anti-virus program did not detect or could not delete.

At The Ultimate Resort, you are introduced to the technical staff who run the mainframe and networking systems. They work in three shifts: morning, day, and graveyard. However, because only three people—Lucia Costa, Izzy Eastman, and Joe Tyler—are responsible for the running of the computers, only one technician is ever there, and when someone gets sick, someone else has to cover that person's shift.

You learn that The Ultimate Resort's management relies on Joe Tyler as backup man, and he is mostly stuck with the graveyard shift. Lucia and Izzy prefer to let Joe do all the work, while they play computer games and do only the daily routines.

Halfway into your diagnosis, you discover some disturbing irregularities. Someone (maybe a group of people) has tampered with the equipment. You uncover subprograms and subroutines that have nothing to do with running the telecommunications array, automatic security alert and surveillance, accounting/payroll, and LAN. You examine the original software and the modifications, and you read the logs. You find nothing out of the ordinary, and yet there are unaccounted-for discrepancies in the programming.

You tap into a subroutine just to see where it will lead you and boom—you see a long, long list of large files. At first this doesn't surprise you, but later, upon reflection, you understand that whoever created this program did not bother protecting it with a password out of sheer arrogance or stupidity. You open a file and find lists of names, account numbers, and other personal information. You open another file and find pornographic images.

Someone has been using this equipment for personal and private purposes rather than for company business. Whoever it is has been downloading and storing pornography in the mainframe memory banks. Furthermore, upon some discreet investigation, you find out that the perpetrator has not only created some sort of exchange in hardcore material but has also made it into a profitable small business.

You figure that every month the revenue generated from selling memberships and pass codes comes to at least $10 000. Moreover, The Ultimate Resort and Spa's accounting program routinely processes the money from credit cards in this illicit scheme and deposits it into a numbered account somewhere in the Cayman Islands. You calculate that this illegal activity has consumed about 15 percent of computer memory and storage space so far, and if your projection is correct this will increase to 20 percent by the end of the year.

You suspect Joe Tyler is the culprit, and you know you must tell Sergei. You document your findings. However, before you can phone your boss, you find a more serious problem.

Because of the nefarious activities, some mean viruses have found their way into the servers and the systems. Some are the run-of-the-mill variety and you quickly dispense with them. However, another one is resistant to standard anti-virus detection and elimination. You catch the irregularity only by accident: The infection blends in almost naturally with the software programs. The virus/worm has created subroutines, and you suspect that someone is controlling them—someone who could be anywhere in the world. The virus/worm is not quite dormant. It replicates itself with every use and attaches itself to the outgoing information transfer. In short, any computer system that has a link with the supercomputers at The Ultimate Resort and Spa is surely contaminated. In a given day, there must be hundreds, if not thousands, of exchanges of data from cable to satellite feed.

What can this virus/worm do? It duplicates information and sends a copy to 100 unidentifiable, secret websites. It has repositories in other servers all over the world. You try all the tricks of the trade you have learned, but this virile infection rebuffs you and almost shuts you down when you attempt to uncover even one mysterious website.

You ponder your options.

1. You phone Sergei Malik and tell him your suspicions about Joe Tyler and the mysterious virus. He says, "Write me a memo outlining what you have uncovered so I have a written record." Write this memo.
2. Sergei also asks you to inform Judy Sedna of Ashimoff Robotics and the general manager of The Ultimate Resort and Spa. Put this information into letters rather than memos.
3. Using this scenario, write a set of instructions or guidelines on computer usage for employees at The Ultimate Resort and Spa or at CyberTel. Use an internal memo to distribute the instructions to the staff.

4. Using a memo, offer some suggestions that may prevent such occurrences from happening again at any of the three companies: The Ultimate Resort and Spa, CyberTel Computronics, or Ashimoff Robotics.
5. Assume you are Sergei Malik. Write letters to the general manager of The Ultimate Resort and to Judy Sedna of Ashimoff Robotics. What will you say to them?

case twelve
The Ultimate Landscape

Six months ago, you graduated from Northern College with a diploma in horticulture and found employment with The Fifth Season, Inc., a company that specializes in landscaping and in installing pools, patios, and driveways. Raj Singh, vice president of the landscaping division, has remarked that you have a crackerjack attitude and will go far in this green thumb business. And you are about to prove him right.

You have just completed a bone-crushing job ahead of schedule and Raj rewards you with a weekend pass at The Ultimate Resort and Spa for some rest and recreation. "You saved the company about $5000. I'd say you deserve a treat at the company's expense."

As you arrive at The Ultimate Resort, you notice construction going on a stone's throw from the main building. Quickly you learn that a swim and gym facility is being built. The building is almost complete; at least the heavy equipment and construction crew have all gone on to other jobs. Only panel trucks and mini-vans dot the location, all belonging to electricians, plumbers, carpenters, and other tradespeople.

You see that the general contractor—the umbrella company that subcontracts out all the work from excavating to landscaping—is Hammer N Chisel, Limited. From beginning to end, the general contractor hires other firms and people to do the work. And the company has not called on The Fifth Season, Inc., the landscaping experts!

Still, you are a career professional, and you give the surrounding terrain a professional appraisal. Another landscaping company has already done some work: the main walkways and paths have all been marked off—most unfortunately in a grid pattern. Even these rough markers reveal a dull, even boring, trek from the main building to the swim and gym facility. Moreover, such a design does not fit into the spirit and ambiance of The Ultimate Resort and Spa.

As you are walking around the construction site, you see two people talking loudly. You cannot help but overhear their conversation.

"Landlubbers and Mowpower, Limited went belly-up! I can't believe it. Just last month they were considered as solid as the Rock of Gibraltar. Now, they've filed for bankruptcy," Jasmine Lopez, vice president of Hammer N Chisel, Limited, says. (You learn her name later.)

You recognize the general manager of The Ultimate Resort and Spa, Gus Daniel. "Don't tell me that Landlubbers and Mowpower were contracted to do the landscaping for us."

Jasmine Lopez nods. "Yes. And yes, I know our contract says we'll complete everything in time for your grand opening."

"We've already advertised. Invitations and publicity have all gone out. This is a pretty mess!"

"Finding another contractor on such short notice—"

This is the point when you jump into the conversation. Even though you have no authority to negotiate a deal or anything, you sense an opportunity too good to pass up.

"Excuse me," you say, "I couldn't help overhearing that you need a landscaping contractor."

"Who are you? And what business is it of yours?" both Jasmine Lopez and Gus Daniel say at the same time. You hand them each your business card.

You inform them that you work closely with Raj Singh, the landscaping division head of The Fifth Season, Inc. Jasmine Lopez murmurs something about having heard of him and about knowing the good reputation of The Fifth Season. Gus Daniel stares at you in a skeptical but admiring way.

Quickly you tell them that The Fifth Season can do the job and on time. You outline what you can do to improve the design of the pathways, the symmetrical patterns of shrubbery and trees, and the placing of plants and flowers. You toss in a ballpark figure, and you have just jumped two notches higher in their estimation of you.

"Look," Lopez says, "I don't usually make sudden decisions like this, but we're in a tight spot. So here's what I can do. You write me a proposal. Give me the general outlay and costs. Our lawyers can hammer out the contract details later. Send it to me—here's my card. Tell Raj I said hello."

You call Raj and give him the good news.

"Jazz and I go way back. She's ex-wife number 2," Raj informs you. "Tell you what, kid. Since you have surveyed the lay of the land, you write the proposal. I'll cosign it so there's no mistake about authorization. Can you do it tonight? Fax me a draft immediately."

1. Write the proposal letter to Jasmine Lopez as she has requested. Her business card gives you this address:

   Jasmine M. Lopez, Vice President

   Hammer N Chisel, Limited

   1750 Lord Tweedsmuir Drive

   Toronto, ON M1B 3P0

2. Assume that you are Jasmine Lopez. Write a brief report in a letter to Gus Daniel, summarizing the problem with Landlubbers and Mowpower, Limited. Provide details about the new contract with The Fifth Season, Inc., and reassure Daniel that he will have his grand opening on time.
3. Still writing as Jasmine Lopez, send an e-mail to Raj Singh. What business details will you share with him? Will you add anything a little more personal to this e-mail?

4. Gus Daniel has requested some designs for the landscaping contract. He has written to Jasmine Lopez, who has forwarded the request to Raj, who asks you to respond.

Daniel wants to know the design of the flowerbeds, the kinds of flowers and plants, and the saplings to line the pathways from the main building to the swim and gym facility. If possible, draw some illustrations to accompany your letter to him.

case thirteen
Not Quite the Ultimate Landscape

It is early spring at The Ultimate Resort and Spa, and you have arrived ahead of your landscaping crew to start planting. This morning two trailerloads of flowers, shrubs, and saplings from Perennially Yours, a subsidiary of the parent company of The Fifth Season, Inc., were delivered, and as junior foreman you are assigned to oversee the completion of the contract.

Raj Singh, your immediate supervisor at The Fifth Season, Inc., was impressed by your initiative that landed this small but significant contract with The Ultimate Resort. As reward and promotion, he gave you the job—a task he does not normally entrust to new employees until they have worked with the company at least five years. "This is your opportunity, kid," Raj said. "Show me that you're better than that horticultural diploma you have hanging on your office divider."

You check your briefcase. The invoices for the plants are all in order. The planting areas at The Ultimate Resort have all been mapped out on paper and photocopied for your crew. Now all you need to do is check that everything has been delivered.

As you count the trays of petunias, pansies, azaleas, and other annuals, you suddenly spot something on a number of plants: whitish, powdery discolouration on the young leaves. Mildew! Not in all the trays and not on all the plants—only the petunias and azaleas seem to show signs of the fungal infection. But you are not sure. After all, you have 1200 trays and each tray holds 6 to 8 plants.

You randomly check the fruit tree saplings and your heart sinks: You find lesions on the apple saplings, blackish spots with a brownish purple border. The Latin phrase *alternaria mali*, the alternaria blotch, comes to mind—a rotting disease that eventually kills a tree. To make matters worse, you discover that the leaves of the oak saplings are scorched. Anthracnose, another blighting fungus, is deadly, especially to oak trees.

Immediately, you call Raj at the head office to tell him about your initial findings. Here is part of your conversation:

Raj: Have you made a complete inventory?

You: Not yet. When my crew gets here, we'll examine every tray and every leaf. As I said earlier, my random check shows only the petunias and azaleas infected. The pansies, impatiens, begonias, and marigolds all seem okay.

Raj: Look, our company can't afford to replace everything. It's not even a matter of insurance. I want you to separate the healthy plants from the diseased ones. Make sure you and your crew don't spread the infection, eh?

You: We know our job.
Raj: Well, make sure everyone takes extra careful precautions. This contract is our foot in the door with The Ultimate Resort.
You: What do you want me to do?
Raj: Plant the healthy ones as planned. Remove and quarantine the infected plants. Write down the batch series, species, and numbers. Same for the saplings. Keep an accurate count. I'll ship you replacements as soon as possible.
You: Raj, I've got a bad feeling about all this. What if the nursery still has more infected plants?
Raj: I'm way ahead of you. Three shipments from Perennially Yours went out the same day to different locations and retailers. Odds are good that those shipments will have diseased plants too.
You: What a mess!
Raj: Listen—with disaster comes opportunity. I'm putting you in charge of warning the other clients about this problem. I'll have my secretary e-mail you the names and addresses.
You: Thanks. More work.
Raj: That's why I hired you.

Raj's secretary e-mails you the following list of company names that have shipments of possibly infected plants:

Northern Plantations and Gardening: npgardening@implants.com
College Pro Planters and Mowers: colproplamow@flowers.ca
The Good Earth Society: goode_soc@horticulture.on.ca

1. Write one e-mail and copy it to the other clients, warning them about your discovery. Include in your e-mail, a short set of instructions on what to do with the diseased plants and how to get replacements.
2. Raj must write a letter to The Ultimate Resort and Spa explaining the problem with the plants. Obviously there will be a delay. But he assures the general manager that all contractual obligations will be fulfilled.

   Unfortunately, Raj's secretary is unavailable to write the letter. So, because of your ties with The Ultimate, Raj gives you the job. Compose a letter explaining what problems you have encountered and what measures you (or your company) are taking to remedy the situation.

   Hint: You may need to design a letterhead and address for The Fifth Season, Inc.
3. Raj needs some documentation for the record. He says it is company policy. Since you were the first to discover the problem, you should write him a memo report about this incident.

You and your crew have finally tallied up the infected shipment from Perennially Yours:

azaleas	35 trays (6 per tray)
petunias	19 trays (8 per tray)
garden heliotrope	10 trays (10 per tray)
evergreen shrubbery	52 pots
apple saplings	25 trees
oak saplings	20 trees
maple saplings	18 trees

4. Bring some of the plants discussed in this case study into class. Working in pairs or small groups, write a clear description of the blossoms or foliage.
5. Prepare a clearly labelled diagram to go with your description.

case fourteen
Ultimate Progress

You are a newly graduated civil engineering technologist who has been subcontracted by JL Boys Construction, Inc. (JLB). JLB, in turn, is one of the subcontractors working on the new swim and gym facility at The Ultimate Resort and Spa.

JLB: How are things going with your report?

You: Haven't completed it yet. Just made an inventory. I went to the site yesterday for one last check, Mr. Boys.

JLB: Call me Jon like everybody else, OK? Look, I don't want to rush you but we're kind of short-handed. You come highly recommended from Northern College.

You: I've gotten a few jobs under my belt since I received my civil engineering technologist diploma. Anyway, let me run with what I have here. Got a minute?

JLB: Sure.

You: The last report you sent in to Bobcaygeon Builders, Inc. was on May 20; that makes it about three months ago—

JLB: Yeah, quarterly reports. Paragraph 3, subsection 2, part of the obligations in my contract with Val. When the report is on her desk, she sends me the interim cheque.

You: I didn't write that earlier report for you. A Nick Prudhomme did it. Seems OK. Your company laid the foundation for the swim and gym facility at The Ultimate Resort and Spa, and—

JLB: Hate to rush you, but I have to take my granddaughter to her soccer playoff. Cut to the chase. Anyway, Val at Bobcaygeon Builders accepted the interim report. Let's stick to this one.

You: The Olympic-size swimming pool is almost complete, and so are the adjacent hot tubs and whirlpools—two of each—and a kidney-shaped toddlers' pool. Only the finishing touches—

JLB: Yeah, my brother and his crew'll put in the linings for the big pool and the small one. Greg got the pumps and filtering system done about two weeks back. You were there yesterday. How's the skylight? Are the Plexiglas domes all fitted in?

You: That's your job too? I thought I saw the guys from ArcAngels Outfitters caulking the inside.

JLB: We subcontracted out. Ahmed ibn Noor was supposed to send me his invoice so I can include it with your report. Wait a minute. Aha! Found it. You can always trust Ahmed to beat the clock.

You: Will I be getting the original or a photocopy of the invoice to include in my report?

JLB: When you hand in the report tomorrow at eight in the morning, I'll attach a copy. Just make a note that ArcAngels Outfitters' invoice is enclosed. Did Jackie finish the tiling all around the swimming pool? When I called her on the cell she said she and her partner were putting in the grout.

You: The grout's in, but the glaze isn't. Jackie Cwiek says she can't do the glazing until the grout dries completely. Something about curing.

JLB: Did my daughter do a good job? I trained her myself. And now she wants to be her own boss. Calls her little company Really Cwiek Jobs.

You: From what I've seen, it's great workmanship. Oh, Jon, I don't have the figures for the labour and materials. I should be including them in this invoice.

JLB: My brother-in-law's the accountant. He'll send the invoice to Val. Your job is to write the progress report. Just put in what's been done since May and what still needs doing. I have a suspicion that the people at The Ultimate Resort are pressing Val for something official. And please make it brief but inclusive, OK?

You: Sure thing, Jon.

1. Write the progress or interim report in letter format to the following:

   Valerie Whitefeather, Manager

   Bobcaygeon Builders, Inc.

   99 Lakefield Road

   Peterborough, ON K1P 2T0

2. Jon Boys of JL Boys Construction calls you five hours later and says the general manager of The Ultimate Resort and Spa wants to know who the subcontractors are and what work they did in the swim and gym facility. Jon wants you to e-mail a breakdown of jobs to Sarah Poole at this address: sp_gm@ultimateresort.com.

case fifteen
Ultimate Arch: Part One

The Ultimate Resort and Spa needed to expand its parking lots since the resort began construction on the swim and gym facility. The management decided not to ruin the woodland area beside the main buildings. That space would make a great hiking and dirt biking trail in some future expansion. So the resort bought 10 acres (4 ha) of property across the four-lane highway to make a parking lot for vans, RVs, and trailers. Then it faced the problem of how the guests would cross the highway safely. The solution was to build a pedestrian footbridge over the highway.

You are part of the construction crew building the footbridge. Even though you have a civil engineering technologist diploma, you feel you need more practical hands-on experience than you got at Northern College. This morning you have just come out of a scheduled meeting on safety.

"Keep your wits about you," the foreman warns everyone. "Accidents are preventable. There's no future in being a client of Workers' Compensation."

As an apprentice labourer, you are given the task of cleaning up after the veteran workers. Today, your job is to take debris and toss it into the wide cylindrical chute that runs down about 15 m to a giant dumpster. All morning, you have been unloading your wheelbarrow of twisted metal, wires, empty containers, and other waste. You enjoy hearing the sounds of tumbling debris and the smashing noises as everything collides in the dumpster. With your mathematical knowledge, you calculate not only the seconds an empty container takes to slide down the chute but also its force of impact.

You make sure to avoid steering the wheelbarrow too closely to the scaffolding and metre-high wooden railings. "It's amazing what powdery concrete dust can do to make you slip and slide. You can twist an ankle, or worse, fall through the safety rails," the foreman's voice echoes in your head.

The noon whistle goes off, and everyone stops to take a lunch break. You are at the top of the chute and want to empty your wheelbarrow before having your lunch. For the past week, the passing lanes of the highway have been closed so the welders can set the 10-m, 5-t beams that join the concrete pillars. The construction workers sit on the edge of one of the beams to watch the cottagers in their RVs, pickups with boats and trailers, and SUVs down below. Sometimes they wave at these impatient people, and sometimes, especially, the women in convertibles wave back. This is one of those times.

Someone lets out a loud wolf whistle.

At that precise moment, you are heaving in the last heavy piece from your wheelbarrow into the chute. You are already off-balance as you let the cinder block go. Without warning, a worker rushes by to satisfy his curiosity and bumps into you. You lose your balance entirely and fall into the chute.

You hear your own echoing curses and screams for help as you slide down the 30-degree incline. You choke on the fine dust, and oddly you are thankful that you are wearing safety goggles, a hardhat, and thick gloves. Before you land in the dumpster, you see the jagged edges of debris. In a daze, you wonder what the force of impact is for someone of your weight and size rollercoastering down on a hard surface.

Moments later, the rescue crew pulls you out of the dumpster. They take you by ambulance to the nearest medical centre. The doctor examines you and finds no broken bones or internal injuries. You have some contusions, scrapes, and minor cuts on your face, arms, and legs that require a few bandages but no stitches. You are shaken up, but you want to return to your job so none of your coworkers will call you a wimp.

When you report for work the next day, your foreman tells you to write an accident report. He will photocopy it in duplicate for the company's files and for the Workplace Safety and Insurance Board.

1. Produce the accident report in memo form. Address it to

   Zeke Nanabush, Foreman

   Zenith and Nadir Construction, Limited

2. Write a list of recommendations about safety on the job based on the elements of this scenario or on your own workplace.

case sixteen
Ultimate Arch: Part Two

The police have restricted the flow of highway traffic that passes by The Ultimate Resort and Spa. Safety barricades form a wide perimeter around the half-built bridge that spans four lanes of highway and a wide dividing median. A huge crane on a flatbed trailer commands attention even on this drizzly June morning. The threat of an electrical storm is real. Today is the day to lift 4 of the 10-m, 5-t girders onto the reinforced concrete pillars that stride the highway.

Much of the ordinary construction has been curtailed for fear of accidents. Only essential workers are there, while the rest are given a half-day off. Because you are a civil engineering technologist, you want to witness heavy-duty construction. It is not every day that you see girders put into place with such professional precision. You just might learn something.

"You know what happens," the safety foreman says to you, "if one of those beams suddenly crashes down 15 m? It leaves a 10-m long indentation across both sides of the highway 20 cm deep. And if you're underneath, they'll need scrapers to—well, you get the idea."

So you watch from a safe distance. You also notice pools of water collecting on the flatbed trailer from the morning rain.

"We sure picked a lousy day to set the girders," the foreman tells you, "but a crane and operator cost about $3000 per day. We can't afford to put this off till the rain stops."

Gusts of wind bring dark thunderclouds and flashes of lightning. You see the tip of the crane become a lightning rod, and the whole crane shudders with the shock. Unfortunately, the delicate hold that the cables have on the first girder shifts at that moment. The girder slams into the reinforced concrete pillar, and chunks of concrete fly into the air. Fortunately, the cables hold, and the damage to the pillar is minimal. However, a large piece of concrete flattens the windshield and top of a half-ton pickup truck.

Even as the rain slashes down and the wind howls, you think you hear someone in the pickup screaming for help. Then you're sure you see a bloody hand waving through the driver's side window.

When it is finally safe to attempt a rescue, you find the driver of the pickup bloodied and badly hurt. Luckily, his hardhat has saved his skull from being crushed. The injured man stares at you blankly: he is in shock. With your first aid training, you know better than to move him. However, you stay with him until the ambulance arrives to take him to the hospital.

The foreman says to you, "You're a witness. I want a report on my desk by tomorrow, OK?"

1. Write a witness report in memo form. Address it to Zeke Nanabush, Foreman. What did you actually see? Do not add conjecture.
2. You learn later that the injured man's name is Morgan Pike. He had been delivering parts to the site. With a small group, research an aspect of workplace injuries and rescue operations, especially in construction accidents. Check statistics and guidelines on workplace safety. Find a knowledgeable person to interview. Write your findings in a short report.

case seventeen
Alarms: True and False

A fire occurs in the gym facility at The Ultimate Resort and Spa about 2 a.m. on June 21, 2002. The local fire department dispatches two pumpers and a tanker, and by 8 a.m. the firefighters extinguish the two-alarm fire. No one is hurt, but there is substantial damage to the newly built facility. The fire marshal is called in to investigate the fire, and he determines that it was accidental. There is plenty of evidence that carelessness on the part of the construction crew contributed significantly to the million-dollar disaster.

Karen Tanaka, your immediate superior at Riehl Inspections, Inc., calls you on her cell phone as you are ordering breakfast at a fast-food franchise. Just recently, because of downsizing of the company, you have moved up from assistant inspector to full inspector. What that basically means is that you are allowed to tackle assignments by yourself, you don't need a mentor to guide your every move, and you can exercise certain powers to get the job done. You don't get a raise in pay though. (You should consider yourself lucky you still have a job.)

"I've arranged with Sid Mendes, the fire chief, to let you into the building," Karen says. "The place is badly scorched and is crawling with people who represent companies or agencies with vested interests of every sort. I want you to represent Riehl Inspections."

"What do you want me to do?"

"Check the alarm system and the sprinklers. Our company got a subcontract from JL Boys Construction, Inc., so we're involved."

"I didn't know we have a service and installation division. I thought we only investigate and inspect," you reply.

Karen lowers her voice enough to let you know she is about to tell you a secret. "JL Boys Construction offered us a deal. If we installed the alarms and sprinklers, then we could get the maintenance contract with The Ultimate Resort. Headquarters has always toyed with the idea of grabbing a share of the maintenance contract business. The company has a junior employee check the equipment once a month and recommend upgrades every few years. It's easy money."

You learn from Karen that Riehl Inspections subcontracted out the installation of the alarms and sprinklers to an outfit named Magnifico 7 International. It is a family business run from their home somewhere in Burleigh Falls.

"Is there anything else I should know before I start nosing around?" you ask.

"I don't want to prejudice you," Karen says. "Just do a thorough job."

At The Ultimate Resort and Spa, you find the gym facility half gutted. The remnants of fire and fire equipment are still evident. You can smell burnt plastic, metal, wood, and other materials. Sid Mendes, the fire chief, introduces you to one of the fire station captains. Sophie Tyler will accompany you in the inspection.

The building is badly damaged. You find the source of the fire, a corner of the building where the boiler room is. The heat was so intense that glass in the windows is either warped or shattered, and metal superstructures sag noticeably and are twisted. The boiler room is 5 m × 8 m in size, and not all required equipment has been installed. Because thick, fire-retaining doors were not yet installed, the fire easily reached the gym.

Using a ladder, you climb up to the fire-retardant false ceiling to check the sprinkler. You use your penlight to see the make of the sprinkler but learn nothing. This sprinkler has no information on it.

"Was the alarm system activated?" you ask Sophie.

"It was installed but not operational," she answers. "We wondered why we didn't get the call until almost half the building was gutted."

"What about the sprinkler system?"

"See for yourself." Sophie points to the ceiling of the gym. "Those drips in the gym are not the result of our hoses."

You find an extension ladder and climb up to the rafters. There is smoke damage and some heat fatigue in the air ducts and fasteners. You are more interested in the model and make of the sprinklers. You rub off the soot, and using your penlight, you find the evidence. Your heart sinks.

Sprink-O-Matic is manufactured in both Indonesia and Korea. It is an imitation of a design made in Canada. The imitation is made of inferior materials and shows poor workmanship. It is also about one-third the cost of the genuine ShowerFire sprinkler. Sprink-O-Matic is known to be unreliable and does not carry the necessary Canadian Standards Association stamp of approval. But it is inexpensive and has flooded the North American market. It seems that Magnifico 7 International has been cutting corners.

Because you are a professional, you check every sprinkler in the gym facility. Five sprinklers did not work during the fire, and three functioned as designed. At the end of the day, you feel you have done your job and given yourself a workout.

1. Karen Tanaka wants your inspection report immediately. You e-mail it to her immediately (make up an e-mail address for her). Consider the hard facts and evidence. Will you include your suspicions in your report?
2. Assume that you are Karen Tanaka. You are angry that Magnifico 7 International has been slipshod in honouring its contract (Riehl Inspections, Inc. specifically stated in the agreement that only approved materials could be used). Write an official letter of complaint. Do not just threaten to sue: Express your company's and your own indignation and outrage, but include evidence uncovered by your investigator. What will you write?
3. Jon Boys of JL Boys Construction, Inc. calls up Karen Tanaka and wants to know what is in the report and whether his company is liable for damages in a lawsuit or in a renewed investigation requested by the management of The Ultimate Resort and Spa. Karen gives you the task of responding to him in a letter.

case eighteen
Ultimate Swipe

As team leader at Virtual Securities Incorporated, you supervise a tightly knit group of research and development experts. Working for you are Tom Sawyer, Dick Tracy, Jane Marple, and Nancy Drew. Your team has spent five years developing a new security card, from inception to the current trials.

The card incorporates a new nano circuitry your team has developed. The strip is slightly wider and thinner than an 8-cm long piece of Scotch tape and is made of reinforced Mylar and Kevlar compound. It is powered by heat, friction, and human saliva. Room temperature or microfriction from a wallet can sustain it indefinitely. Unlike the standard black magnetic strip on plastic cards, this strip is translucent and can retain half a megabyte of information.

Designed to replace the existing magnetic strip, the VirtuSecure strip can help reduce the size of personal and business devices such as cell phones and swipe machines. For example, with VirtuSecure, a consumer has a universal card for health care, driver's licence, charge/debit transactions, and other functions.

Virtual Securities Incorporated has spent five years and many millions of dollars on research and development of this invention. Now it is time for trials. Will it stand up to everyday use and abuse? Will business and individual consumers buy into this product? Your team is very excited.

Tom Sawyer is monitoring the first two weeks of controlled trials. He has met with some problems. The adhesive does not bond well. Depending on the frequency of swiping, the circuitry strip detaches itself from the plastic card. When the strip is jarred loose, it often gums up the swipe slots. This in turn causes damage to the swipe machines. If someone should use a magnetic strip card right after, the VirtuSecure erases all the codes from that card.

Jane Marple faces a different problem but quite a worrisome one for the project. On March 15, 2002, she noticed attempted security breaches in the group's computer system. Someone or some company was trying to hack into the data. She reported to you then that the hacker was unsuccessful, but vengeful, because that person left several nasty viruses. She was afraid to open files simply because a virus might slip into the system and wreak havoc. Fortunately, she was able to sweep the system clean, but this took up valuable time. Three days were lost.

Bob Cratchit, vice president of R&D at Virtual Securities calls you from The Ultimate Resort and Spa, where he is taking a short vacation. He has investors in Vancouver interested in VirtuSecure strips, and he wants your team to impress them.

"Sure, Bob," you say with confidence, "I'll have a demonstration ready for next Tuesday. The stockholders and investors will be impressed."

"Glad to hear that," Bob replies. "Oh, yes, drop me a progress report. Something for the files, okay? Nothing too long."

Right after you hang up, Nancy Drew rushes into your office. She is resigning from the project as of this minute. Her letter of resignation cites personal and family reasons, but you know better. Nancy has just been offered the vice presidency of CyberSafe Enterprises, a rival company that is also developing a nano strip. You see the implications immediately: You may be able to stop Nancy from taking disks from the office, but you can't wipe out the information in her head. After all, she helped develop the technology. Now you regret not having had everyone on the team sign a nondisclosure contract that would effectively prevent them from revealing the data to another company. And where Nancy goes, the others are sure to follow.

You groan inwardly. Just this morning you phoned your stockbroker to buy 100 000 shares at $3 a share in Virtual Securities, all your life savings.

1. Write a letter on company letterhead and fax it to Bob Cratchit care of The Ultimate Resort and Spa, Suite 213 (705-555-9876). Explain to him the various problems with the strip and with your (disintegrating) team. You do not need to worry about confidentiality because The Ultimate Resort has bonded employees and a secure fax connection. However, you will need a cover sheet for your fax.
2. Bob Cratchit is not pleased with your progress report. However, instead of firing you, he wants you to write an internal memo to upper management explaining the situation and offering some guidelines on how to keep future inventions and company secrets from being pirated by former employees.
3. Write Nancy Drew's letter of resignation.
4. Tom Sawyer and Jane Marple have decided to leave Virtual Securities Incorporated. They have each asked for a letter of recommendation. Write a recommendation letter for Tom or Jane on company letterhead.

case nineteen
Ultimate Sewer Inspection

The Ultimate Resort and Spa has called on Riehl Inspections, Inc. to do a field investigation of drainage and runoff into the wetland about half a kilometre from the resort. For the last month, there have been complaints from both clients and staff about foul smells coming from that area. The smell gets worse when the westerly wind blows in the direction of the resort. Karen Tanaka, vice president of Riehl Inspections, gives you the assignment.

"We're short-handed, or I would have sent a team of three," Karen says. "If we do a good job here, we may get the contract to do the drainage as well. The Ultimate is thinking of developing a dirt bike and hiking trail in the woodlands nearby."

It is early May, and the runoff from the melting snow has subsided considerably. You go in prepared: a hardhat; industrial-standard, knee-high vulcanized boots; a backpack of specimen-gathering equipment; a heavy-duty flashlight; and other portable equipment.

Instead of whiffs, the foul smell hits your nostrils with a powerful acrid sting. By the time your boots meet water, you are forced to put on your industrial-strength air-filter mask. A thick scum of pollutant gathers in pockets about 5 cm deep on top of the shallow but vast pond. When the sun's rays hit the wetland in a certain way, you see an unnatural spectrum of colours. You try to identify the smell, but the closest parallel is that of human waste. Your rubber boots crush branches, garbage, small dead animals, and other debris that was not flushed out in the spring runoff. You take some samples of the stagnant, polluted water.

You follow the shoreline of the long pond for about 1.5 km. Every once in a while you take more samples and label them, and occasionally you photograph the area. In your mini-recorder, you take notes: "The pollutants are no longer just liquid. I can identify feces. This mask is not filtering out the smell. Seems to be coming from the northwest."

Half a kilometre later, you see the source of the foul runoff. A concrete drainage pipe about 2 m in diameter is obscured by shrubs. You immediately identify the steady flow from it as raw sewage. The storm sewer is old, and the crumbling cement reveals the mesh of metal reinforcements. From its construction, you recognize the pipe as part of an abandoned runoff system. However, now someone is using it illegally to dump raw sewage and other chemical wastes.

When you were travelling to The Ultimate Resort this morning, you noticed a factory farm in the next county. You recall the Heritage Farms, Inc. sign prominently displayed. Could it be that this corporation is illegally dumping swine effluvia?

Because the drainage pipe is large enough for you to enter, you snap on your flashlight. The echo of flowing effluvia bounces around the cylindrical walls. The stench of feces and decomposition makes you gag.

As you bend down to gather samples, you trip on a tree branch or a fallen, slimy concrete boulder (even later, you aren't sure which). Your hardhat falls off with a clang, and you hit the left side of your forehead against the side of the drainage pipe where there is exposed metal. To steady yourself, your right arm instinctively snaps out. The polluted water splashes up, and you immediately feel not only wetness but also a noticeable sting on your cheek. Then there is darkness. You have dropped your flashlight, and it is not waterproof.

"What am I going to do now?" Your voice reverberates through the long tunnel.

Fortunately, you remember that your penlight is attached to your keyring. With it you find your hardhat, now covered in gunk. You check your equipment: nothing else is damaged or missing. You make your way out of the storm sewer.

The blood has already caked over the cut on your face when you check yourself in the car mirror. At the Peterborough medical clinic, you learn that the gash requires five stitches, and you also need a tetanus booster shot in case of infection. You take some ASA for the headache and pain.

Next day, you tell Karen Tanaka about your experience. She says: "Put it in writing, OK?" Then with a wicked grin, she asks, "So, are you game to find the source?"

1. Karen is in a hurry for the inspection report. She is willing to wait for the long report next month, when the results of your samples come back from the laboratory, but now she wants something brief but official for the management at The Ultimate Resort and Spa. You are to send the original letter to Sarah Poole at The Ultimate. Karen also wants you to send her a memo about your injury for the file and the Workplace Safety and Insurance Board.
2. Karen receives a preliminary report of the effluvia samples, and it confirms what you have already deduced. In consultation with The Ultimate Resort's management, she tells you to write to the provincial Ministry of Health about your findings. Include a series of ancillary elements in your formal report. Karen will cosign your report.
3. Write up a set of instructions for future inspectors so that they will not experience the problems that you have had.
   - Use your knowledge of safety procedures from the courses you have taken. Apply them to this situation.
   - Warn others of the dangers. Use Warning and Caution boxes where necessary. Remember to explain as well as advise.
   - Put your signature at the end of this set of instructions.

case twenty
Health Club Woes

The health club at The Ultimate Resort and Spa does not have a full-time receptionist at present, since guests staying at the resort can use the in-room messaging service for all their requests. People living in the surrounding community, however, hear the following message when they call:

> Hello. Thank you for calling the Health Club at The Ultimate Resort and Spa. We offer many opportunities for fun and relaxation, including our indoor heated pool, a complete gym and weight room, and squash courts. Please leave your name and telephone number, and someone will return your call.

During the average day, the club receives up to 40 messages from outside callers. These calls are picked up twice daily by one of the front desk operators and passed on to the appropriate department or individual in the health club. During the past few months, there have been many complaints that telephone calls are not being returned.

1. Describe the problem here using the language of communication theory, and recommend some ways to solve it. Keep in mind that cost is always a factor. Organize your solutions, beginning with the one that's most cost-effective.
2. Prepare a short memo directed to the recreation supervisor that describes the problem and offers at least two possible solutions.
3. Prepare a revised message for the voice mail system so that callers will understand what they should do.

Index

C

D

E

F

G

H

I

J

L

M

N

Q

R

S

T

U

V

W

Y